James J. Hill

The Oklahoma Western Biographies
Richard W. Etulain, General Editor

James J. Hill

EMPIRE BUILDER
OF THE NORTHWEST

By Michael P. Malone

UNIVERSITY OF OKLAHOMA PRESS : NORMAN AND LONDON

Library of Congress Cataloging-in-Publication Data

Malone, Michael P.
    James J. Hill : empire builder of the Northwest / by Michael P.
Malone.
        p.   cm. — (The Oklahoma western biographies ; v. 12)
    Includes bibliographical references and index.
    ISBN: 0–8061–2793–7 (alk. paper)
    1. Hill, James Jerome, 1838–1916.   2. Great Northern Railway
Company (U.S.) 3. Businessmen—United States—Biography.
I. Title. II. Series.
HE2754.H5M35   1996
385'.092—dc20
[B]   95–36518
                                                                 CIP

James J. Hill: Empire Builder of the Northwest is Volume 12 in *The Oklahoma Western Biographies*.

Copyright © 1996 by the University of Oklahoma Press, Norman, Publishing Division of the University. All rights reserved. Manufactured in the U.S.A.

1   2   3   4   5   6   7   8   9   10

For
Richard B. Roeder
Historian, Colleague, and Friend of a Lifetime

Contents

Illustrations

PHOTOGRAPHS

MAPS

Series Editor's Preface

JAMES J. Hill ranks among the great organizers and managers of the American West. Born in Canada in 1838, Hill moved nearly two decades later to the Twin Cities, where he quickly exhibited the tireless energy and foresight that characterized his entire career. By his early forties he had helped organize major new transportation systems in Canada and the upper Midwest. Within the next decade, he took control of the Great Northern Railroad and drove it relentlessly west to the Puget Sound in one of the memorable engineering and financial feats of the "Great West." Not satisfied to rest on his laurels, Hill continued to expand and dominate his mushrooming empire until his death in 1916.

But, as Michael P. Malone clearly and thoroughly notes in this smoothly written and lively biography, Hill alienated colleagues as often as he inspired them. Arrogant, self-righteous, sometimes too ambitious, and frequently a blatant bully, Hill lashed out at managers and workers alike who failed to meet his taxing demands of production and loyalty.

Counterpoising these brilliant and dark sides of Hill's character, Malone furnishes a balanced portrait of an enormously controversial western figure. Saluting Hill's hard work, his unsurpassed managerial abilities, and his shrewdness, the author also points to Hill's excessive pride and his willingness to blink at questionable actions that benefited him and his projects. Although Hill's family and friends often respected and admired his drive and perseverance, few wholeheartedly loved him.

This revealing biography of Hill also illustrates Malone's large talents as western historian and intellectual. Well known

as a leading authority on twentieth-century western political
and economic topics and the author of major books on Montana and the modern West as well as of dozens of significant
essays, Malone has also served as an energetic senior administrator at Montana State University in Bozeman for nearly two
decades.

Finally, Michael Malone achieves the two major goals of
volumes in the Oklahoma Western Biographies series. His en-
grossing study of James J. Hill illuminates the life of a notable
westerner even as it explicates important events and trends in
the development of the larger American West. Scholarly and
general readers alike will enjoy this powerful and intriguing
story of James J. Hill, empire builder of the American West.

RICHARD W. ETULAIN

University of New Mexico

Preface

THIS brief volume purports to be neither an exhaustive nor an "authoritative" biography of James Jerome Hill. The man's long and multifaceted career would demand a volume many times longer than this. Rather, my purpose—consistent with the series of which this book is a part—is to attempt a succinct, interpretative biography of a most fascinating and significant man. Given this aim, I have used the large collection of Hill Papers at the James J. Hill Reference Library in Saint Paul only selectively, emphasizing instead the growing volume of historical literature relating to the Northwest.

Furthermore, my purpose here is neither to glorify nor to defame this obviously complex man but to depict him objectively in the full range of his many interests and activities. Clearly he accomplished more than all but a few of the other leading figures in the history of American industry and regional development and was, in fact, a man of remarkable abilities, determination, and drive. Just as clearly, however, he could be quite ruthless, overbearing, and politically domineering. A true picture of the man can emerge only from an attempt to envision all facets of his complex life and personality, and that I have tried to do.

Several good people have offered me special assistance in this endeavor, which was made more difficult by the fact that halfway through it I assumed the duties of a university president. Series editor Richard Etulain, both a close friend and a distinguished regionalist, offered me critical support and many key insights. I owe a special debt of thanks to Dr. W. Thomas White, the capable and dedicated director of the James J. Hill Reference Library, whose help and friendship went far beyond what anyone could rightfully expect. Special thanks also go to Dr. Dale Johnson, director of the K. Ross Toole Archives of the University of Montana, who helped me considerably in making accessible their manuscript copy of the Great Northern history written by Ralph W. and Muriel E. Hidy. Thanks also are due the staffs of the Montana Historical Society (especially Dave Walter and Lori Morrow), the Renne Library at Montana State University, the University of Washington and Washington State University libraries, the Minnesota Historical Society, the Library of Congress, and to Sue Fair of the James J. Hill House staff of the Minnesota Historical Society. A special thanks goes to Shari McCoy, Daphne Ahrendes, Marlene Mazuranich, and Scott Levandowski, of my staff at Montana State University, for all their help as I prepared the manuscript. And finally, I especially thank my wife, Kathleen, for her interest and involvement in the project and for her understanding and acceptance of the time it has claimed.

MICHAEL MALONE

Bozeman, Montana

James J. Hill

CHAPTER I

The Road to Saint Paul

PERHAPS no other generation in all of American history played so fascinating or central a role in national development as the one that, born in the 1830s and 1840s, came to maturity in the Civil War crisis of 1857–67. For this was the generation that not only forged the modern American nation but also worked the industrial-commercial-transportation revolution that formed its modern economy and society. Most of the men involved in this revolution—whether they are called "industrial statesmen" or "robber barons," each title simplistic and misleading—did not fight in the war, choosing instead to pursue their own acquisitive interests. But all of them seized the sudden and unprecedented opportunities the new age presented to them. Some left little behind besides personal and family fortunes and sullied reputations. Others built commercial empires and philanthropies that long outlived them.

One of the latter was James Jerome Hill. As the following pages will reveal, Hill was indeed a speculator, sometimes a predatory one; and many, in his own time and later, considered him an exploiter and a villain. Still growing in eastern Washington wheat fields is a nuisance variety of mustard that old-time farmers call "Jim Hill," after the man their ancestors considered an overlord and a rate-gouger. As a boy, I worked that region many years ago, and I remember one farmer who, in moments of exceptional rage, would proclaim: "By Jesus H. Chee-rist and James J. Hill!"

But there is no denying Hill's remarkable abilities and accomplishments in the "opening" of the Northwest, and the shadow of his historical presence looms heavily even into our own time, eighty years after his death. At the close of his novel *The Great Gatsby,* F. Scott Fitzgerald had his narrator deliver the following benediction for Gatsby: "If he'd of lived, he'd of been a great man. A man like James J. Hill. He'd of helped build up the country." To this day, a crack Amtrak passenger train that runs in part over former Great Northern Railway tracks from Seattle to Chicago bears his title: the "Empire Builder." And tourists daily marvel at the grandeur of Hill's restored mansion on Summit Avenue and the beauty of the James J. Hill Reference Library, both in Saint Paul. On the other hand, most beneficiaries of grants and donations from the Northwest Area Foundation, formerly the Hill Family Foundation, do not even realize that his wealth and foresight made such philanthropy possible in the first place.

Hill was born on September 16, 1838, in the small town of Wellington, near Guelph, in the Canadian province of Ontario. He was named simply James Hill, like the many James Hills who had preceded him in the family. Although rocky and forested, his homeland provided good crops and lay poised in Canada's southernmost extension, between Lake Huron on the west, Lake Erie on the south, and Lake Ontario on the east. Toronto was fifty miles east, but Buffalo, New York, was only slightly farther away to the southeast. And in fact, although his Scots-Canadian roots would always figure largely in his makeup, Hill's later move to the nearby United States would prove easy and natural.

Looking back on his life, Hill once recalled his father's boasting that the Hill family tree could be traced back sixteen generations through Scotland and Ireland. The Hills offered a classic instance of how the Anglo-Scots-Irish hegira contributed to the making of both the United States and Canada. His mother, Ann Dunbar Hill, was born in 1805 in County Tipperary, Ireland, the daughter of Scots Presbyterians who had joined the flight of their brethren from religious persecution in their homeland. Her granddaughter Clara Hill, Jim's daughter, remembered Ann for her "quick wit," her strong will, and her energy and concluded that her son, Clara's father, strongly "resembled her." In 1832, Ann Dunbar moved with her family from Ireland to Ontario.

Clara, the chronicler of the Hill family, passed on the group memory of her grandfather James as a man of "strong physique and iron will," in other words, a typical Scots-Irishman. He died before any of his grandchildren could know him. A descendent of Anglican missionaries who intermarried with the Irish and Scots-Irish, James Hill was born in Armagh, Ireland, in 1811. The earliest of his English ancestors, James Rogers, had been burned at the stake in the mid-seventeenth century. In 1829, this James Hill traveled with his parents to join an uncle who, as a veteran of the Napoleonic wars, had acquired a land grant in Ontario.

Here he met Ann Dunbar, and in 1833 the two married, settling on a hardscrabble, fifty-acre tract four miles south of Rockwood, a one-street village of several hundred people. Typical frontiersmen, they produced four children in quick succession. A son, inevitably named James, died in infancy. A daughter, Mary Elizabeth, arrived in 1835. A second son, again named James and the subject of this study, came in 1838; and the youngest, Alexander Samuel, was born in 1839.

The growing family led a characteristic frontier existence. James Jr. later recalled that his father "was not very prosperous," and he remembered lying awake nights staring at the moonlight beaming through holes in the roof. Only a year apart in age, Jim and his brother, Alexander, were inseparable and spent much of their time hunting and fishing, which remained favorite hobbies of James's throughout his life.

When he was nine, his hunting avocation led to a tragic accident. A bow that he had made snapped, lashing the cocked arrow sharply back into his right eye and prying it from its socket. The family doctor, with classic backwoods ingenuity, managed to return the agonized boy's eye to its socket and restore its muscular control so that the damage would not be evident. But the eye was rendered almost entirely dysfunctional, evidently envisaging nothing more than dark shades. In a counterstroke of good fortune, however, the left eye proved over the ensuing years to be very strong and would serve James faithfully through a long lifetime of intensively close reading and reckoning.

The Hills adhered closely to the Anglo-Scottish culture they had inherited. Their religious affiliations were surprisingly ecumenical, with the father preferring the Baptists, the mother favoring the Methodists, and a number of Quaker neighbors in Rockwood also having a lasting influence on the children. But for all that, they took their religion as seriously as the next family; and the children could never head out to play on Sundays until the biblical recitations had been finished. Interestingly, however, even though young James carried from his youth a strong appreciation for religion and its value to individuals and society, he did not mature to become a devout or even a routine churchgoer.

James Sr. fervently hoped that his namesake would become a physician, and both parents instilled a love of reading and tradition in their children. The children would sing Scottish ballads to the tune of their father's flute, and all through Hill's years, one of his favorite times would be singing around the campfire or roaring out one of his favorite numbers solo while one of his daughters played the piano. He became a voracious reader even before school days, dwelling on the staples of the nineteenth century and the British tradition: the Bible, Shakespeare, Plutarch, Byron, the poems of Robert Burns, and the chivalrous novels of Sir Walter Scott. He remembered that one of his best escapes occurred when he borrowed a copy of *Ivanhoe* and devoured it in one sitting.

The children's schooling was rudimentary but typical of the time and place. For the first grades, the two boys hiked the several miles back and forth to Rockwood, sometimes seeing wolves en route. In 1849, when James was eleven, his father enrolled him at the Quaker academy in Rockwood; and here he attended classes, sporadically, for the next three years, sometimes boarding and doing chores for reimbursement.

The master of the academy, William Weatherald, had a major impact on the boy, implanting in him a love of literature and the essentials of mathematics and other practical sciences and fostering more than a little of the gentle religiosity of Quakerism. Hill's fondness for and indebtedness to Weatherald formed one of his few lasting bonds to his homeland. Years later, James would introduce the schoolmaster to the Canadian Pacific board of directors by stating, "It is to him I owe what little scholarship I possess." After becoming wealthy and successful, Hill took the old man on train trips and gave him gifts and endowments for his expanded academy. In letters, James unfailingly addressed Weatherald as "My Dear Old Master," and when the schoolmaster died, Hill took a special train to his funeral.

Although Hill often told listeners about the inadequacies of his education—"I never went to school a day after I was fourteen years and three months old," as he told journalist Annabel Lee in 1915—the fact is that he had quite a good education by the minimal standards of that time. He could deftly read, write, and reckon; and more important, from an innate intelligence and the fostering of family and teacher, he loved to learn.

To many, Hill always seemed the embodiment of cold and analytical practicality; but even as a boy, he revealed how realism and romanticism can coexist in the same mind, how in fact the interaction between the two can form the personality. History offers other such cases, like that of Robert Goddard, who was not only a great "rocket scientist" but also an avid reader of science fiction. Like so many other nineteenth-century youths, young Jim Hill fell under the spell of Bonapartism—the fetish of strength of will, the power of one dynamic individual to change the world, the conquering hero. He became so enamored that, no doubt avoiding the name Napoleon as being too pretentious, he gave himself instead the middle name of Jerome, Napoleon's brother. His sister shared these ideas, eventually giving five of her children Bonaparte family names.

For years, well into his maturity, he shared with others another manifestation of his robust romanticism, namely his dream of an imperial career in the Orient. He talked all his life of his youthful idea of building a fleet of steamboats on the Ganges and other legendary rivers; like Alexander the Great or Charles "Chinese" Gordon, he hoped to find his destiny in the fabled lands of the East. As time would prove, this was more than mere pipe-dreaming. His eventual move to Saint Paul was initially intended as the first leg of a journey much farther westward. As Henry Nash Smith demonstrated in his classic *Virgin Land*, Jim Hill—in his vision of creating a destiny reaching across the Pacific to Asia, of carrying a newer and better rendering of civilization around the world to its initial birthplace—shared a dream with many Americans of his time. All through his years, he would quite literally be a dreamer as well as a doer.

In 1848, James Hill, Sr., quit his hardscrabble farm and moved his family into Rockwood, where he bought and managed a roadside inn. Suddenly, his children found themselves in a populous, gregarious, and sometimes raucous environment; it may be that James Jr.'s lifelong moderation in drinking, smoking, and other forms of relaxation and socializing stemmed from what he saw and learned during the next four years. In any event, on Christmas Day of 1852, his childhood, which had been relatively secure and uneventful previously, suddenly ended with the death of his father, after an illness so brief that James Sr. barely had time to have Weatherald draw up a will. This will deeded the farm to his sons, but in fact, the days of family togetherness now came abruptly and tragically to an end.

No longer able to stay in school, the fourteen-year-old James had to go to work. In the spring of 1853, he gained employment "in a general store at the crossroads" of Rockwood owned by Robert Passmore; he earned one to two dollars weekly plus board by performing clerical duties, keeping books, and also milking cows and cutting wood. Here began his first lessons in the knacks of dealing with customers, making ledgers, and handling merchandise; and he proved himself highly industrious and adept at them all. Through the mists of reverie he later wrote, "I was dissatisfied, and yet, when I look back to those days, it was very pleasant."

Also in 1853, eighteen-year-old Mary Elizabeth Hill married a Rockwood-area farmer and began raising a large brood of children; and in the following year Ann Hill, never an effective manager, gave up on the inn and moved with the two boys to the nearby, larger town of Guelph. Here James took up similar employment in a grocery store and then knocked around at various tasks as he approached maturity. Unlike his brother and sister, however, who were content to remain in the Rockwood-Guelph area the rest of their lives, farming their lands and raising a host of children, James dreamed of larger worlds beyond and became restless to leave. Clearly, a rich imagination and a driving ambition were fundamental parts of his nature.

One of Hill's favorite stories involved how, as he approached age eighteen in 1856, he decided to leave the nest. An itinerant trader from Saint Paul, Minnesota, took a liking to the lad after he had voluntarily watered the man's horse. Handing him a tattered copy of a New York newspaper captioned "Splendid Chances for Young Men in the West," the trader said, "Go out there, young man—that's the place for you." Jim carried the copy around, reading and rereading it, until it fell to pieces, and now he finally focused his dreams of adventure on a real decision.

The next day, he cut the last of the wood he had been chopping at the time. Years later, someone left a sign at the spot— "The last tree chopped by James J. Hill"—which remained there long afterward. His brother, Alex, could look after his mother, and thus he could leave. And once he did leave, he would seldom return or look back. He did provide for his mother until her death at age seventy-one in 1876, and later he generously helped his poor brother and sister raise their families over the years, at one point forwarding each of them fifteen thousand dollars to purchase farms. But otherwise, his break with Ontario, once it came, would prove to be definitive.

With the close of winter in 1856, seventeen-year-old James Hill left the known world behind and headed eastward by train to Toronto and then across upper New York State. He carefully planned his itinerary to look over the heartland of the Middle Atlantic states but probably had it in mind from the start to end up at Saint Paul, Minnesota, at the head of navigation on the mighty Mississippi. Saint Paul formed the natural point of embarkation northward to the Canadian prairie frontier for both Americans and Canadians, since the Canadian regions north of the Great Lakes were too rocky, rugged, and lake-strewn to afford easy transit from the east. A number of his friends and acquaintances from Ontario had gone there, some staying and others returning to sing its praises as a land of opportunity.

He left Guelph with six hundred dollars in cash, his life savings, and another ten dollars borrowed from a farmer friend,

James Fairview—money he later handsomely repaid in the amount of five thousand dollars—but seemingly with little else. Alone in the world, he carried all his worldly goods in a simple valise. Actually, he took with him all the tools he would need to succeed in America: a quick intelligence, self-sufficiency, genuine courage, an engaging personality, a fierce ambition, and a remarkable work ethic.

His odyssey of a lifetime took him eastward to Syracuse, where he paused to work for several months on a farm and enhance his finances. Then, on July 4, he headed south to marvel at the wonders of New York City and also to get his pockets picked of some, but not all, of his money. In Philadelphia, he thrilled to the sights and sounds of the opera; and then he traveled on farther south to Baltimore, Richmond, Charleston, and Savannah. He may have been looking for opportunities, but more likely he was mainly sightseeing, sizing up a new nation that had grown mightily but was about to descend into recession—the Panic of 1857—and was about to fall into the maelstrom of the Civil War. Soon he was en route by rail back north to Pittsburgh, Chicago, Dubuque on the Mississippi, and then by steamboat upriver to Saint Paul. He arrived in midsummer 1856, still with most of the six hundred dollars in his pocket.

In selecting his new home, the young man chose wisely, for Saint Paul stood at the pivotal threshold of the dynamically expanding northwestern frontier, a new city barely fifteen years old and already boasting over ten thousand energetic inhabitants. A classically raw frontier city, with hastily built homes and businesses along rolling hills and bottomlands denuded of their natural timber, it occupied one of the most strategic locations in interior America—the head of navigation on the great Mississippi River. It lay on the east bank of the river, near Minnesota's east-central border with Wisconsin.

Just to the west, the Mississippi's great upstream tributary, the Minnesota River, entered the mainstream below the Falls of Saint Anthony. Several miles farther to the west, above the falls, Saint Paul's future "Twin City" of Minneapolis was still in embryonic form, only now anticipating its rise as a water-power and flour-milling center. Just as the Mississippi upstream to the north beckoned toward the vast forestlands of northern Minnesota, the Minnesota River beckoned west and northwest. For beyond its headwaters, along the territory's western border, ran the Red River of the North, which coursed northward to Lake Winnipeg in Canada through a broad and incredibly fertile valley.

The river city teemed with activity. Fort Snelling, a major facility nearby at the mouth of the Minnesota, still held a military garrison. More important, except for the five months of winter when the river lay frozen, hundreds of commercial "packet boat" steamers chugged upstream to city docks and levies. They hauled in all sorts of cargoes for transshipment north and west and carried down such ladings of unprocessed wealth as the furs that Canadian Métis traders brought down from the Red River valley in their big carts with the famous screeching wheels and axles. This was, in fact, the heyday of river commerce. The railroad had just reached the Mississippi downstream at Rock Island, Illinois, making for a shortened transit upstream by boat. Some boats also shuttled from above the Falls of Saint Anthony upriver toward Saint Cloud. Only a few years in the future, railroads would enter the Twin Cities themselves, reducing the river traffic and the levies of Saint Paul to lesser importance, but few thought of that now.

Minnesota Territory continued to evolve rapidly, even under the impact of the Panic of 1857. Two years after Hill's 1856 arrival, it became a state, by which time it already had nearly eighteen thousand farms and ranches and five hundred thousand acres devoted to agriculture, most of them in the state's southern half. Interestingly, the new state, soon to become the flour-milling capital of the world, was still importing flour at this time and only beginning to export. With little competition yet from Saint Anthony, the millers of Saint Paul ground their spring wheat during the winter, warehoused it, and then shipped it downstream with the spring thaws.

Like all the Mississippi River towns, Saint Paul had the reputation of being a tough place, where violence and even murder happened not infrequently. Some still called it by its old name, "Pig's Eye." In fact, it was a remarkably vibrant and cosmopolitan little city. In addition to French-Canadian and mixed-blood Métis traders from Manitoba, other Canadians like Hill drifted in from the Lake Plains region, and many now headed on toward western Canada. Numerous Irish Catholics, refugees from the potato famine, also arrived. Offsetting to a large extent the tempestuous southern border-state immigrants who came upriver, the "Yankee" immigrants, coming across the Upper Midwest, also figured largely, building churches and schools and attempting to force temperance on a hard-drinking populace.

The confident young man who strode into this environment in mid-1856 now pretty well bore the appearance he would keep into middle age. In his youthful prime, Hill was short, solid, and taut, weighing 135 pounds with a twenty-nine-inch waist. With his long torso and short legs, he looked—and was—burly and strong. As he put on 30 more pounds approaching middle age, he kept his powerful demeanor but of course became more stocky and squat-looking, a not unfashionable figure in those days.

By the time Hill was in his early twenties, his hairline had receded sharply. His piercing, darting eyes, accented by a high forehead, held people's attention as he engaged them in characteristic rapid-fire, highly animated conversation, gesturing expansively and driving home his point with jabbing motions of his hands—the embodiment of high energy. Naturally gregarious, he easily made the transition, which had begun at Guelph, from small to large town, and he soon had many acquaintances. As his friend Harlan Hall later remembered, everyone around the Saint Paul levees came to know "Jim" Hill, his name usually rendered as one word, "Jimhill," a man who always seemed up on anything and everything that went on.

It may well be that, as Hill later told countless listeners, he planned to head west or northwest from Saint Paul, to pursue his dreams of oriental or at least far western adventure. But hard reality intervened, and he had to make a living; so he soon changed his plans. Jim found employment where so many others did, on the levees along the Mississippi, the focus of the city's

James Jerome Hill, 1878. Courtesy of James J. Hill Papers, James Jerome Hill Reference Library, Saint Paul, Minnesota.

economic livelihood before the 1860s. Over eight hundred chug-ging steamers coursed to these levees during the busy warm months of the year. His first employer was the firm of Brunson, Lewis and White, who served as local agents for the Dubuque and Saint Paul Company's fleet of Mississippi steamboats. He carried the title of "shipping clerk," and he did maintain the books. But his duties also included handling the incoming and outgoing freight and therefore involved much manual labor on the docks and in the warehouses.

The youth who had known the long hours of loneliness on the farm took naturally to the camaraderie of the levees, and the variety of the work and people suited well his high-energy nature, as did the fact that he could work with little supervision. Consigning and expediting freight, he naturally learned quickly who was doing what and how things worked. He learned, for instance, how the steamship companies could price-gouge local consumers because of the lack of winter service. Only weeks after arriving, he wrote his grandmother back home: "I like this country very well. . . . I am in the Commission and Shipping Business. My salary is twice as much as I could get in Canada."

Over the next several years, he worked for a succession of employers: Brunson, Lewis and White, then the Temple and Beaupre Company, then four years with the firm of Borup and Champlin, a well-regarded organization that handled local business for the powerful Davidson and Galena Packet steamship lines. Borup and Champlin were prominent wholesalers of groceries and many other products and were heavily involved in merchandising and forwarding. Hill worked for them through the hectic Civil War years.

In fact, he came to be regarded locally as the prime reason for Borup and Champlin's reputation for efficiency. He worked incredibly hard, sometimes laboring late into the night, falling asleep at the desk, then getting up for a swim in the river and a cup of black coffee, then going back to work. As he saw it in retrospect, these years formed his apprenticeship, and he learned much more than bookkeeping. He learned how to extract favorable rates from shippers, how to beat back their attempts to inflate rates artificially, how to purchase commodities cheaply and undercut competitors, how to deliver efficiently, and how to cultivate and maintain the loyalties of customers by voluntarily anticipating and looking after their every wish. These lessons would serve him well when he switched over to the world of transportation.

If ever there was a born entrepreneur, it was Jim Hill—highly intelligent, highly motivated, highly acquisitive—and it was only a matter of time before he went into business on his own. He made his first moves in this direction during the long and quiet winters of these early years, when the frozen river halted shipping and when warehouses filled with ladings for the spring, leaving him time to work on the side. He procured oats for sale as horse fodder, including deliveries for the cavalry horses at Fort Snelling, and marketed firewood from the retreating forests around the city. This latter activity took him on journeys around the area, increasingly acquainted him with the hinterland, and soon led further into the fuel business, which became one of the cornerstones of his future fortune.

During 1863–64, he made his first, tentative moves into the Red River trade northward to the faraway and isolated communities of Manitoba, Canada, particularly Fort Garry, the future Winnipeg. Norman W. Kittson, a flinty, tough, and shrewd Scots-Canadian of typical reserve and dour visage, was a veteran of the old, transnational fur trade that had centered at Pembina, on the Minnesota-Manitoba border. A generation older than Hill, Kittson was now one of Saint Paul's leading businessmen and wealthiest individuals, a forwarding agent there for the Hudson's Bay Company (HBC) and a one-time mayor of the city. He also brokered hides and furs brought south by Métis and other non-HBC traders and in turn forwarded merchandise northward to them.

When the all-powerful HBC began frowning on Kittson's work for these independents, he made an arrangement to turn this business over to Hill as an erstwhile partner. The young man had worked hard at befriending Kittson, as he would other older, established men of power later in his career, and the old Scot became much impressed by him. By 1866, Jim found himself more and more heavily involved in the Red River trade, brokering furs for shipment out and consigning the movement of finished products northward to the frontier, and this trade would soon lead him naturally into the actual transportation business northward. Kittson became his close friend, mentor, and longtime business associate. Jim would name his firstborn son James Norman in the older man's honor.

In *Hear That Lonesome Whistle Blow,* Dee Brown characterized the young Hill as "a shaggy, muscular, brawling, two-fisted fighter." This description, nearly total in its inaccuracy, may have derived from an incident that occurred a little over a year after his arrival in this tough town, when he and a friend were walking along one evening and were accosted by a group of inebriated Irishmen who insisted that the two join them for a drink. Provoked and angered, Hill wrote that he "hauled off and planted, one, two in Paddie's grub grinder and knocked him off of the side walk about 8 feet." Another of the hooligans pulled a knife and slashed both Jim and his friend, wounding Hill below the ribs. The police arrived in time to avoid further injury and took away the drunks; Hill's wounds proved to be superficial and soon healed. This was as close as he ever came to being a "brawling . . . fighter."

In fact, Hill drank little, worked hard, and mainly confined his evening and weekend socializing to respectable settings. During these early years in Saint Paul, he seemed to find boardinghouse life much to his liking. As always, he read incessantly. A compulsive joiner in the best tradition of the nineteenth century, he joined and enjoyed the Pioneer Guard militia unit and turned out to be a very good shot, despite the fact that he had only one good eye. Hill also relished the uniformed and ceremonial camaraderie of the local volunteer fire department, namely Minnehaha Engine Company No. 2, particularly the competitive drills and the thrills of racing to fires while appreciative audiences watched. When the Civil War broke out in his adopted country, Jim, with apparently sincere enthusiasm even though he was not a U.S. citizen, joined in forming the First Minnesota Volunteers and was evidently disappointed when his injured eye disqualified him for actual service. Here again, fate had intervened to protect him, since the First Minnesota was badly shot up at Gettysburg; and James J. Hill, like other budding capitalists of the new generation, escaped the horrors of war.

As the years passed, his roots sank deeper into Saint Paul society, and the fragile bonds to his Ontario boyhood frayed. During the winter of 1860–61, he journeyed home to sell the old family

THE ROAD TO SAINT PAUL

farm to a neighbor, giving his mother the eight hundred dollars he received as his part of the profit. After that, he seldom went back again. The final visit came late in 1876 to bury his seventy-one-year-old mother, Ann Dunbar Hill, who died after his early successes but just before his truly dramatic rise to wealth and power.

In selecting a wife, Jim Hill seemed to display the same sort of careful analysis that he employed in his businesses. Notably cautious, he had written a friend back home in 1860, "I am not married yet and am not prepared to say when I will be." He soon began to weaken, however, after meeting Mary Theresa Mehegan, who had been born to newly arrived Irish immigrants in New York City in 1846. Four years later, her father had moved the family to a farm near the Falls of Saint Anthony and then moved once again to Saint Paul soon after. He failed to prosper, and then on Christmas Eve of 1854, he suddenly died—a tragedy eerily similar to that which had fallen on Hill at about the same time. Several years later, her mother entered a second marriage that evidently proved to be unhappy, and her two daughters were raised in Catholic convent schools.

When Jim first met her, around 1860, Mary Mehegan was in her mid-teens. Strikingly Irish in appearance, she had a pretty, roundish face and tended slightly toward plumpness. Naturally reserved, she shied away from the jocularity of frontier Saint Paul and was intensely religious, as she always would be. She counted among her closest friends John Ireland, the future highly influential Catholic bishop, and his sisters. Evidently, she first caught Hill's eye while working as a waitress in a local hotel restaurant, and they struck up a friendship and then a courtship that met all the standards of contemporary decorum. Her confidant Father Caillet advised her forcefully to pursue a future with this promising young fellow, to continue to educate herself "to be his companion."

She did exactly that, apparently with financial help from Hill and his friends, traveling to newly opened Saint Mary's Institute in Milwaukee, which was run by the Sisters of Notre Dame. Here, she studied not only the French and music that would

Mary Mehegan Hill, 1867. Courtesy of James J. Hill Papers, James Jerome Hill Reference Library, Saint Paul, Minnesota.

make her a refined lady but also such practical pursuits as sewing, tapestry, and needlepoint. And here Jim visited her and, on carefully chaperoned walks, asked her if she could bring herself to accompany him "if he should organize a line of steamboats on the Ganges River," the old chimera that lingered on.

His peculiar romantic musings evidently set well with her, for in June 1864 they became engaged. And on August 19, 1867, they became husband and wife, wed in the bishop's home rather than the church because Hill would not agree to become a Catholic, although he did agree that the children would be raised Catholics. The ceremony was a simple one, with only the bride's family and Hill's close friend Stanford Newell present. They took the train to Chicago and Milwaukee for their honeymoon and returned to their new home on Pearl (later Grove) Street in Saint Paul.

They formed an exceptionally close bond, and the couple remained harmoniously dedicated to one another throughout their long life together. Both of them held strongly traditional views about marriage and family, and no scandal or even accusation ever arose about their relationship. Even by Victorian standards, Mary Hill was a very conservative woman, and those women closest to her commented often about her deference and even subservience to her iron-willed, occasionally insufferable husband. Her world centered on him, on the many children that soon arrived, and on her home and faith. If she did in fact kowtow to James J. Hill—so did nearly everyone else in time!

The Hills wasted no time in beginning what soon became a large, happy, and highly regarded family. Their firstborn, Mary Frances ("Mamie"), arrived the year after their marriage, 1868, followed by James Norman in 1869, Louis in 1872, Clara in 1874, and Katy in 1875, eventually to be followed by four more daughters—Charlotte, Ruth, Rachel, and Gertrude—and by a final son, Walter, whose birth finally rounded out the family in 1885. Frail from birth, little Katy died a year after her birth, the only one of their many children who did not live to maturity. Hoping to console his bereaved wife, whose own health was fragile after childbearing, Jim Hill took her east that fall to view the wonder of the day, the Centennial Exposition at Philadelphia.

During his first decade as husband and father, Hill provided an ever-rising standard of living for his growing family. At the time of his marriage, he had figured that once he had amassed $100,000—a modest, little fortune in those days—he would retire and devote himself to a life of study, philanthropy, and fatherhood. But like other ambitiously driven entrepreneurs of his time, he soon abandoned that dream. Eleven years later, at the time he entered the world of railroading, he would count assets of $150,000, and this would prove to be only a modest beginning.

In 1871, the Hills purchased a small home in Saint Paul's "Lowertown," on the corner of Ninth and Canada Streets, next door to his close friend Henry Upham, who became president of the First National Bank. Then, five years later, Jim razed this home and, acting as his own contractor, began building at the same site a substantial mansion. During construction, the family moved temporarily to a country place outside town at Dayton's Bluff. The mansion, into which the family moved in 1878, was built of white brick from Wisconsin and rested in one of Saint Paul's best neighborhoods, with close family friends all around. It boasted stained-glass windows, a coal furnace, and a third-floor classroom where the older children were privately tutored by a church-sanctioned scholar, August Chemidlin, as well as servants' quarters and facing stables. Sadly, this once choice site is now a vacant lot near the Interstate 94 loop in downtown Saint Paul.

By the mid-1870s, the Hills were living in relative luxury according to the standards of the time, with fine horses and teams, a grand piano in the living room, and a large diamond ring for Mary. To escape the sultriness of Saint Paul summers, James sent his wife and children to retreats like Lake Elmo and Lake Pepin, down the Mississippi, joining them on weekends.

On Sundays he would, in these early days, accompany his family to mass, then head to the office in the afternoon and return home for dinner, with everyone formally attired. As his daughter Clara recalled, "Neighbors lived in close relationship with each other, and childhood was passed in a very stable world." Soon Hill began skipping mass and heading directly to work. The only thing that Hill refused to give his family was more of himself, for he labored long hours into the night with only partial respites on weekends. Aside from rides behind his horse teams and occasional bird hunting, he permitted himself few diversions in his relentless drive to achieve wealth and status.

In the spring of 1865, as the Civil War finally ground to an end, and still two years before his marriage, Jim Hill began a series of career thrusts that moved him decisively away from employment for others and toward independent entrepreneurship. Aided by William Wellington, yet another well-established, older friend, he secured the Saint Paul agency for the powerful Northwest Packet Company, which had gained a near-monopoly over an upper Mississippi steamboat trade that was already beginning to lose its hegemony to the newly arriving rails. Working also as an independent agent, Hill applied his well-established contacts and knowledge of the local marketplace to serve not only the freight and passenger needs of the packet line but also those of its close affiliate, the Milwaukee and Mississippi Railroad.

A year later, in partnership with Wellington and George Blanchard, he proudly formed the firm of James J. Hill Company. He negotiated an exclusive arrangement as forwarding agent for the Saint Paul and Pacific Railroad whereby his firm would transfer produce from riverboats to this firm's rails that pointed westward to Minneapolis and up the Minnesota and Mississippi Valleys. The railroad, which Hill would one day command, leased him a superb riverfront location, on which he built a large warehouse that served as a transfer facility. Within the walls of this one, 350-foot-long building on the levee on Silbey Street, his employees could buck cargoes directly up from a lower level that faced the docks to an upper level that faced the rails. This arrangement drastically reduced the costs of transfer, which had earlier necessitated loading goods onto wagons to move up the steep slope from boat to train.

Agent Hill would simultaneously book cargoes headed north by train to Saint Cloud and from there on by cart or wagon. In addition, his warehouse could handily store manifests for seasonal distribution, such as cordwood cut in the summer for sale in the winter or flour ground in Minneapolis in the winter for shipment downstream in the spring. Competition made business tough in 1866, but conditions improved markedly in 1867, and his joint businesses were soon prospering.

As his business expanded rapidly in the latter year, Hill reorganized his enterprise with the title James J. Hill and Company.

Hill's warehouse facility on the Mississippi, 1867. Courtesy of James J. Hill
Papers, James Jerome Hill Reference Library, Saint Paul, Minnesota.

He brought in as his partner, in charge of the transportation side
of the firm, Egbert Litchfield, whose two half-brothers both exercised key roles in the leadership of the fledgling Saint Paul and
Pacific Railroad. This move, of course, pulled Hill more closely
into the orbits both of the railroad and of this powerful Minnesota
family, which evidently helped finance his warehouse. The warehouse became a beehive of activity as natural products ranging
from flour and fuel to hay moved through its doors, headed both
south downriver and north and west up the railroad.

    Meanwhile, Jim Hill vastly expanded his fuel business. In 1869
he and partners Chauncey Griggs and John Armstrong created a
concern called Hill, Griggs and Company, concentrating at first
on the cordwood business that he had been interested in for
several years. Logging primarily off forestlands to the north, they
sold heavily, once again, to the railroad, and also to the large
home and commercial markets in the fast-growing Twin Cities.

But here, as elsewhere by the early 1870s, coal was crowding fuelwood from the market; and as usual, Hill quickly got out in front of the emerging trend.

Hill's rise to the top of a burgeoning local coal business is interesting not only because it formed a cornerstone of his career and generated venture capital for later investments but also because it revealed for the first time his instincts toward what friends would call vertical and rational integration of an industry and what foes would call ruthless monopolization. Thoroughly immersing himself in the details of the business through reading and correspondence, he worked with Chicago agent Robert Law to purchase mass tonnages of high-quality anthracite coal.

Then, as the size of his shipments and thus also his bargaining power grew, he remorselessly leveraged railroads to deliver the coal from the Chicago and Milwaukee areas at preferred rates— learning in the process skills that would serve him well when he ended up at the other end of the transportation bargaining table. In 1872 he formed a purchasing "pool" with two other large Twin Cities firms; and two years later, Hill, Griggs and Company loomed over all of its competitors, selling five thousand tons of anthracite yearly.

Hill and his competitors brought in increasing cargoes of coal by rail from the East, so that coal became a major component of westbound freights on what would become the Chicago and Northwestern. They also imported coal via large steel freighters across Lake Superior to Duluth and then south to the Twin Cities via the Lake Superior and Mississippi Railroad. By 1873, Hill and his partners controlled nearly one-third of the forty thousand tons traveling this route annually, and he formed with the Great Lakes shipping magnate Mark Hanna a business relationship that would bear fruit long into the future. Hill, Griggs and Company built large dock-loading facilities in Duluth and a big weatherproof storage facility at trackside in Saint Paul. Eventually, Hill bought up his own sources of soft coal at Fort Dodge, Iowa, one hundred miles to the south, and would one day build a line to connect to them.

In his coal dealings, as in others to come, Jim Hill proved

himself a tough, relentless, and driven taskmaster and, frequently, a hard man to get along with. Convinced that Griggs did not measure up, he forced a parting of the ways in 1875 and formed a new partnership with his associates Armstrong, George Acker, and Edward Saunders. When Colonel Griggs went independent, Hill ruthlessly employed his influence with the railroads to keep Griggs from getting preferred rates on shipments.

Ever the pragmatist as well as the tough competitor, Hill also eventually presaged another future characteristic when he abruptly changed course and parleyed with his chief competitors to bring peace to the area coal industry by joining together in a market-sharing consortium. In the spring of 1877, they formed the Northwestern Fuel Company, capitalized at $100,000, with Hill as president and Griggs as vice-president; the company was a highly efficient, integrated organization that served its customers very well. Within little over a year, Hill would depart the independent coal business to devote his full energies and attention to railroading.

But he would remain in the coal business, as it related to railroading, for the rest of his long career. It had taught him much and had demonstrated a salient fact of his entirely pragmatic business personality. When competition suited him in entering a market, he competed fiercely. But when competition became wasteful to him, he hesitated not a whit to end it, even if this meant joining with old enemies and creating an unblushing situation of monopoly.

The breadth of the young entrepreneur's business activities seems quite remarkable. He frequently bought up machinery and buildings at foreclosure sales and resold them for tidy profits, items as diverse as iron foundry equipment and saloon furniture. Sometimes he failed, but other times he profited handsomely, learning in the process more and more about ever-widening ranges of endeavor. In truth, he represented an especially virulent example of the ever-vigilant frontier merchant, always watching for the main chance. By the 1870s, the star of opportunity beckoned more from the north—from the broad Red River valley and the expansive Canadian prairies.

The Red River of the North, heading in a succession of lakes that form the current Minnesota–South Dakota border, is often confused with the turbid river of the same name that forms the Texas-Oklahoma boundary, far to the south. Flowing north to Lake Winnipeg, the northern Red forms the border between Minnesota and North Dakota and drains a broad, well-watered, and nearly treeless alluvial plain of twelve thousand square miles. Extending well into both western Minnesota and eastern North Dakota, as well as across southern Manitoba downstream, the valley in the early 1870s was only beginning to demonstrate its deceptive fertility but was about to become one of the world's great granaries. During the period 1878–84, according to historian Stanley Murray, it would attract "more land seekers than any [other] area of comparable size in North America."

North of the forty-ninth parallel boundary, the modern Canadian state was only now beginning to coalesce. When Great Britain had enacted the British North America Act in 1867, it had created the Dominion of Canada, the locus of which lay in the four eastern provinces of New Brunswick, Nova Scotia, Quebec, and Ontario. In the vast, nearly unpopulated regions northwest of the Great Lakes, the plains area hitherto known as "Assiniboia" came into the fold with the Manitoba Act of 1870, and faraway British Columbia followed the next year.

As the old Hudson's Bay Company surrendered its authority over these lands to the new dominion, the plains expanses northwest of Minnesota seethed with unrest. The scattered populace, dominated by French-Indian Métis, feared a future devoid of their old HBC business partner and dominated by a new and unknown government. Led by the fiery Louis Riel, the plains Métis rebelled in 1869, and a thoroughly frightened Canadian government sent out the nation's most senior HBC officer, Donald A. Smith, to calm the situation. These events, and Smith particularly, would figure large in Jim Hill's future.

A truly self-made man, Smith had come to Canada as a penniless Scottish immigrant back in the 1830s and had slowly climbed the HBC ladder through years of hard service. Year after year of lonely work at remote locales such as Labrador and Winnipeg and miles of travel through frozen wastes had failed to dampen his enthusiasm and had underscored his abilities. In 1869, the frenetic, hard-driving little man got his reward with selection as overseas governor of the entire Hudson's Bay Company.

Although Hill had first become interested in the Red River–Canadian trade in casual partnership with Kittson several years earlier, he did not venture down the valley and into Manitoba until March 1870. On this trip, he aimed both to look over the land and, voluntarily, to size up the situation following the Métis revolt at Fort Garry (Winnipeg) for Canadian Provincial Secretary of State Joseph Howe. The winter journey, which he understandably loved to recount for the rest of his life, involved hard travel by dog train, horseback, and even river raft. It tested both his resolve and his stamina, and it amply demonstrated his grit.

On the journey, near Pembina along the Canadian border, he first met Smith; in long conversations, the two highly energetic men discovered that they had much in common, including a belief that the Canadian government must move quickly to assert its authority in the West. The trip home in April proved equally challenging, particularly when Hill had to design a makeshift lever-pulley with a wagon wheel, rope, and forked stick to force the dislocated shoulder of his mixed-blood guide back into its socket.

As a result of this reconnaissance, and others that soon followed, Hill became convinced of the wonderful fertility of the Red River valley, and with his partners he now moved energetically into the trade. The route to the intermittently navigable Red headed northwestward from the Twin Cities via the Saint Paul and Pacific Railroad. It then extended by wagon to the head of navigation—at Breckenridge, Minnesota, just north of the current North Dakota–South Dakota border, during high stream flows and at points north in the drier months—all the way up to future Grand Forks, North Dakota, where the Red Lake River flows into the Red.

From Breckenridge and points north, flatboats could easily course all the winding way north down the sluggish river to Fort Garry; and one lone steamer, Kittson's *International*, working for the HBC, navigated both ways. Railroads soon spanned all the way to the Red, making the journey much simpler. The Northern Pacific, coming west from Duluth, soon reached the river downstream at Moorhead. And then the Saint Paul and Pacific, out of the Twin Cities, connected upstream in 1871 to Breckenridge.

The firm of Hill, Griggs and Company began rafting on the Red River in 1870, with Chauncey Griggs's brother Alexander, a veteran of Mississippi steamboating, brought into the firm. Early in 1871, the partners took the decisive step of having a shallow-draft steamboat built, which they launched on the Red as the *Selkirk,* directly challenging the monopoly of Hill's erstwhile partner Kittson. With Hill aboard, the steamer moved downriver in April, carrying 115 passengers and 150 tons of freight. Fort Garry was not much to see: the future Winnipeg consisted of just under 250 people and a meandering array of crude saloons, saw-mills, and trading posts. But within ten years, Winnipeg would be the queen city of the prairies, with over 8,000 inhabitants. And by the time the *Selkirk* finished its second journey, it had already repaid the costs of its construction. During 1871–72, as the HBC presence steadily dwindled, Hill and his partners competed head to head with former HBC-man Kittson for the fast-growing river trade. Watching the young Saint Paul merchant's aggressiveness, Donald Smith, Kittson's superior, concluded: "Hill must be a very able man. We must not be caught napping."

Yet this commerce was merely a final phase of the era of steamboat traffic. Although profits could soar, they were also highly seasonal. The Red lay frozen for over half the year, and the steamers sometimes stood frozen in place throughout the winter along the bends of the muddy river. Once railroads reached the Red, all they needed to do to eliminate river traffic altogether was stretch their tracks northward parallel to the river, providing year-around, all-weather service. The Saint Paul and Pacific, reaching the river in the same year that Hill launched his steamboat, now performed what Hill biographer Albro Martin aptly terms the classic function of a frontier railroad: it joined the heads of navigation on two great waterways. For the next nine

years, a depressed hiatus period in which rail building was dormant, the steamers on the Red served as tendrils or forward
extensions of the stalled rails.

Although the greater share of Hill's warehousing-forwarding
business still centered in the Twin Cities area, during this brief
period the Red River trade captured his imagination and began
to take more and more of his time. He fretted over low water
levels and muddy and snowy roads before the rails reached the
Red, and he matched the rough, rate-cutting tactics of Kittson
blow for blow. Bulky cargoes of hide and fur still constituted a
major part of the ladings, but agricultural production in the
valley was increasing geometrically and clearly laid claim to the
future. To Hill, it became ever more clear that the entire valley,
all the way to the shores of Lakes Manitoba and Winnipeg, was
about to become one giant wheat field.

In this enterprise, just as in the fuel business, Jim Hill's behavior foretold future and larger happenings. He quickly moved
from tough, all-out competition to an accord with the opposition. In 1872, Hill, Griggs and Company quietly merged with the
Kittson operation to form the Red River Transportation Company, a $100,000 firm whose two steamboats soon grew to five.
The accord rationalized the business but soon also led to complaints about monopoly. Other outfits, on both sides of the
boundary, attempted to compete with the company during the
several years it was in operation, but they were ruthlessly sup-
pressed.

For instance, when angry Winnipeg businessmen formed the
Merchants International Steamboat Company to break the monopoly, Kittson and Hill slashed rates to the point of loss; and,
wondrous to tell, the *International* even "accidentally" rammed
and sank their vessel. The Red River Transportation Company
thus maintained its hold on the river and its high rates. Even
when the firm did lower rates with its streamlined organization,
the Canadians downstream protested constantly, loudly, and jus-
tifiably about the "monopoly" that was gouging them.

Steamboating on the Red had only a few years to go. By the
close of the 1870s, advancing rails would seal its doom. This

might have meant that James Hill's move into the business would prove to be a dead end, but in fact, it proved to be quite the opposite. His enterprises now bracketed the stalled-out Saint Paul and Pacific Railroad on both ends. In Saint Paul, his ware-housing-merchandising business buttressed the railroad at its base of operations. Even by 1869, Hill figured that his agency was providing the road with fully 30 percent of all its traffic.

On the Red, his steamboating-forwarding business served as the advance staging arm of a railroad temporarily too weak to move forward to its natural termini. Unlike most Minnesotans, who viewed the Saint Paul and Pacific as a near-worthless dere-lict, Hill viewed it as a miracle waiting to happen, a potentially wondrous enterprise simply lacking competent leadership. He studied the road constantly, reading every scrap of information he could find about it and boring anyone who would listen with endless detail as to what it could one day be. Thus would his move into river transportation lead naturally to an incredibly promising career in railroading.

As he approached the climactic year of 1878, the year in which he would cross the threshold from local to regional and ulti-mately national significance, James J. Hill—now in his late thirties—could take considerable pride in what he had already accomplished. He had amassed a modest fortune. He provided his growing family with an enviable life-style and enjoyed the reputation of being one of his city's leading businessmen, a man to reckon with.

The young entrepreneur who would now attempt his leap into the big time brought some highly impressive assets to the en-deavor: a well-established and respected area business, a breadth of financial interests that ranged from warehousing and broker-ing to fuel and transportation, and a knowledge of the regional economy that was probably unparalleled. Unlike most pioneer railroad executives, he knew from the outset how cleverly and tough-mindedly shippers and clients operated, how they went about extorting "rebates," for example, from the railroads—even on the ladings of competing shippers—in return for large contracts with the carriers. In short, as railroad historian Julius

Grodinsky comments, he possessed a priceless advantage compared with most other nineteenth-century rail titans. Rather than coming from the outside world of finance, as most of them did, he arose from the inside world of freighting and transportation, and he knew this world in all its complexities. He was about to demonstrate how certain well-established, regional capitalists on the frontier could challenge and even best larger eastern interests.

CHAPTER 2

The Manitoba

THE railroad that became the life mission of James J. Hill, and that would one day evolve into the Great Northern, came into existence in the surge of new rail charters of 1853–57, a period that coincided with Hill's arrival in Saint Paul and that also formed a seedtime of American rail construction. Bearing a typically grandiose title, the Minnesota and Pacific Railroad was chartered by the territorial legislature in 1857 to span Minnesota on an east-west axis. From Stillwater on the Saint Croix River, the territory's eastern border with Wisconsin, its charter pointed westward to nearby Saint Paul.

From there, its "Main Line" aimed on to the west through rich, partially forested hill country toward Breckenridge, the upper-end head of navigation on the Red River, the territory's western boundary with Dakota. A second, "Branch Line" projected northwestward upstream from the Twin Cities along the east bank of the Mississippi toward Saint Cloud and beyond to Crow Wing and ultimately to far-off Saint Vincent, where the Red River crossed the Canadian boundary in far northwestern Minnesota. However, as events eventually unfolded, the Branch Line would instead bend northwest from Saint Cloud, paralleling the Main Line and eventually joining it beyond Alexandria and Fergus Falls at Barnesville in west-central Minnesota. From that point on, the combined lines would descend the Red River valley, heading straight north to Saint Vincent. As Ralph Hidy and his coauthors note in their authoritative corporate history of the Great Northern Railway, the Minnesota and Pacific could legitimately claim to be the state's first active railroad, evolving to offer a southeast-northwest route linking the head of navigation on the Mississippi with the head of navigation on the turbid, meandering Red.

One of the hoariest, and most mischievous, of all the many

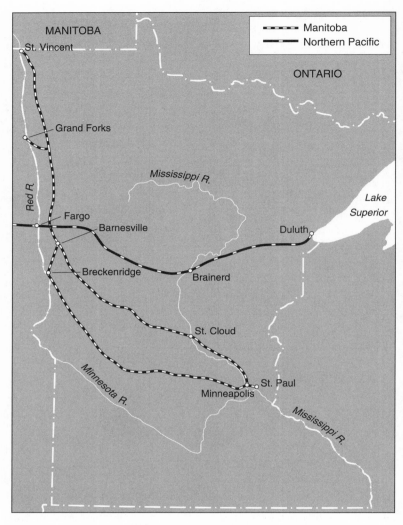

Minnesota: The Northern Pacific and the Saint Paul, Minneapolis, and Manitoba Railroads, 1878–79.

legends surrounding Hill is the story, still widely repeated today, that rhapsodizes about how he built a great transcontinental line without the benefit of a federal land grant. This is considerably less than a half-truth. In fact, the Minnesota and Pacific received an initial grant of 2.46 million acres from the territorial legislature, lands that the legislature in turn had received from Congress. Typically, the Minnesota and Pacific grant lay in a checkerboard of alternating private and public sections, first six and then ten sections per mile of track.

Reaching only as far west as the valley of the Red, this land grant appears rather puny when compared with the huge swaths given to transcontinentals like the Northern and Southern Pacific lines or with the total of more than 175 million acres bestowed on all railroads by the federal and state governments between 1850 and 1871. However, as economic historian John B. Rae notes, the Minnesota and Pacific grant ranked "seventh largest of the original seventy-five railroad grants and the largest of those in which the land was given to a state rather than directly to a railroad company."

Equally significant, unlike the lands bestowed on the transcontinental roads, lands that consisted heavily of far-off and arid stretches, this grant lay near at hand, mostly in the humid and fertile Red River valley. Thus did the roots of the great Hill fortune sprout, like those of so many other "self-made men" who "built the West," from the rich seedbed of federal subsidy. This is not necessarily an opprobrium; it is simply the truth. The land grant presented a wonderful opportunity, and he and his associates had the grit to seize it.

Like many another frontier railroad, this one got off to a fitful start. Speculators, who came to include even that New York prince of rail plungers Russell Sage, milked it of its resources and potential profits and left very little accomplished. Among the tricks they employed was the use of construction companies that overcharged the railroad, thus drawing excess profits, and left both the road and its owners holding the bag, a device later made notorious in the building of the Union Pacific transcontinental. Construction on the Minnesota and Pacific began in the autumn of 1857, and in the following year the legislature ponied up a $5 million bond issue to support it. But in 1860, amid a rising chorus of criticism, the road defaulted and failed. The state foreclosed the Minnesota and Pacific's mortgage and purchased its assets for $1,000.

In the wartime tempest of 1862, the state legislature reorganized the road as the Saint Paul and Pacific Railroad Company. Finally, later that year, trains pulled by the pioneer engine "William Crooks"—a funnel-stacked 4-4-0 American locomotive that would become a sort of mascot of the corporation as the first engine to operate in the region—began chugging along the key ten-mile stretch between Saint Paul and Saint Anthony.

To help the road break out of its financial miasma, the legislature gathered its existing properties into a separate firm, called the First Division of the Saint Paul and Pacific Railroad. Speculator E. B. Litchfield gathered up the stock of the firm and pressed ahead, with his main emphasis on the more strategic Branch Line, which did not at first require the expense of bridging the Mississippi. Rails extended northwest to Sauk Rapids, just beyond Saint Cloud, on the Branch Line by 1867, but construction west via Minneapolis on the Main Line proceeded only at a snail's pace. Building ahead of demand, these typical rail speculators succeeded mainly in indebting their road.

Over the next several years, as the nation began its recovery from the Civil War, the Saint Paul and Pacific made little further progress. By 1871, the Main Line reached westward only to Benson, far short of the Red River, and the end of track on the Branch Line remained where it had been four years earlier. The road had procured deeds on its land grant for fewer than nine hundred thousand acres. To agitated Minnesotans, pining after the rails that would link them to national markets and hasten the immigration already coming their way, the road seemed a sorry proposition: "two streaks of rust and a right of way." Some of them casually helped themselves to the piles of wooden ties, lying along the unfinished track, for fenceposts and firewood.

While Minnesota's oldest railroad thus languished, the attention of the Northwest riveted on the mighty Northern Pacific

(NP), chartered by Congress in 1864. This transcontinental system was projected to link the westernmost arm of the Great Lakes—Lake Superior at Duluth—to some harbor on Puget Sound on the Pacific; it was also authorized to build a western branch track to Portland, near the mouth of the largest of western rivers, the Columbia. Unlike the original transcontinental, the Union Pacific–Central Pacific system to the south, whose charter preceded it by two years, the NP received no subsidy package of federal loans. But it got instead what amounted to the greatest subsidy Uncle Sam ever bestowed on a private entity: a land grant of twenty sections per mile of track in the states it crossed and forty sections per mile in the territories, constituting a vast, forty-seven-million-acre checkerboard of alternating public and private sections sprawling across the "northern tier" of the American West.

The NP offered an indescribably rich prize to potential builder-investors, but equally important, its charter also bore grave liabilities regarding its future as a viable and competitive carrier. Whoever undertook its construction would naturally build westward as rapidly as possible in order to meet the time lines for receiving the federal land grants. They would have little incentive to build well or to construct the all-important "spur" lines that would funnel regional traffic to the road and guard it from flank attacks by competitors. In any case, the railroad charter shortsightedly limited the ability to build and manage such spurs.

Another simple but critical weakness involved the eastern terminus of the railroad. Duluth made a seemingly natural eastern hub as a Great Lakes port; but the fast-growing Twin Cities—the clearly evolving center of regional economic activity and the natural base for the railroad—lay far to the south of its trunk line and would be accessible only by a branch. In sum, this key railroad, like its predecessor, would be a predictable target for speculators, would be hastily and poorly constructed far ahead of demand, and would be naturally entangled with the road that did reach northwest from the Twin Cities—the Saint Paul and Pacific (SP&P).

After several false starts, construction of the NP surged forward in 1870 under the guiding hand of Jay Cooke, of Philadelphia, who had risen to the forefront of American banking as the leading financier of the Union cause in the Civil War. Over the next three years, its rails reached both westward from Duluth to Bismarck, in central Dakota Territory on the westward-bending Missouri River, and northward from Kalama, in Washington Territory on the north bank of the lower Columbia River, toward the NP's new port city of Tacoma on Puget Sound. Meanwhile, Cooke and his associates ballyhooed the road so extravagantly that its route became known jocularly as "Jay Cooke's Banana Belt," where a mild climate and fertile soils guaranteed good crops and the good life.

During this first burst of NP construction, certain of its executives, particularly George Wright and William Moorhead, saw clearly the wisdom of acquiring control of the SP&P and thus locking up a potential rival. A northern spur of the Branch Line out of Saint Cloud, when completed along the Mississippi, would connect with the NP at Brainerd in central Minnesota, offering their road a natural route into the Twin Cities.

And farther west, the combined Main and Branch Lines, when completed and melded together at Barnesville, projected a critically important extension, due north along the east side of the Red River, all the way to the Canadian border. This Saint Vincent Extension also crossed the NP, at Glyndon, just east of Fargo-Moorhead, the new sister cities that bestrode the Minnesota-Dakota border. Naturally, the planned Saint Vincent Extension of the SP&P proved highly enticing to the NP, offering it potential spurs north and south that could control the Red River valley.

Frustrated at their lack of progress in advancing the SP&P, both its president, George Becker, and E. B. Litchfield, the contractor who with his brothers was the main investor in the road, agreed to deliver majority control of their operation to the NP when Cooke authorized an offer. In December 1870, the NP bought control of the First Division of the SP&P. Having made this wise decision, however, the NP arguably erred in not placing its main emphasis on building the SP&P's Branch Line quickly to

Brainerd, or in not building tracks of its own along the west bank of the Mississippi, and thereby bringing the Twin Cities into its orbit. The problem was, consistently, that the NP simply lacked the cash to do all the building that it needed to do.

It focused instead on building rapidly westward toward Bismarck, Dakota Territory, and thus securing its land grant as rapidly as possible. As it moved west after 1870, the NP concentrated what little capital it did pump into its SP&P subsidiary mainly into completing the Main Line to Breckenridge and the Saint Vincent Extension, which now had a land grant of its own, bringing the total for the road to nearly three million acres. Thus the NP developers, motivated by a federal land-grant policy that encouraged reckless building, isolated the Twin Cities.

Herein lies one of the most interesting "might-have-beens" in the history of the Northwest. Had the NP built more conservatively and soundly, anchoring the SP&P as its eastern matrix, it would probably have dominated the entire region permanently, and there would never have evolved a competing Great Northern system. But both the NP and its promoter had become impossibly overextended in all of this, and in 1873 both fell into bankruptcy. Cooke's fall, in turn, precipitated the so-called Panic of 1873, the worst depression the United States had yet seen. The NP lay dormant and discredited through the mid-1870s. So too, of course, did its subsidiary the SP&P, now once again destitute but no longer the creature of the NP.

All of this appalled Minnesotans and Dakotans, who considered both railroads to be run by derelicts at best and thieves at worst. Jim Hill, probably the best informed of all outside observers, agreed with this low opinion of the management of both roads. But he realized better than others that the SP&P had great potential—if, that is, its lines could somehow be completed before the deadlines expired for completing the trackage and securing the land grants. As a steamboater on the Red, he knew the potential value of the farmlands lying along the Saint Vincent Extension, many of these lands the potential property of this railroad. And as a freight-warehouse-fuel merchant in the Twin

Cities, he knew well what the SP&P meant to the cities and what the cities meant to the entire rail system of Minnesota.

To the casual observer, certainly, the SP&P seemed now more than ever hopelessly in disarray, like many other regional "streaks of rust" reddening and flaking away in the wake of the 1873 Panic. Majority control of its stock lay in the hands of E. Darwin Litchfield, the brother of E. B., who had regained control after the failure of the NP. But the majority of the bond issue of the First Division, now badly depreciated, belonged to a consortium of Dutch investors, who had begun purchasing it during Sage's machinations, figuring to cash in big. Since Litchfield owned majority control of the stock and the Dutch bondholders held first claim on the railroad's assets, both sides parried with one another, desperate to get some return on their endangered investments or to get out of them altogether.

Far removed from the situation, and poorly informed, the Dutch investors hired a prominent New York City banker, John S. Kennedy, to represent them. Kennedy, yet another reserved, laconic, and hard-nosed Scot, was a prosperous man who was about to become very wealthy and was also due soon to become one of James J. Hill's closest associates. One of New York's most prominent bankers and a close friend of J. P. Morgan's, the fastidious Kennedy had a wealth of experience in railroad finance, and his Scottish-American Investment Company lent him ready access to venture capital.

Mainly due to Kennedy's influence, the district court had appointed Jesse P. Farley, of Dubuque, Iowa, as the receiver in charge of managing the bankrupt SP&P and its further construction under a board of trustees. Farley seemed then, and seems now, a peculiar, even suspicious choice for Kennedy and the court to have made as a railroad receiver and manager. Approaching old age, he was dim-witted, contentious, and obviously avaricious. The Amsterdam investors knew he was "uneducated," and Kennedy himself once referred to him as "stupid." During three years of his management, the SP&P spent only $100,000 on building and maintenance and seemed headed merely to oblivion.

However, at least two other men agreed with Jim Hill that the

SP&P offered intriguing possibilities. On their travels up and down the Red River and across the flat valley floor, Hill and his stoic, old partner Norman Kittson got to know the railroad very well and became intimately acquainted with Farley and his lazy modus operandi. In 1873, their shrewd and frenetic Canadian friend Donald Smith, of the Hudson's Bay Company, dropped by, and the three of them soon began evolving a remarkable scheme. Smith brought a good deal to the exchange, more in any apparent sense than the other two. He was, in fact, one of Canada's most prominent men, not only as chief commissioner of the Hudson's Bay Company but also as a director of the Bank of Montreal and an outspoken, Conservative member of the general dominion parliament in Ottawa as well as the provincial assembly in Winnipeg.

Smith had been a key participant in the political debates and struggles surrounding the projected, transcontinental Canadian Pacific Railroad, an idea that had earlier run aground and was now very contentious. Like Hill and Kittson, he knew the extreme difficulty of trying to run an all-Canadian line westward from the Saint Lawrence Valley through the rocky, lake-strewn, and nearly unpopulated lands north of the Great Lakes. Rather Smith, Hill, and Kittson saw that the natural passageway to western Canada lay southwest across Ontario, Sault Sainte Marie, and Lake Superior to Duluth and then northwest through American territory in Minnesota to the Red River and on north to Winnipeg—in other words, in a southern loop that avoided the forbidding Canadian Precambrian Shield country.

Winnipeg, the gateway to the Canadian plains and the entire Canadian West, was the key. And so, therefore, was the SP&P Railroad, which naturally formed the western end of the arc west from the Great Lakes region to Winnipeg, touching, as it did, the Canadian border less than two hundred miles south of that city. It would be an easy matter for Canadian investors, such as Smith, to build a connecting line from Winnipeg south to meet the SP&P at the boundary, thereby making Winnipeg the staging point for a future Canadian Pacific aimed westward toward the Pacific. And so an alliance was born.

Each of the three men was wealthy, but not amply so, and it would require great wealth as well as herculean effort to secure even a chance at such a large property. In fact, such an enterprise seemed impossible. For one thing, the Minnesota legislature had enacted a law making the transfer of the SP&P land grant to any new company illegal. For another, the deadlines for completion of the road in order to gain the land grants drew ever nearer. For yet another, E. Darwin Litchfield, whom members of the group were soon genially calling "the old rat," was ornery, obstreperous, and quite determined to keep his stock and complete the railroad himself. And yet, as Hill, who knew the road better than anyone else, including Farley, constantly argued to his friends, the potential prize defied description. Indeed, he seemed completely fixated on the project. Many years later, his banker friend Henry Upham recalled that Jim had spoken of it to him "probably several hundred times" during the mid-1870s.

As Albro Martin points out in his close analysis of the man, Hill calculated the transaction in the following manner. The depreciated $15 million in bonds, most of them in the hands of the Dutch, had to be acquired, at rates—depending on the class of issue—ranging from eleven to eighty cents on the dollar. This would require about $4.6 million. Over $900,000 more would be needed to build the Main Line on to Saint Vincent and to finish incomplete sections in between and meet the terms of the land grants, for a total investment of slightly more than $5.5 million.

The assets, real and potential, that this investment could acquire were awesome: $11.4 million in trackage, $1.2 million in various equipment and property, $200,000 in townsites, and over 2.6 million acres of prime land conservatively valued at $6.7 million. Thus, if properly done, an investment of $5.5 million could yield a near-term return of $19.3 million. And this was only the beginning! As Hill well knew, even under the tutelage of someone like Farley, the SP&P clearly showed marked earning potential; and as the economy began improving in the mid-1870s, more and more immigrants were steadily moving into western Minnesota. He assured his partners that, properly run, the road could quickly show annual increased earnings of $600,000–$800,000. Here stood the kind of opportunity that came only with the opening of a new frontier, once in a lifetime—once in many lifetimes.

Unfortunately for the threesome, however, the princely sum of $5.5 million lay far beyond their collective means in this age of good, hard dollars worth several times their descendants of to-day. They needed far more capital than they had, or even than they could borrow, and thus they must look for others to join them. Smith's cousin George Stephen began to show promise as a fourth "associate" as Smith worked month after month to warm him to their plan.

Unlike his cousin, who was eleven years his senior, Stephen was a natural aristocrat, a "man of parts," as they said in those days. Tall and slender, with soulful eyes, he was polished and reserved in dress and demeanor, a very private person whose stoicism masked a driving ambition and a genuine if well-founded arro-gance. Like the others, Stephen was of Scottish ancestry; he had made good money in dry goods, steel, and banking and in 1876 became president of the Bank of Montreal. He ranked, even at a young age, as one of Canada's foremost financiers; and as his cousin Smith began telling him of the potential of the SP&P, he would soon become, along with Hill, one of its two driving forces.

Through 1874 and 1875 and into 1876, the threesome gradually evolved into a foursome and steadily became more committed to what still seemed a long chance. For Hill, the least wealthy or prominent of the group, it proved to be one of the most critical and nerve-wracking times of his life. Devastated by the death of his young daughter Katy in the summer of 1876, he nevertheless pressed his compatriots on. He was far better informed than any of the others as to the state of the railroad. He summarized well his feverish hunt for whatever knowledge he could gain: "I com-menced to get all the information that I could find, copies of the mortgages, of the complaints, and paper books published in con-nection with the lawsuits, records in the court, and such infor-mation as I could gather from parties who were likely to have information as to the situation in Holland, as to the situation

George Stephen, Lord Mount Stephen. Courtesy of James J. Hill Papers,
James Jerome Hill Reference Library, Saint Paul, Minnesota.

with the bondholders, and their relations to the Dutch Committee, the position of the several lawsuits, the grounds, so far as I
could learn, upon which the lawsuits were brought, and with
counsel discussed the merits or probable merits of those cases."
Hill communicated directly and individually with the leading
Dutch investors, had his attorney, R. B. Galusha, monitor all the
relevant cases, and even subscribed to an Amsterdam newspaper
to track the Dutch bond market.

Hill knew that E. Darwin Litchfield not only would not cooperate with them but also harbored designs of his own, attempting an accord with the Dutch bondholders whereby they would together reorganize, own, and complete the SP&P. Just the preceding year, bondholders of the defunct NP had similarly begun reorganizing their corporation, which threatened once again to co-opt its smaller rival. If either of these efforts met quick success, the "associates" would face little chance of going far. It is a fair measure of Jim Hill's grit and ambition that he now staked everything he had, his entire career, on the gamble for the SP&P. In the spring of 1876, as his obsequious "official" biographer J. G. Pyle wrote, he began cutting back on any new commitments and moving out of the rail freight business in Saint Paul to devote his full attention to acquiring the road. He was crossing the Rubicon, and if he failed, he might end up broken.

Both Hill and Kittson devoted considerable time and attention to cultivating the court-appointed receiver, Jesse Farley. Just how far they went with this we shall probably never really know, but clearly Farley freely gave them the most intimate details about the road and its construction. They came to understand that although he had managed to build only eighty-seven new miles of road between 1873 and 1876, the grading and terminal work he was doing in the Twin Cities was adding value to the railroad that was less obvious to the casual observer and that the prospects for new farm traffic were in fact most promising.

On the darker side, Farley would later claim that he had colluded with them directly to keep the property looking shabby and to talk down its value in order to frighten the bondholders into selling cheaply. In return for this dereliction of his duties as receiver, Farley claimed, they had promised to make him a director of their new corporation and to give him a major share of the profits as an investing partner.

Thus, with Farley's open cooperation, the trio of Hill, Kittson, and Smith began probing to see what sort of offer might be sufficient to interest the Dutch bondholders, who were understandably nervous about their jeopardized investment. Late in 1876 their spokesman, Johan Carp, came to Saint Paul, accom-

panied by "Captain" John Barnes, a representative of their New
York counsel, John S. Kennedy. Hill and Kittson laid out their
strategy to Barnes, balancing their dismal report on the condition of the road with their optimism about what they might do
with it. Farley aided and abetted their strategy.

Clearly skeptical about what these locals might be able to accomplish in the midst of a stultifying depression, Carp also knew
that they might be the best, even the only, chance that he and his
friends had to salvage anything on their investment. Late in
January 1877, Hill and Kittson tendered a formal offer to Carp of
$3.5 million and then fleshed out more details with a further
mailing in May. They knew this offer was far too low, but they
succeeded in their objective of opening a dialogue that continued as both sides jockeyed for advantage, with Kennedy the inter-
mediary serving as the Dutch investors' counsel.

One reason the Dutch were anxious to deal was a mounting
antiforeign sentiment in Minnesota and throughout the West, a
feeling that these speculators would do anything for a quick buck
except build a decent railroad. This bias found ready reflection in
the state legislature and helped Kittson and Hill get the facilitat-
ing legislation they needed. After all, both men, long established
locally, had many friends there, and the legislators themselves
desperately wanted the road completed soon.

Rumors abounded that the two associates were bribing or
otherwise offering cash favors to legislators, an admittedly common practice in those days of unsophisticated lobbying. For instance, the long-hostile *Winnipeg Times* commented, "The wily
Jim Hill had to 'grease' other interests, legislative, judicial and
private to the tune, it is said, of a million." Clearly, Hill and
Kittson lacked any such resources, and on the record, at least,
there is no evidence that bribes were either offered or taken.

In the spring of 1876, the Minnesota legislature passed legislation allowing foreclosure sale of railroad corporations and assets
without forfeiture of their land grants. At the same time, the U.S.
Congress, faced with a number of similar situations, enacted a
law permitting mortgage foreclosure on land-grant railroads
without loss of their tax immunity on the granted lands.

Then, in May 1877, the state legislature again proved amenable to the arguments of Hill and Kittson, who had cleared away the NP's opposition to their schemes by assuring the NP that they would give it the Brainerd extension. The lawmakers reestablished the time lines for completion of the SP&P, allowing a new builder reasonable deadlines to gain the granted lines. Whoever they might be, the builders of the SP&P would have until the beginning of December 1878 to complete the Branch Line section from Melrose to Alexandria, until the beginning of 1880 to complete the Extension to Saint Vincent, and until the beginning of 1881 to complete the Branch Line linkage to the Saint Vincent Extension from Fergus Falls to Glyndon.

Now, in the spring of 1877, began a momentous rush of events. That month, Jim Hill headed north to meet with Smith and Stephen in Montreal. An ill Kittson remained behind; and in any event, as he grew older, Kittson tended more and more to follow the lead of his trusted young friend. In this, their first meeting, Hill and Stephen hit it off well; the two very strong personalities thus began a long lifetime of friendship and give-and-take.

After Hill once more spun his rhetorical web about what the risks in store might gain them, Stephen decided to come fully aboard. They agreed that Stephen, as the leading man of finance among the four, would travel to England that autumn. Confidently, he predicted that with his many contacts as president of the Bank of Montreal, he would have no problem raising a major share of the $5.5 million they would need to buy the bonds and to foreclose on and complete the road.

In June, Hill traveled to New York and met Kennedy, a man who would figure as largely in his future as would Stephen, for the first time. Once again, the Scottish bond seemed to work its magic, and they readily formed a lifelong friendship. He and his associates now learned that the Dutch seemed to be responding favorably to the proposal that he and Kittson had tendered them. Then in September, Stephen came to Saint Paul, accompanied by his cohort, Richard B. Angus, general manager of the Bank of Montreal, yet another tight-fisted Scot who was destined to play a large role in the coming enterprise. Farley took the group out on a tour of the completed tracks. Though dismayed by the sweep of the prairie and the devastation clearly wrought by drought and locusts, Stephen seemed heartened by Catholic Bishop John Ireland's successful colonizing activity in the Red River valley. Radiating optimism, he headed off to England to raise the investments needed.

Reality intervened harshly when Stephen failed to raise the investment capital in the financial markets of England, which were gripped, like those in America, by depression. Once he returned, however, Stephen showed his mettle by calling his colleagues at once to Montreal at Christmas of 1877 and taking over leadership of the enterprise. His failure in England did also have its positive side. It clearly demonstrated to the Dutch bondholders that, with capital this tight in tough times, their own options were severely limited as well. As for the associates, they now faced the hard choice of either giving up the plan altogether or, by grasping at every source of credit they could find, attempting to entice the Dutch to sell out on credit, with only a down payment.

The four men proceeded at once to draw up a modified proposal, keeping the basic purchase offer for the bonds and coupons at $3,753,150, with added, associated costs of foreclosure suits and reorganization tacked on. For down payment and earnest money, subject to loss if they failed to meet their terms, they offered to give Kennedy, the Dutch investors' agent, $125,000 in cash on signing. The associates would eventually have to come up not only with more than twice this much earnest money but also with much more for other construction and related investments. The grand total would come to about $125,000 *apiece,* immediately.

In return, they asked the Dutch to accept an agreement on credit, paid at 7 percent interest, until foreclosure of the mortgages and transfer of title to the new owners. Within six months of that occurrence, they agreed to pay the full purchase price, either in cash or in bonds of the new company valued at 6 percent. To entice the Dutch to take the bonds instead of cash, they threw in a bonus of $250 in preferred stock for each $1,000 in bonds thus purchased. These terms were, primarily, Hill's work. His worshipful biographer Pyle grew rhapsodic at what Hill had put over on the sellers: "How the eyes of the Dutch Committee would have bulged if they could have seen the prospective purchaser's estimate of what he was going to get!"

Having reached this moment of truth, the four men now formalized their earlier agreement about commitments and rewards. They divided their expenditures and profits into five equal shares. Each of the four would have a one-fifth share, with a "fifth fifth" going to Stephen on the understanding "that one half of the said two fifths interest so set off to the said George Stephen" would "be held by him for the purpose of securing the necessary means to carry out and complete . . . said agreement."

In other words, they gave Stephen this share to use, at his discretion, to bring in yet another partner to help shoulder the crushing front-end burden of investment. To carry them through, Stephen and Angus quietly opened a line of credit from the Bank of Montreal to the individual partners. This was touchy business, since stockholders could easily argue that these two bank executives were diverting resources of the organization toward their own personal profit. This situation naturally brought Angus into the heart of the team, and he would eventually end up a minor partner on a par with Kittson.

Thus prepared, after a frenzied holiday season, the foursome, along with their Saint Paul attorney R. B. Galusha, headed to New York early in January of the fateful year 1878 to meet with Kennedy and his associate Barnes. They found Kennedy eager to close a deal with his Dutch clients, for he genuinely believed this offer to be the best they were likely to get. On January 5, 1878, having come to terms on the precise wording of the offer, Kennedy mailed it to Holland, with the deposit now raised from $125,000 to $280,000.

The plot was thickening considerably, and it is impossible to know for sure what happened. Clearly, however, Kennedy, while representing the Dutch bondholders and advising them to take what they could get from the four associates, at the same time joined up with the associates and thus became the fifth partner. Actually, the syndicate was never quite that simple in composition. Stephen's man Angus and Kennedy's man Barnes also participated, and Kittson did not stay in at the full rate of his three original partners. As for Kennedy, even by the easy moral standards of the Gilded Age, he obviously had a glaring conflict of interest on his hands.

Evidently, Kennedy saw the main chance easily enough: that these chaps had a wonderful opportunity and the ability to seize it. But Stephen also helped him make up his mind by inviting him into the group, offering him the "fifth fifth." One would assume that the other three associates participated in this decision, although Smith later claimed, "We did not ask Mr. Stephen to account for it." Heather Gilbert, in researching her biography of Stephen, seemed to find the answer to this very large question in a letter that he wrote, years later, to Sir Arthur Bigge. With characteristic self-congratulation, Stephen claimed: "Kennedy was very useful to me. To reward him I gave him $\frac{1}{5}$ interest, making him equal to Hill, Kitson [*sic*] Smith and myself & that is how he became the Scotch millionaire." Before this occurrence, Kennedy had been worth only $500,000.

Gilbert has a point in observing that Kennedy could defend his behavior, since he got the Dutch the best deal in sight and since they were in fact pleased with it. But Kennedy could hardly run with the hares and the hounds at the same time. After all, his man Farley had worked hand in glove with Hill and Kittson to convince the Dutch that the road was a loser. And by buying in with the associates, he gained a part of every dollar his clients sold short. Contemporary wisdom had it that the Dutch investors got bilked, a perception that bothered few locals, since foreign speculators ranked low on their list of favorite people anyhow. Later historians, like Dee Brown, have simply passed on this generalization. It is perhaps an overstatement and simplification of a complex situation, but surely it is at least a half-truth.

Even with Kennedy aboard, and with his invaluable ability to join Stephen in raising investment capital, the associates faced severe strains as they assessed what lay ahead of them if the Dutch accepted their offer. These tensions erupted publicly as the group took their leave of Kennedy in New York. When Stephen stated, quite abruptly, that Hill and Kittson must come up with their full share of the hard cash at once, Hill spoke back heatedly to him. Realizing the danger of their relationship coming apart, and their embarrassment of Kennedy, Hill wrote soothingly to Stephen in mid-January: "My hesitation was solely due to my desire that neither Mr. Kittson or myself should undertake to do what was totally beyond our power, while at the same time we are ready and entirely willing at all times to risk everything we have got in the world upon our faith in the property . . . but we cannot alone furnish our share of the money. . . . I will never be wanting in mutual cooperation and loyal confidence in those who are my associates, and once having assumed any responsibility or duty you will never find me looking back."

Such strains were natural enough: Hill and Kittson had a close bond on one side of the boundary, Smith and Stephen on the other; but neither twosome had such close ties to the other. Yet with so much at stake, they worked it out. Both Hill and Kittson proceeded to sell off most of their stock in the Red River Transportation Company, which was garnering huge profits carrying immigrants and railroad construction materials downriver. And Hill sold out his entire holding in the Northwestern Fuel Company in June for $21,500. All of this, the greater part of their net worth, they sent to Stephen to apply toward payment of the loan he had secured from the Bank of Montreal, a loan that he was anxious to extinguish, since it could embarrass him severely.

Late in February 1878, they received the exhilarating news that the Dutch committee had accepted their offer for all classes of bonds. On March 13, they gathered once again in New York to sign the formal agreement. It was a truly momentous occasion. The Dutch seemed happy enough. Ironically, in view of who really came out ahead in the transaction, they showed their appreciation of Stephen by giving him a handsome bowl that featured a rendering of a Dutch victory over the British! But after all, the associates' triumph would become real only if they could complete the lines on schedule. If they did, those Dutch who took bond options in the new firm would be very glad that they did.

The door to success and wealth that had seemed tightly shut now swung open to the five associates. However, their greatest challenges still lay immediately ahead. Of these, the most formidable would be to meet the construction deadlines imposed by the Minnesota legislature. This responsibility would fall naturally on Jim Hill, the youngest, least wealthy, and most dynamic of the partners and the one who, on the spot, knew the road best.

They also had to come to terms with the First Division stockholders, particularly the Litchfields but also the NP, which not only held stock in the SP&P but also wanted, naturally, to control its growth and direction. Stephen, working closely with Hill, took the lead in these tasks. As for the three other associates, Kittson remained largely passive. Kennedy became more actively involved, working closely with Stephen on the financial side and more closely with Hill in the actual management of the road. Heavily and contentiously involved in Canadian politics, Smith would make only secondary contributions.

Strategically, they had to make several important things happen in unison. Most important, they had to extend the Branch Line west from Melrose to Alexandria by the first of December, en route to its linkage with the Main Line at Barnesville. And they had to forge the Saint Vincent Extension all the way from Crookston north to Saint Vincent on the Canadian border by the end of December. Unless these legislative deadlines were met promptly, they would forfeit the land grants and be unable to gain possession of the railroad through bankruptcy foreclosure. At the same time, Stephen negotiated the building, by Canadian contractors, of the Pembina Line, linking Winnipeg south to a connection with the Saint Vincent Extension at the border. The associates would have liked the contract to build this line themselves, but Canadian politics—particularly the controversiality of Smith—meant that the Pembina Line must of necessity be an allied, not a directly owned, property.

Kennedy, as the trustee overseeing management of the bankrupt SP&P, directed Farley as receiver to proceed with construction, and he advanced the funds, to be repaid later by Stephen and the associates. In May, the federal court permitted Farley to issue "receiver's debentures"—a form of bond that could be collected only when and if the property was completed—at a rate of up to $10,000 per mile of track, secured by a first lien on the railroad, to finance construction.

In Saint Paul, James J. Hill faced a myriad of tasks and problems, all orbiting around the central issue of assisting—actually pushing—the slow-moving receiver along until they could secure outright ownership of the property. Shepherding building materials, for instance, posed a major challenge. Kennedy had a long-standing involvement with the Cambria Iron Works of Pennsylvania, and he used it to secure huge orders of high-quality rails, which were purchased with the promise of the debentures and which Hill then dispatched west and north for construction.

As for the actual construction, Hill and Kittson tightened their personal control over two small railroads tied to the SP&P—the Red River and Manitoba, and the Red River Valley Railroad— and they set out to contract with the receiver, Farley, to do the actual construction. Farley, however, had his own ideas on the subject, despite Kennedy's proddings to turn over much of the work to Hill and Kittson, and he convinced Judge John Dillon that he could bring it off himself. Herein lay a potentially lethal problem, for Farley's ineptness was matched only by his greed, flightiness, and orneriness.

The associates' relationship to Farley raises some very troubling questions. As noted earlier, he would later claim that he had colluded with them, unethically and illegally, in misleading the Dutch as to the true value of the railroad and in managing the property as receiver in the interest of the associates rather than in fidelity to the court. In return, he maintained, they had promised him a directorship in the new corporation and a sizable share in its ownership. It is impossible, from this vantage, to know precisely what did happen between them. Beyond a doubt, though, the associates did promise him something, which Stephen referred to as a "bonification." In this relationship, Farley clearly violated the law, by his own admission, and the associates themselves were at least skirting the serious matter of "influencing" a court-appointed officer. Although admittedly they had to deal somehow with this unsavory character to get him moving, they also raised a moral and legal cloud that would hang over their heads for years to come.

As the construction season began in the spring of 1878, Kennedy stroked Farley, assuring him that Kittson and Hill spoke of him in the "very highest terms," that they wanted him to work closely with them, and that they "both could and would make it worth [his] while to do so." Kennedy added, "They have no idea of superseding you but mean you to remain in full charge and with full power and authority." But in a matter of only weeks, it became clear that the aging and dilatory receiver, frequently absent from the job, would never get the tracks completed in time. Impetuous and impatient, Hill crowded the old man remorselessly and began taking on more of the tasks of management himself, as well he had to. Dangerously, he also brushed aside the receiver's demands for some consideration of reward.

Soon, Farley was in high dudgeon. He wrote Kennedy late in May: "I have had some sharp talk with Mr. Hill. If he persists in his Present course to ignore all my claims to Share in the honours or profit to some small degree, He may have cause to Regret it." Kennedy soothed him, but increasingly to little avail. By summer, it seemed likely that if Farley remained in place, the construction deadlines would not be met. He absented himself from the job for days at a time and worked at a snail's pace when there.

Finally, through some combination of convincing, cajolery, and perhaps promises, the associates persuaded him to stand aside and allow Hill—who was already handling supply and other matters—to take over the supervision of construction. Assigning the direct work to a favorite contractor, David Robbins, Hill now entered one of the most dynamic phases of his life, for the first time engaging in the work of railroad construction. Well equipped by his background and his remarkable astuteness and energy, he would prove remarkably good at it, demonstrating a rare ability to muster and command men and materials and to control both a broad strategy and a myriad of details.

As summer turned to fall, Jim Hill worked and worried by day and night, now at his Saint Paul office, often until after midnight, and then in the field, driving himself to the limit and seeing little of his family. He found it imperative, he said, "to be where the money was being spent." In close communication with Stephen and Kennedy, he fought especially against delays— delays of supply materials, particularly the steel rails from Cambria, and delays of the Canadian contractors who were proceeding south from Winnipeg at a niggardly pace. The associates had a bad scare when the Cambria Iron Works had a massive shutdown, forcing them to buy supplemental rails from another vendor. Nevertheless, Hill soon had the workers laying rails at the rate of more than two miles per day, over twice the pace Farley had made earlier.

Out in the field of western and northwestern Minnesota, Hill seemed to be everywhere, and the mystique of his dynamism now took form. Autumn came early in 1878, bringing with it both snows and floods, which delayed construction, and equipment failures, such as windmills that locked and deprived locomotives of water for motive power. Keeping work crews in the field, not to mention keeping them working at capacity, proved especially difficult. Hill alternately cajoled and coerced them.

He learned many of the men's names and would walk along the grades calling out to them familiarly, even spelling them at their picks and shovels while they retired for a cup of hot coffee, a gesture he would employ for the rest of his career. On the other hand, he routinely fired shift bosses when they failed to perform to his satisfaction. When one whole crew rebelled, he faced them off and fired the entire entourage. He then brought a new work crew into the tense situation, posting solemn guards to forestall aggression from either side. "The work," he said, "seems to drive and control everybody in place of being controlled and driven."

Meanwhile, the partners had to deal with their old nemesis the Litchfields, the primary stockholders in the First Division, and with the reborning NP, which once again sought to suppress the

SP&P and whose president, Charles Wright, also held a large bloc of stock in their road. Luckily for them, however, the new NP executive group found itself still divided, predictably, on strategies. One faction, led by Frederick Billings, wanted to make an accord with the associates so that the NP could devote its full energies to building west and quickly securing the giant land grant and the earnings from its sales. Another group, including Wright, wanted to secure their Minnesota base through headlong competition with, and suppression of, the SP&P.

The members of this group proposed to build one line down the west bank of the Mississippi from Sauk Rapids to Minneapolis and to construct a major depot there, a thought that warmed the hearts of Saint Paul's budding rival sister city. They also projected constructing another line up the west bank of the Red, to compete for the Manitoba trade, and perhaps even building on to Winnipeg. The NP further harassed the SP&P by trying to make common cause with the two eastern roads linking the Twin Cities with Chicago: the Chicago and Northwestern; and the Chicago, Milwaukee, and Saint Paul. But Hill, who had already extracted favorable rates from these carriers on the mass shipments of materials for his road and its Canadian counterpart, held them at bay, playing them off against one another and offering them the valuable use of his terminal facilities in Saint Paul.

Hill held the NP group in utter contempt, as a bunch of eastern speculators who did not have their act together; and, increasingly characteristic of this hard-shelled man, he made little effort to disguise his opinion. As he commented to Stephen, "Depend upon it, there is not a more dishonest and insincere lot of railway men in the whole country, and I do not think they ever had any business with other lines, that they did not by some sharp dodge take a mean and unfair advantage." He also knew that the NP crowd could not both build west rapidly and consolidate their Minnesota base and that, when pressed, they would head west for the land grant.

"We do not think," he wrote Stephen in June, "the No. Pac. people intend to build any road in Minnesota either in the Minnesota Red River Valley or from Sauk Rapids to Minneapolis. If they have any money they would be more apt to build west of Bismarck and save their land grant." He sized them up correctly. In any case, Hill had a potent, warlike counterthreat, which he spelled out to Wright. As he recalled the conversation to Stephen in September 1878: "If he persistently attacked us we would make a struggle for life and would not come off second best. . . . [W]e would at once survey a line from Grand Forks to Fort Buford at the mouth of the Yellowstone which was on as good and easy line all the way, through a country as good for agriculture as the very best portions of his road, and we would ask Congress for half of his grant to the Rocky Mounts, &c., and that he knew there were strong interests opposed to him who would be only too glad to help us."

Angry and accusatory, Jim Hill became so inflamed in his dealings with the NP group that the more politic Stephen had to step in and take over the negotiations both with the NP and with the Litchfields. In early November, through the use of arbitrators, he concluded a "protocol," dubbed by some the "Great Treaty of Peace," which was very advantageous to the SP&P. The NP backed off from its threats either to build a west-bank line along the Mississippi to Minneapolis or to intrude within twenty miles of the west bank of the Red with a parallel line. And it agreed to support Stephen in his effort to come to terms with the Litchfields.

Clearly, Billings's strategy of placing top priority on westward extension had prevailed, and in fact, this NP faction that looked west got something in return. The SP&P granted the NP use of its Saint Paul depot, along with ten acres there for a freight facility, and use of its Branch Line tracks into the city. The NP could now muster all its energies for the great thrust to the Pacific. All parties arguably won, except for Minneapolis, which saw its hopes for a separate and competing railroad dashed.

Coming to terms with the stubborn E. Darwin Litchfield took a while longer. He demanded a full share in the associates' enterprise, since by his reckoning, his agreement with the Dutch bondholders to run the First Division remained in effect. When he demanded a cool $1 million as his price to sell out, Hill once again lost his temper. And once again, coming to his rescue, Stephen proved his diplomatic abilities. Early in February 1879, the Litchfields accepted Stephen's offer of $200,000 in cash and $300,000 in bonds of the new railroad corporation about to be formed to replace the old one, in return for the surrender of all of their SP&P bonds and almost all of the stock, along with a promise to cooperate in the foreclosure suits soon to occur.

In the meantime, with Hill now fully in charge of construction, the SP&P proceeded to meet its legislative trackage deadlines quite comfortably. The tracklayers reached Alexandria on November 5, prompting the *Saint Paul Pioneer Press* to exclaim: "The Saint Paul & Pacific company are entitled to gratitude of the State for the liberality and enterprise displayed [in getting this done]." And the Saint Vincent line was finished shortly thereafter. On November 10, the first through train ran from Saint Vincent to Saint Paul, towing two luxury sleeper cars—the Saint Paul and the Minneapolis—with Farley, Hill, and a full entourage of their friends and supporters aboard.

Gaps in the line still remained to be built, but the victory was theirs. Hill quickly rushed his crews north to help their Canadian counterparts complete the Pembina Line, and the last spike there was driven home on December 2. Service now opened all the way from Winnipeg to Saint Paul, leading the *Saint Paul Daily Globe* to revel, "It brings an empire to our very doors." As witnessed by new stations along the line handsomely named Angus, Kennedy, and Stephen, the Scottish associates were making their enduring mark on the land and on history; and an imposing engine-shop facility arose at Crookston, just east of Grand Forks, Dakota, where the Red Lake River joins the Red, a location that future years would prove to be highly strategic.

The last two months of the climactic year 1878 marked a frenzied time in the life of James J. Hill. In November, his wife, Mary, once again pregnant, contracted a serious case of pneumonia and for a time hovered near death as the family watched helplessly and frantically. She soon recovered, however, and the family enjoyed an especially happy Christmas, basking in the joy not only of her recuperation but also of the successes of the father, which meant an even grander standard of living for them all. Then, in January 1879, Mary gave birth to yet another daughter, Ruth.

As the associates wrapped up the legislatively mandated construction of SP&P lines, they could now tie together the package of ownership and come to terms with the NP and the Litchfields. At the end of December 1878, they finally succeeded in getting a slow-moving Judge Dillon to issue the debenture certificates with which they could begin paying their mounting bills. They had run up construction and agreement settlement bills that aggregated well over $1 million, above and beyond their Bank of Montreal loan for the deal with the Dutchmen.

On the positive side, however, the SP&P First Division showed net profits by the end of the year of well above $500,000, indicating what a vast earning potential it truly had, as farmer-immigrants poured onto the fertile lands it was opening. Among the associates, only Hill had fully anticipated the road's true strength. For, in poring over its books, he had perceived that nearly $200,000 in First Division expenditures that had been spent on construction had been improperly charged to operations, thus understating the true profit capacity of the road. Finally, beginning in March 1879, came the crucial series of rulings in the Minnesota District Court and in Judge Dillon's U.S. Court in Iowa; these rulings proscribed the foreclosure sales and the prices to be mandated for the various classes of bonds. At last, the railroad of destiny was nearly theirs.

Accordingly, the original four associates met together in Saint Paul on May 23, 1879, along with Barnes, representing both himself and Kennedy, to form the new corporate entity that would now take over the foreclosed properties, which they formally took possession of the following month. They named it the Saint Paul, Minneapolis, and Manitoba Railway Company and made Stephen its president and Kittson its vice-president. Capitalized at $31,486,000, the "Manitoba" would have $15 million in common stock, initially levied in 150,000 shares at $100 each, and an initial bond issue of $8 million in 7 percent, first-mortgage classification, soon to be followed by another issue.

The majority of these issues went to the associates and their partners for past and future investments and expenditures, each receiving stock worth $2 million. Much of the rest went to pay for the properties now brought under the control of the Manitoba—the Red River and Manitoba Railroad, which had been the instrument of the Dutch investors, and the little Red River Valley Railroad and the Winnipeg and Western Transportation Company, which was the heir of the old Red River Transportation Company. These purchases, along with the earlier, main acquisitions at foreclosure sale, rounded out the corpus of the fledgling Manitoba Railway.

Several days later, the associates further assembled their organization. They created an executive committee, on-site in Saint Paul, composed of Hill, who was now formally designated general manager, Kittson, and their highly competent attorney, R. B. Galusha. Hill would receive the respectable salary of $15,000 per year. Their first task was to complete the trunk line construction from Alexandria to Barnesville and from Fisher's Landing west to the Red River crossing at Grand Forks, Dakota. To raise funding for further building, the partners advanced to the corporation $2.7 million in collateral bonds. By the end of 1879, they had brought this mandatory work to completion and were proceeding to make improvements and to begin the lateral, spur lines that would funnel traffic to their road.

As the situation of the railroad became more clear in the autumn, the associates continued to structure their finances. They placed a second mortgage on the Saint Paul, Minneapolis, and Manitoba to issue a further $8 million in 6 percent bonds. With these, they settled accounts with those Dutch investors who wanted to invest in the new property rather than take cash. With the remainder, they both provided for further construction and issued themselves the first real, immediate profits they had yet seen. Now, they could actually distribute the stock of the Manitoba among themselves, and this was an extremely delicate process. From Montreal to Saint Paul to Winnipeg, many eyes had been watching them, to see how much they would attempt to "water" the stock and otherwise manipulate the organization to their own gain. The latter two cities already buzzed with gossip about what they were doing.

Jim Hill, evidently, pursued the capitalization of the road most aggressively. After all, among the partners, he not only was working the hardest but also was making the most spectacular ascent from a modest fortune to a great one. Years later Smith, who viewed himself as "a man of moderation," recalled that Hill's sweeping ideas on the subject had caused him "considerable perturbation." Late in November 1879, the associates divided up the stock certificates, each receiving 29,993 shares, with Stephen receiving two sets of this amount. Most of this latter "fifth," as noted earlier, ended up in the hands of Kennedy. As for Stephen's cohort Angus, who had done so much to handle the delicate situation of the Bank of Montreal loan, he received 5,500 shares, which came from 1,100 assessed to each of the five associates.

At the time, of course, no one could know the potential value of these securities. On the face of it, the associates had laid out a total of $10 to $11 million and become primary owners of a corporation capitalized at $31,486,000. As the road developed under expert management, though, it naturally increased sharply in value and earned handsome profits. As Albro Martin noted, a full one-fifth share, held until the mid-1880s, would have been worth $4,970,000. But not all the associates held on to their shares. Kittson, aging and insecure, soon sold his. The others held on, and each of them became fabulously wealthy and remained heavily involved in the Manitoba enterprise.

Of course, the associates had to plow much of these earnings into paying off the debts they had incurred during 1878, but they also had other sources of profit in addition to the initial stock and bond issues. From the very beginning the earning power of the railroad exceeded even Hill's expectations, and then, of course, there was the land grant. As we shall see, they rapidly sold off these properties in the boom atmosphere of the early 1880s, and in so doing, they earned over $13 million in further profits.

Thus was born the great Hill fortune and the fortunes of his friends as well. Stephen and Smith would soon use their newly acquired riches to build the Canadian Pacific Railroad. Hill would join them for a while, but the Manitoba would always remain the focus of his career and his investments. The associates gloried, of course, in their spectacular success, the product of enormous risks and efforts. But as they looked toward a rosy future of building their property, one ugly cloud hung over their heads—the problem of old Jesse Farley and his nasty accusations.

Jim Hill wasted little time, after gaining full control of the Saint Paul, Minneapolis, and Manitoba, in sending Farley packing. Hill showed little sensitivity to the old man's ego, to his greed, or to his clear ability to retaliate. When Farley confronted Hill in the spring of 1879 with the impossible demand that he be made a director of the new corporation and a full partner in its ownership, Hill dismissed him contemptuously. With his usual broken English and lack of class, Farley then wrote Barnes, bemoaning the fact that he had been "left out in the cold." He said: "[Hill is] such a Lyer cant believe him. . . . He is notoriously known to be the biggest lier in the State." Farley added, "You must Not blame Me if I should try to get even with Jim Hill before I leave here." Farley even stated that he pitied anyone having "to breath the foul air connected with everything Jim Hill [had] anything to do with."

Evidently, the associates had intended to reward Farley for his services as receiver, despite the obvious impropriety of so doing, but they had neither the intention nor the legal ability to meet these sorts of demands. Barnes implored Kennedy to confront the aging rooster and "cut his comb." But he also conceded that Hill was "such a loose talker and so inclined to make messes of negotiations" in which he had "no special experience" that this could lead to a truly dangerous situation.

Farley obviously believed that a promise of great reward had been made to him and now lay broken. He complained to Kennedy that either Kennedy or Stephen should have told him that he could not be a director of the Manitoba and that he had agreed to take the receiver position only after Kennedy had promised him a large remuneration. More pointedly, he told Kennedy: "I have in my possession the names and amounts paid by him [Hill] to bribe the Minnesota legislature." However, he never produced any such list. Barnes commented in June 1879, "I think the old man has gone crazy with jealousy and spite."

It is unclear what the associates had actually promised Farley. Promising him anything at all was wrong and illegal but admittedly necessary if they were to get the job done. In any case, they could not give him what he now demanded; and so, frustrated and enraged, Farley went to court, charging that the associates had broken their oral contract promising him a one-fifth share in the Manitoba. The cases—*Farley* v. *St. Paul, Minneapolis & Manitoba Railway et al.*, *Farley* v. *Kittson et al.*, and *Farley* v. *Hill et al.*—wound their way through the state and federal court systems for years.

Farley first failed before the Minnesota Supreme Court in 1880 and then the U.S. District Court in 1882. In the latter ruling, Judge Samuel Treat, who gained national fame soon afterward for his ruling in the "Wabash Case," found not only that Farley could not prove his point but also that he came before the court self-indicted. His very accusation rested on the admission that he had violated his duty as court receiver to manage the property in the interest of its owners.

Farley, however, pressed grimly on and appealed his case to the U.S. Supreme Court. To the chagrin and mortification of Hill and his partners, the court agreed to review it. Both sides employed top-flight counsel. Senator William Evarts, who had earlier been chief counsel for President Andrew Johnson in his impeachment defense, joined Hill and Kittson's attorney George Young. Farley employed Senator George Edmunds to represent him. The associates received a hard blow in February 1887, when the Supreme Court, employing a highly convoluted and technical argument, remanded the case to federal district court for a full and open trial. This was bound to be embarrassing, for sentiment in the Twin Cities ran against the millionaires, who had grasped such an enormous prize, and in favor of the "little guy," who claimed that they had manipulated him.

The trial in U.S. Circuit Court for the District of Minnesota, Judge David Brewer presiding, began in the spring of 1888. Brewer would soon advance to the U.S. Supreme Court. It proved to be a terrible ordeal for both sides. Stephen, Smith, and particularly Hill testified at great length, reflecting on the early days in the Red River valley. Kittson did not testify, for he had died of heart failure while en route by train to the trial. The stress of the situation probably contributed to his demise, for the Twin Cities rumor mills had it that he would have bribed Farley on his arrival there. Once again, Farley told his tale of how Kennedy had secured his appointment as receiver, of how the partners had orally promised him a partnership and directorship in return for his betraying his trust, and of how they had cast him aside. They, in turn, again denied the entire claim.

The anxious litigants had to wait until September 1889 for Judge Brewer's verdict. When it came, it gave the associates all they could have hoped for. Brewer ruled that Farley could not demonstrate with finality that an oral contract had been made, and he expressed his doubt that any agreement of such importance would not have been put in writing. It had simply been Hill's word against that of Farley and his nephew. The judge commented that Farley's contentions were "absurd," in that the partners were clearly pressing Kennedy to get him to hurry the pace of construction in the first half of 1879. If Hill and Kittson were, as alleged, collaborators with Farley, why would they have been put in this outwardly contentious situation? Why would he not simply have turned the work over to them from the outset?

The logic here may well have been flawed, for Farley may simply have been attempting to keep his oar in the water in an uncertain situation. But the fact remained that the old gent had no written agreement, and that was that. Case dismissed. Yet, an element of uncertainty remained, since the U.S. Supreme Court had to ratify the lower court decision, and this did not happen until December 1893—fifteen years after the events in question. By this time Hill had become a national figure. But, as was obvious at the time, the Brewer decision effectively ended the matter.

After the great victories of 1878–79, the *Farley* case, grinding on for so long, cast a dark pall over the lives of the associates. What does one conclude about it? Beyond debate, Farley was a self-convicted felon. Nearly as obvious, however, is the fact that the associates colluded with him. Kennedy not only played fast and loose in representing his Dutch clients but also rather clearly manipulated the receiver, an officer of the court. It is reasonable, up to a point, to argue that the associates *had* to deal with Farley, since this was the only way in which they could finalize their control of the railroad.

In the last analysis, it seems certain that Kennedy, Stephen, Hill, and Kittson did offer Farley a substantial reward—maybe even hinting at a full partnership—in return for his cooperation and betrayal of his trust. The rumors that Kittson offered him a bribe and that Hill then elbowed him aside may well have been true. Whatever happened, the Farley episode tainted the creation of this soon-to-be-great railroad empire and left a stain, like the mark of Cain, on the lives and reputations of those who gave it birth.

Of course, during the glorious months of 1879, most of this problem still lay in the future. Meanwhile the associates had won the great, hard-fought victory that brought them the railroad that became the Manitoba. For each of them, but for Jim Hill especially, the frenzied months of 1878–79 marked a true watershed, the hinge of a lifetime. With the stocks and bonds of the Saint Paul, Minneapolis, and Manitoba came the exhilaration and sudden transition in status from being comfortably well-to-do to being a multimillionaire at the young age of forty—at a time when several millions represented a truly great fortune. In completing the railroad, he had demonstrated his toughness, his stamina, his unflinching ability to discipline and to fire people, his competence in controlling large work forces, his quickness in mastering the intricate details of finance—in other words, he had proven his mettle. James J. Hill had "made it."

CHAPTER 3

Expanding Horizons

HAVING met the terms set by the Minnesota legislature and completed the basic trunk lines of the Saint Paul, Minneapolis, and Manitoba Railway, the associates now faced an intriguing choice of options, not unlike those earlier posed to their NP rivals. On the one hand, their most natural course lay in cementing their hold on the heartland of western Minnesota and northeastern Dakota. This meant concentration on building an infrastructure of lateral spur lines and the accompanying grain elevators, depots, and towns and of course on selling off their land grant. But on the other hand, as fate would have it, they too now saw looming before them the prospect of a mighty transcontinental railroad. This, the prize of what for most of them was their homeland, was the Canadian Pacific (CP). For George Stephen and Donald Smith, the CP would become the royal road to the highest ranks of Canadian and British society; but for James J. Hill and John S. Kennedy, it would prove to be a diversion and a cruel disappointment. Hill and Kennedy, and eventually Stephen and Smith as well, would find that their future would continue to lie with the Saint Paul, Minneapolis, and Manitoba.

The Pacific railroad issue formed the most central and emotional question in Canada during the years following the 1867 creation of the dominion. Without such a bond of union, in fact, the fragile, embryonic commonwealth might not survive. When far-off British Columbia on the Pacific entered the confederation, it did so only with the government's promise that the railroad would be built within a decade. But such a mammoth undertaking presented a formidable challenge to a federation numbering fewer than four million people.

Conservative Premier Sir John A. Macdonald made the first attempt in 1873, placing the wealthy steamship entrepreneur Sir Hugh Allan in charge. The whole enterprise collapsed soon after, however, when the "Pacific Scandal" erupted over the fact that Allan, a cohort of Jay Cooke's of the NP, had also been investing heavily in politicians, including Macdonald. As a result, the Macdonald government fell and was replaced by that of the Liberal Alexander Mackenzie. The Pacific railroad project made no more progress during the mid-1870s than did its counterparts in the United States.

Macdonald, one of the true builders of Canada, then returned to the premiership in 1878, the same year that the associates were building north toward a connection with the line running south from Winnipeg to the boundary. By now in Canada, as in the United States, railroad fever was running at fever pitch, with British Columbia threatening secession if it did not gain linkage to the East. Beyond this, the premier also realized that the NP, or some other American railroad near the border, could easily siphon off the commerce of western Canada by building spurs northward. The very future of his nation could be undermined. And he knew further that the transcontinental must be an all-Canada line, not merely a connection with some line bending north from the midwestern United States, such as the Manitoba.

Realistically, the all-Canada railroad could start new construction from the northern shore of Lake Superior at Thunder Bay, then head northwest toward Winnipeg. In terms of political reality, this road would have to be a true transcontinental, wedding to an eastern trunk line at this Great Lakes point of embarkation and then crossing the difficult wilderness of lakes and rocks north of the Great Lakes, thus joining Winnipeg—the gateway to the plains—with the population centers of the Saint Lawrence Valley.

To build the Pacific railroad, the conservative Macdonald administration turned naturally to the same sort of arrangement that its U.S. counterparts favored: private investors abetted by federal subsidies. While several groups of potential investors vied for this mighty contract during 1879–80, only one had the demonstrable means and credentials that measured up to the task. That was the group headed by George Stephen, of the Bank of Montreal, a group that came to be known in Canada as the "Saint Paul Syndicate" and that had just proven its abilities in

building the Manitoba. To Stephen and Smith, the Canadian
Pacific enterprise promised nationalist fulfillment as well as
profit. It also promised them, and Hill and Kennedy as well, a
western transcontinental linkage to their American railroad and
access to huge new markets.

Stephen, Smith, Hill, and Kennedy each pledged $500,000 to
the Canadian Pacific endeavor. So did R. B. Angus, who was in
effect replacing the retiring Norman Kittson as a full-fledged
"associate." Under Stephen's aegis, a number of other prominent
investors joined the consortium: Duncan McIntyre of Montreal,
who led the Canada Central Railway, which linked the Ottawa-
Montreal area with Lake Nipissing, the northern inlet to Georgian Bay and Lake Huron; the prestigious, Paris-based firm of
Kohn, Reinach, and Company; and the prominent London investment house of Morton, Rose, and Company. Of necessity,
most of the investment capital in the CP came from Great Britain
and the United States, with less than 20 percent of it coming
from Canada. And political sensitivities had to be looked after.
Smith, for example, again had to remain in the background,
much to his chagrin, since he had just lost his seat in parliament
amid charges of political chicanery.

For Macdonald, dealing with the Stephen syndicate presented
genuine problems. He detested Smith, and the western Canadians
bristled at the monopolistic implications both of the current
Manitoba-Pembina line and of the projected Canadian Pacific.
But he had little choice, since these were probably the only men
who could do the job, and so he pressed ahead with the "Pacific
Bill." As it passed parliament in February 1881, the legislation authorized the Canadian Pacific Railroad to link with the Canada
Central Railway at Callander, near Georgian Bay, and to run westward to some Pacific port in British Columbia. Generously subsidized with $25 million in direct support and a twenty-five-
million-acre, checkerboarded land grant, the road had a ten-year
allowance for construction and was granted monopoly protection in that no competitor would be allowed to build to the
south between it and the American border.

Stephen faced even more severe tests of his diplomatic skills in meeting the Canadian Pacific contract than he had in securing the Manitoba. Smith deeply resented having to stay in the background, and the activities of Hill and Kennedy also had to be understated, since they were Americans building the lifeline of Canada. The roles each played closely resembled those they had performed earlier on the Manitoba, with Stephen handling finance and governmental relations, assisted in this and at the Bank of Montreal by Angus. Kennedy also assisted him on the financial side, and Hill weighed in as the expert in construction and operations, an expertise he had demonstrated in building good Minnesota lines in a hurry.

For Jim Hill, this reconfigured arrangement caused several nearly impossible problems. For one thing, he could spare precious little time from what, as we shall see, had to be his first concern—continuing to develop the Saint Paul, Minneapolis, and Manitoba. He came aboard the Canadian Pacific project because of loyalty to his partners, the obvious chance for further profit, and the clear possibility that the CP could become a westward extension for the Manitoba, via Winnipeg. He knew that, for political reasons, the Canadian government had to walk softly on the issue of an all-Canadian railroad. But unlike the stoical Stephen, he could never silence his criticism of the wasteful impracticality of building through the Precambrian Shield region north of the Great Lakes, a rocky and lake-strewn wilderness that made both for difficult construction and for a small supporting population.

Economically realistic but political naive, he entered the project believing that wisdom would eventually prevail. And wisdom would mandate that the CP direct its main course across the Great Lakes from either Detroit or Sault Sainte Marie onto American soil in Minnesota, thence via the Manitoba and the Pembina extension to Winnipeg. In this manner, the Manitoba and the CP could become profitable partners.

Once again, the syndicate turned dynamically to its task. Along with financing, which Stephen handled, the selection of their route and the organization of contractors first occupied their attention. On the eastern end, Hill continued to argue against the need to build the tortuous 650 miles along the north shore of the Great Lakes, from Georgian Bay to Thunder Bay; the segment from Thunder Bay northwest to Winnipeg would be equally difficult and futile. Hill's vantage, for now, focused on the staging point of Winnipeg, to which the Manitoba could easily and profitably carry materials for building westward. To the west lay two distinct zones: 850 relatively easy miles of prairie; but beyond that, 400 hard nautical miles of mountains. Unlike the northwestern United States, where an arid plain opens between the Rockies and the Cascades in Washington and Oregon, British Columbia is one vast mountain region, where the Rockies intermingle directly into the Coast Mountains beyond.

Looking at the projected westward route of the CP, Hill saw that it aimed to cross the plains well to the north of Winnipeg. It would traverse the old, established explorer-trapper route of the North Saskatchewan River—the "fertile belt"—which would bring the CP to the Pacific to the north of Vancouver Island. This long bend to the north struck him as not only expensive but also dangerous to the new Canadian state because it would leave the southern prairies open to invasion by American railroads just across the border. Such a development could mean the American colonization of western Canada, even the secession of this area from the union. Such was the geopolitical vision and power placed in the hands of Stephen, Hill, and their colleagues that they were now in the heady position of determining the destiny of a nation. It is a true measure of Jim Hill's talents, and also of his self-confidence, that, far from flinching from such awesome responsibility, he eagerly reached out and grabbed it. Loving the excitement of rail and community building in his adopted country, he would now apply what he had learned to his homeland.

Immediately, in February 1881, Hill sent Major A. B. Rogers to scout potential mountain crossings beyond Kicking Horse Pass, an already known cleft in the Continental Divide west of the headwaters of the Bow River, an upper fork of the South Saskatchewan. Rogers was a bona fide frontier legend, a small, tough, and exquisitely profane man who was said to be able to subsist on a diet of chewing tobacco and pork rinds, but he was also a born explorer. Always impetuous, Hill did not even wait the long months for Rogers to return but instead forged ahead to convince his partners of the wisdom of the southern plains route, assuming that a workable pass would surely turn up.

Several weeks later, three of the four members of the syndicate's executive committee—Hill, Stephen, and Angus, with McIntyre absent—met in Saint Paul and arrived at a truly momentous decision. With them sat botanist John Macoun, a government explorer who had traveled the broad plains drained by the South Saskatchewan. Like contemporary American railroad promoters, Macoun fervently argued that earlier dismissals of the plains as desolate arid lands were entirely wrongheaded. Rather, he implored, the basin of the South Saskatchewan was a beckoning farmland, potentially the "Garden of the whole country."

The true nature of this area, here just as south of the boundary, lay somewhere between the stereotypes of desert and garden. But Hill, the born promoter, fervently agreed with Macoun, who later recalled that at one point the railroader slammed his hands on the table and exclaimed, "Gentlemen, we will cross the prairie and go by the Bow [Kicking Horse] Pass if we can get that way." Stephen and the others readily agreed.

It was a bold move, a classic example of Hill's audacity; and once ratified by parliament, the decision became policy. In fact, it was a reckless move; for if no feasible passes were found west of the divide, it could mean the impossible expense of winding rails through the endless canyons of the hairpin-bending Columbia or Fraser River systems. Was it the right move? It dashed the hopes of the cities along the "fertile belt" of the North Saskatchewan, particularly Edmonton, and it took the railroad through regions that were drier and over passes that would prove higher than those to the north. But the decision clearly had much to recommend it.

By following the Fraser River to the Strait of Georgia, this route took the CP to the excellent seaport site of Vancouver, which afforded easy access to the open sea via the Strait of Juan de Fuca. It allowed the CP to avoid the speculators and established towns along the northern route and to determine its own

city sites, for example Brandon, Regina, Moose Jaw, and especially Calgary. It offered better access to coal, and of course,
it placed the road in a better geopolitical situation to keep the
American interlopers south of the border. And, as Canadian
writer Pierre Berton notes, it meant that the great Rocky Mountain tourist potential west of Calgary, at Banff, Lake Louise, and
nearby locales, would be fully realized.

Throughout the remainder of 1881, Hill marshaled as much
time as he could from the demands of building and managing
the Manitoba to prepare for the big construction campaign
slated for the following year on the CP. On the west side in
British Columbia, an independent American contractor, the capable Andrew Onderdonk, was already at work, employing Chinese labor. Onderdonk's involvement reassured the western Canadians not only that they would have a piece of the action but
also that rails would actually be built there.

Meanwhile, far to the east, the CP partners freighted huge
stores of rails and other materials to Winnipeg via the Manitoba
Road and hired two Minnesota contractors, R. B. Langdon and
D. C. Shepard of Saint Paul, to do the building. Shepard, who had
already begun a lifelong relationship with Hill, impressed James as
being exceptionally capable and loyal, as in fact he was. When Hill
saw that Shepard's bid was too high compared with another, he
conveniently left the competing bid lying open on his desk so that
Shepard could see it and thus resubmit one that was acceptable.

It soon became clear that, given all the crushing demands on
his time back home, Jim Hill simply could not devote enough
time and effort to the CP enterprise. He did not have to look far
to find the man he now recommended to step in as general
manager to Stephen, replacing the slow-moving A. B. Stickney
and eventually to replace himself. This was William Cornelius
Van Horne, the general manager of the Chicago, Milwaukee,
and Saint Paul. As Hill wrote Stephen: "You need a man of great
mental and physical power to carry this line through. Van Horne
can do it. But he will take all the authority he gets and more, so
define how much you want him to have."

In securing the appointment for Van Horne, Hill accomplished two ends at once: gaining a highly competent general manager for the CP and removing a powerful rival from the Milwaukee Road. The two men—one a Canadian who came south and the other an American who went north—had much in common. They even looked alike—stocky, barrel-chested, and bald—and both were hard-driving and tough administrators, with stamina that became legendary. Van Horne, however, played as hard as he worked, whereas Hill's socializing was more conventional and restrained. Van Horne could reportedly drink and play poker all night, then get up and work all day. His big cigars became his trademark, and a brand of them eventually carried his name. When the two men soon became heated rivals, Hill would rue the day he recommended Van Horne for the job.

Van Horne quickly took hold of the CP, building the same sort of relationship with Stephen as financier that Hill had earlier. Just before Van Horne's arrival in Canada, Major Rogers returned, at the close of 1881, from the snow-clogged Rockies. After a long, harrowing experience, he had found the Selkirks crossing (now named Rogers Pass) to be wholly workable, and a return journey in 1882 verified his judgment. Stephen lived up to Hill's promise with a check to Rogers for $5,000, and the proud old man framed rather than cashed it.

Van Horne then moved, with Hill's full support, to sack former Confederate General Thomas Rosser as chief engineer, since Rosser had been shamelessly colluding with town builders and land speculators along the route. With the opening of the construction season in 1882, the big army assembled by Hill and his partners forged rapidly westward. Van Horne's crews laid four hundred miles of track by January 1883, and by August of that year, the CP reached all the way from Winnipeg to Calgary on the Bow River, where the Canadian prairies sloped upward to the towering, beautiful, and foreboding Rockies.

Inevitably, Van Horne's aggressiveness quickly began to fray the fragile bonds holding together the old team of associates. As Hill had written Angus, even before 1882: "The only reason for going into the scheme was for the purpose of benefitting the St. Paul, Minneapolis & Manitoba Railway, but now it assumes the position of a deadly enemy. I sincerely hope I am all wrong, but I fear the result much more than I can tell you." At the bottom of this feeling was what had troubled Hill all along: the determination of the Macdonald government, regardless of practicality, to forge an all-Canadian line across the Shield country north of the Great Lakes. It now became clear that Stephen and Van Horne—good "Canadians" both—would press ahead with this construction. They had to, regardless of their own opinions, to salve the nationalist sensitivities of their countrymen.

Hill's ire mounted steadily as he saw that the Canadian government and the CP were making an irrevocable decision: to build the Nipissing–Thunder Bay main line along the north shore. Such a line, he argued, "would be of no use to anybody and would be the source of heavy loss to whoever operated it." He had logic on his side in arguing that the better route should run from Callander Junction on Lake Nipissing to the Great Lakes at Sault Sainte Marie, via water to Superior-Duluth, and on to Winnipeg by the Manitoba. But, simply put, nationalism prevailed over economics, as it often does, and his argument lost out. Later developments would prove him correct, when the CP would acquire the Soo Line along this very path, over American soil, in order to secure a competitive advantage.

Jim Hill's relationship with the CP steadily worsened through 1882 into 1883. He fumed over Van Horne's hard-nosed approach to the division of traffic and revenues between the CP and the Manitoba and over his decision, even before the north shore tracks were completed, to haul construction materials over the Great Lakes rather than via the Manitoba. At one point, Hill swore to get even with Van Horne, even if he had "to go to Hell for it and shovel coal." Stephen and Angus tried, with little success, to keep peace between the two; but in fact, their squabbling simply reflected the gulf widening between two railroads that were evolving into natural and national competitors.

The formal parting of the ways came in mid-1883, when both Hill and Kennedy resigned from the Canadian Pacific board of directors and sold their stock in the enterprise. Smith, who had lurked unhappily in the background, now stepped onto the CP board and diminished his participation in the Manitoba board. As for Stephen, like Smith he remained on the Manitoba board, similarly distracted from much participation; and both he and Smith kept intact their highly remunerative investment in the Minnesota railroad. Outwardly, relationships between the two roads and their managers remained cordial. When the last spike was driven, in November 1885, west of Revelstoke, Hill was there; and a month later, Stephen assured him that the CP would offer the Manitoba trackage to the West Coast.

Behind the scenes, however, the old camaraderie and trust that had held the associates together now gave way to acrimony. Hill's closest associate and mentor, the aging John Kennedy, bristled at Stephen's criticism and condescension, particularly his "cruel, base, and unfounded accusations" that the old New Yorker was not up to the demands of the new age of finance. Like Kennedy, Hill increasingly came to resent Stephen's apparent lack of interest in Manitoba affairs and his failure to attend board meetings. Writing in October 1886, Hill reminded Stephen that he had earlier promised to leave the board, if such seemed in order. Hill then came to the point, "I have to ask that you will before you sail [for England] send me your resignation as a member of our board, to be used in case I find it necessary for the reasons I have stated."

Once again, though, Stephen remained coolheaded when Hill fulminated. He hedged and, in the end, both remained on the board and maintained his Manitoba investment. As he wrote Hill in mid-1888:

> Let me say what I dare say you are not aware of, that is that we each [Stephen and Smith] have a greater pecuniary interest, in one way & another, in the St.P.M.&M. than we have in the P.P.R. [the CP] but if it were otherwise & we had no money in you [sic] road, we should still take the greatest pleasure in doing anything we could to secure and increase its prosperity. Our feelings towards the Manitoba road must always be of the most friendly character, even if we had not a cent in the property, and . . . nothing could give greater pleasure than to find some way of working these two lines in harmony with you.

Admittedly, the actions of the CP did not always bear out Stephen's soothing words. But in fact, both he and Smith would eventually become disenchanted with the CP and the government policy regarding it over the years and would in fact maintain their ties to the Manitoba. As for Hill, he would soon be glad they did.

For Smith and Stephen, the CP nonetheless proved the adventure of a lifetime, the avenue to great fortune and status. Stephen would later depart Canada for the British Isles, where he bought a Scottish castle and entered the peerage as Lord Mount Stephen, borrowing his title from the mountain named for him in western Canada. Smith followed him soon after, adopting the cumbersome title Lord Strathcona and Mount Royal. In contrast, Hill had become just as avid an American as Van Horne had a Canadian, formally establishing his U.S. citizenship in 1880. For him, the CP venture represented a regrettable diversion, a diversion from what was becoming—ever more clearly each year—his life mission: the building of the Saint Paul, Minneapolis, and Manitoba Railway.

With the dawn of the 1880s, that great boom decade of western rail construction, the Minnesota heartland of the Saint Paul, Minneapolis, and Manitoba Railway surged with activity. Looking eastward toward Chicago—the greatest rail hub in America and, like Saint Louis, a major "gateway," where trunk lines from the East bridged to lines serving the rest of the continent—three strong carriers reached toward the Twin Cities. These were the "Granger Roads," so called because they prospered by serving the rich agricultural heartland of the Upper Midwest. The Chicago, Milwaukee, and Saint Paul had at one point aimed to capture the Manitoba but could not afford it and would now attempt to invade the Red River valley itself. The Chicago and Northwestern worked more to the south of the Twin Cities and offered the Manitoba little trouble. And the Chicago, Burlington, and Quincy, profitably controlled by Boston financiers, aimed directly at Minnesota and would soon arrive with its Chicago, Burlington, and Northern subsidiary.

As the economic doldrums resulting from the Panic of 1873 began to lift in the late 1870s, however, the main focus of attention riveted once again westward, on the giant but stalled Northern Pacific transcontinental. Under the tutelage of Frederick Billings and his group of investors, the NP construction crews forged westward from Bismarck, aiming toward the Yellowstone River valley of southern Montana, beginning in 1877. A large cloud of uncertainty hung now, as it had several years earlier, over the western terminus of the railroad.

Would it be Commencement Bay on Puget Sound, where the NP was developing the city of Tacoma, which meant crossing the high Cascade Mountains of western Washington? Or would it be the queen city of the Pacific Northwest, Portland, Oregon? This handsome city had the advantage of controlling a water-level route down the Columbia River to the sea, but it also had the serious disadvantage of a poor harbor at the sandy mouth of the ebbing and flowing river. A third possibility, also troubling to Portland, involved a combination of the two above choices: running the main line to Portland and then northward to the better harbor on Puget Sound, so that Portland would basically be only a way-station en route to the principal harbor.

The key to Portland and the Columbia River route lay in the Oregon Steam Navigation Company, a powerful and resented outfit that monopolized first steamboats and then the strategic tracks that ran along the south bank of the river eastward from Portland into the arid interior of Oregon. In 1879, the Oregon Steam Navigation Company came under the control of Henry Villard, a wealthy German immigrant and a charismatic promoter who had invested heavily in Oregon railroads and in the city of Portland. Villard, in turn, reorganized the company under his Oregon Railway and Navigation Company (OR&N) and completed the laying of rails northeastward into the fine farmlands of southeastern Washington. Now, he faced both a threat and, conversely, an opportunity posed by the advancing NP.

Casting their lot with Portland, the Villard group could prevail only if the NP chose to meet the south-bank tracks of the OR&N and thus to use this line as the final western leg of the transcontinental. Thus members of the Villard group set out to occupy key strategic points to block the alternate north bank of the river in Washington. But, like Portland itself, they knew that the Billings faction aimed to build directly over the Cascades in southern Washington to Tacoma; and they therefore concluded that their only hope lay in seizing control of the NP itself, ousting Billings, and reversing his strategy. In 1881, Villard engineered a daring coup by aggregating what he termed a "Blind Pool" of $8 million—wherein investors who did not even know his purpose gambled on his reputation and put their money behind him—and with these resources Villard bought control of the NP and assumed its leadership.

Driven both by the compulsion of the land grants and by the profits and glory that would come with completion, Villard's crews built hurriedly from each end of the road during 1881–83. On the same day, September 8, 1883, the gold spikes were driven home on the main line near Gold Creek, in western Montana, and on the line running from Portland to Kalama, on the north bank of the Columbia, and on to Tacoma. Jim Hill watched with a stiff upper lip as citizens of the Twin Cities erected a grand arch symbolizing their state's gateway to the NP's "Main Street of the Northwest" and as they threw flowers over Villard's triumphant parade through the arch. The entire Northwest seemed to be Villard's oyster. Four trains headed west for the ceremony at Gold Creek, bearing thirty-six senators and congressmen, nine governors, nine generals, fifty reporters, and former President U. S. Grant. The northern transcontinental was a reality, and if the Twin Cities were not its eastern anchor, they were still linked to it.

Many observers would later compare Hill with Villard. The comparison was inevitable. The historian Julius Grodinsky, for instance, commented, "While Hill was building carefully and checking his costs minutely Villard built in ignorance of costs." Like other transcontinental plungers, Villard did in fact build rapidly and poorly; and like the pioneering Union Pacific–Central Pacific, much of his main line would later have to be torn up and rebuilt. He had rushed to get the massive land grants and to secure his West Coast investments. Amid mounting deficits and acrimony, Villard was then forced to resign the presidency of the NP in 1884.

To Portland's dismay, his successor, Robert Harris, then proceeded to build the NP's Cascade Branch westward from Pasco-Kennewick in Washington over Stampede Pass to Tacoma and Puget Sound. As of the mid-1880s, therefore, the NP stood as a land-rich but financially strapped trunk line, desperately in need of renovation and spurs. It now reached Portland only via a line it did not own, whereas to the north of its port on Puget Sound lay a bustling little city, Seattle, hungry for a railroad of its own and angry at the NP, which had spurned it in favor of its own seaport, Tacoma.

Portland did, however, soon receive its own direct transcontinental connection from yet another main line, the old Union Pacific. Built in the late 1860s as the eastern end of the original transcontinental, the Union Pacific reached from Omaha to Ogden, Utah. It then found itself in an incongruous situation, since it relied on an independent line, the Central Pacific, for transit on to the Pacific at San Francisco Bay. Paralleling the Central Pacific westward made no sense. So, the Union Pacific constructed what it called the Oregon Short Line on a northwestern course from Granger, in southwestern Wyoming, along the bending Snake River through southern Idaho, thence across northeastern Oregon.

At Huntington, Oregon, in 1884, it joined to the tracks of the OR&N, which was now divorced from the bankrupted NP. Thus, by the mid-1880s, the Far Northwest had two transcontinental lines, one connecting to the mouth of the Columbia and the other to Puget Sound. Contemporaries believed, wrongly as events would prove, that no more would be built, since Congress had soured on the idea of support of railroads by the bestowal of any more land grants, which the public believed had benefited speculators more than the people.

Finally, even as Hill watched the CP, the NP, and the Union Pacific transcontinentals lay their tracks ever onward to the Pacific Northwest, yet another new line arose to complicate his life right in the midst of his Minnesota heartland. This road, popularly known as the Soo Line, was the Minneapolis, Saint Paul, and Sault Sainte Marie; it emerged from a marriage of interests between the CP and the booming flour-milling industry of the Twin Cities.

Before the 1880s, the wheat raised in the Upper Midwest had passed primarily to Buffalo, New York, situated strategically at the eastern edge of the Great Lakes, for milling into flour. Buffalo ruled as the national capital of the flour-milling industry. The opening of the Minnesota and Red River valleys not only flooded the market with new wheat but flooded it with a new variety: hard spring wheat, which suited this harsh climate better than the traditional, fall-planted winter wheat.

Spring wheat posed severe problems to millers, however, since it dirtied the flour with "middlings," the hard residues of shattered hulls. Meanwhile, Minneapolis was producing a remarkably industrious group of millers, attracted to the waterpower provided by the Falls of Saint Anthony. And over time, these entrepreneurs developed technologies that overcame this problem: the "middlings purifier," which used air blasts to sweep out the hulls, and other purifying and regrinding techniques that produced a "New Process" flour well suited for baking into bread.

The Minneapolis flour millers were already producing $7.5 million worth of product by 1870, and in 1876 they came together in the Minnesota Millers' Association. By 1890, the twenty-four area mills grossed $60 million annually: seven million barrels per year, which made Minnesota the largest flour-producing area on earth. Huge grain elevators loomed along the rolling, wooded skyline; and Minneapolis now rose up to displace Buffalo, since vastly better transportation systems made it sensible to ship finished flour eastward by rail or water rather than to ship bulky cargoes of wheat. Although firmly entrenched in Saint Paul, and sometimes resented for it, Hill and his associates took a keen and appreciative interest in Minneapolis. They invested in waterpower at the Falls of Saint Anthony and in a giant grain elevator facility in the booming rival city to the west.

The barons of the new industry became major forces to be reckoned with, including William Washburn and C. A. Pillsbury, who had completed by 1883 the largest flour mill in the world. In modern parlance, as Minneapolis thus superseded Buffalo, Minnesota flour milling escaped the frontier condition of economic colonialism and was "adding value" to its rich agricultural production in a big way. Under the leadership of Washburn, the Minneapolis millers naturally took an intense interest in the railroads hauling their product, prompted also by the belief that their hometown had been slighted by the roads in favor of Saint Paul. A direct eastbound route to Sault Sainte Marie would provide them with ready access to eastern markets, access preferable to lake steamers, which were locked in by ice during the winter months.

Indeed, this was the very same route that Hill had advocated to the CP as its best transit of the Great Lakes country. In addition to the Soo Line along this path, the millers also projected a "Minnesota and Pacific" line northwestward into the wheat country, some of whose product was bypassing the Twin Cities and their mills along a northern corridor to Duluth and Chicago-Milwaukee. All of this was upsetting to Jim Hill, particularly the idea of a line heading westward in direct competition with the Manitoba.

But much worse, Hill learned that Stephen and the CP had a direct hand in the Soo. When confronted, Stephen admitted that they had invested $750,000 in the road but swore that the CP had no intent to become involved in operations west of the Twin Cities. Naturally, this acquisition intensified the already brewing trouble between Hill and Stephen and Smith. Hill angrily wrote Kennedy, now his closest confidant, "It would seem unfortunate that our Montreal friends should have affiliations with the only people who are giving us trouble in Minnesota." In the years ahead, intermittent warfare would erupt, both east and west of the Twin Cities, between the emerging CP–Soo Line and the Hill railroads.

Within this context of railroad expansion in the early 1880s, James J. Hill devoted most of his days—and nights—to enhancing and expanding the newborn Saint Paul, Minneapolis, and Manitoba Railway. He faced a myriad of challenges: raising the necessary investment capital and fleshing out the infrastructure of the system, military-style campaigning against competing railroads, attracting settlers to the road's hinterland, and reconciling the associates' divergence of interests that arose from the CP venture.

As both the CP and its associated Soo ventures gained momentum, Hill and Kennedy, on the one hand, and Stephen and Smith, on the other, pushed and pulled at their fraying relationship. In the end, self-interest and the resilience of their bond would serve to hold them together, barely. Clearly Jim Hill, as general manager of the Manitoba, was forced to carry an inordinate, unfair share of the load, whereas Stephen and Smith continued to profit from their investment even while they increasingly devoted their energies to what was becoming a rival road.

Stephen attempted to make things right by sending his suave and politically astute right-hand man, R. B. Angus, to Saint Paul to help Hill shoulder the burden. But this could not work. It technically placed Angus as Hill's superior; and in any event, Angus still spent most of his time in Montreal, whereas the imperious workaholic Hill held firmly to control. The partners soon ended the arrangement, and Hill, in turn, took the title of vice-president under Stephen's continuing presidency, a title that Hill would soon see change yet again.

With each passing month, as the attention of his fellow associates wandered, Hill's became ever more focused, and his authority over and control of the Manitoba became nearly absolute. Matching incredibly long hours at his big rolltop desk with frequent forays into the field, he built up a remarkable command of the details of the railroad, its infrastructure, its operations, and its hinterland. Indeed, his knowledge of the railroad, in even the most minute detail, quickly became a matter of legend. For example, while standing on a Dakota rail siding one day, he spotted an engine numbered 94. From that recognition, Hill astounded the engineer by walking up and addressing him by name—Roberts—and noting that the engine had just been in for repairs. At the same time, Hill learned the industry itself—its parameters, problems, and potential. His genius lay precisely in his ability to master detail while fashioning broad vision and strategy. Only his rival-to-be Edward Harriman ever even approached him in this regard.

This same intensity and drive made him a very difficult man to work for and with; as his responsibilities mounted, so did his persona as a demanding, even raging autocrat. John F. Stevens, a highly self-motivated employee, remembered him fondly as "a rather hard taskmaster," given to "occasional sarcasms." In fact, he drove his office employees mercilessly, banning even coffee breaks; he second-guessed them and often bypassed them by intervening personally and unannounced into their affairs.

As time went on, he gave way to occasional fits of shouting and acrimony, even of throwing books and other objects near at hand. He could be absolutely unforgiving; for example he fired a station master simply because he could not bear the man's name—Spittles! One day, while riding one of his trains that was exceeding the posted speed limit, he queried the engineer about it. When the poor fellow, who did not recognize the boss, casually admitted the transgression, Hill summarily fired him. Jim Hill was not a man to disappoint, anger, or cross.

Nonemployees also experienced the infamous Hill temper and retribution. The plush community of Wayzata on handsome Lake Minnetonka, just west of Minneapolis, complained loudly about the commotion his switch engines made during the night. Even though such influential families as the Pillsburys and Lorings lived there, Jim Hill peremptorily closed the passenger station and thus forced the locals to board his trains a mile away. The first of his trains to pass through town did so with such speed as to start a fire with sparks from its engine. Only many years later, after numerous pleadings, was the Wayzata station reopened.

Since Stephen was preoccupied with the CP, John S. Kennedy in New York came increasingly to manage the finances of the Manitoba. He did it conservatively and well, and the bond between him and Hill grew stronger. The younger man's letters to the older were unfailingly deferential, even obsequious. Even after the patriarchal old Scot gave up the presidency of his bank to his nephew J. Kennedy Tod in 1883, he stayed on as vice-president and board member of the railroad.

Kennedy did his friend a great favor by helping him straighten out his personal finances, which had gotten hopelessly intermingled and confused with those of the railroad, to which Hill had even extended personal loans. Interestingly, Hill resembled his contemporary John D. Rockefeller in that he usually did well only by investing in his main area of focus; his many side forays into other projects quite often failed. The one truly notable exception, as we shall see, was his investment in iron ore.

In his Saint Paul office, Hill relied first on a system in which he delegated supervision of trains to General Superintendent E. B. Wakeman and of shipping and passengers to W. S. Alexander. Still, he clearly needed an executive-level assistant. After Angus gave up on their unworkable arrangement, Hill became vice-president of the Manitoba in charge of operations. On the recommendation of a Chicago friend, meatpacking baron Philip Armour, he finally prevailed on the veteran general superintendent of the Chicago and Rock Island, Alan Manvel, to take this position. When Hill rose to the vice-presidency, Manvel became general manager.

Manvel proved to be capable, although also cautious and plodding. His frustration, due both to overwork and to Hill's ungovernable tendency to overrule and skirt his authority, steadily mounted until he announced that he could no longer endure it. Eventually Manvel gave in and agreed to stay aboard, but his problems continued. Undaunted, the boss forged ahead, flanked by two Saint Paul assistants, one handling Manitoba details and one dealing with Hill's personal finances and affairs, and by his capable man at the 40 Wall Street office in New York, Edward Nichols, who similarly split his time between railroad affairs and Hill's personal matters.

The associates maintained the property under their own close control. When one group of Boston investors considered buying in, for instance, they had second thoughts, reckoning that the Manitoba was "too much of a family party for general investors." Even though only Hill in Saint Paul and Kennedy in New York kept a hand in the direct management of the Manitoba, Stephen and Smith kept their stock and, as we have seen, remained on the board. After buying out old Norman Kittson, who was growing tired and cautious, in 1881, the foursome held nearly half the stock in the property.

Supported by other large and allied stockholders, such as Angus and then new directors like D. Willis James and Samuel Thorne of New York and powerful Chicago merchant-king Marshall Field, they had no trouble commanding the destiny of the road. Hill found Field too preoccupied to contribute much and later cajoled him off the board, but both James and Thorne provided strong leadership. James, a financier and steel man, respected Hill but sometimes criticized and fought with him; Thorne, on the other hand, was a fellow railroad man and usually served as a friendly supporter and peacemaker. Hill, in turn, rose steadily toward leadership both of the Manitoba and of the group. When Stephen surrendered the presidency in 1882 to devote his full energies to the CP, Hill naturally—almost anticlimactically—assumed the presidency of the Manitoba.

The Manitoba associates managed the finances of their railroad in a highly conservative and prudent manner. They were neither plungers nor reckless speculators but were in the business for the long run. Unlike such vaunted manipulators as Jay Gould or Henry Villard, Jim Hill took the opposite tack from speculative practices such as milking a railroad of its land grants and its resources and dumping oversold stocks and bonds on a gullible public. Instead, he and his three key partners advocated and practiced a policy of plowing large percentages of profits directly back into the property, knowing that the best defense against invading railroads was a better-built system that could operate at lower rates.

The partners generally avoided the watering of their stock and worked hard to fend off the bears and the bulls who increasingly pursued it as its reputation grew. And they did so in an age when the watering of rail stocks was so common that New York wags spread the rumor of a statue being erected depicting Cornelius Vanderbilt with a waterpot in hand and when Henry V. Poor estimated that one-third of all railroad capitalization consisted of H_2O.

Thus when, in mid-1883, a pack of "bears" staged a raid on Manitoba stock, the foursome mounted an elaborate defense. The concerted selling by the bears drove down the value of the stock from 120 to 80, and this sort of instability threatened not only severe, long-term losses but also a loss of reputation. So the associates formed a large stock-buying pool, with Hill personally throwing in $250,000, and drove the values back up, pegging them at just over $100 per share. Also in 1883, the Manitoba board of directors made a sweeping financial reorganization.

During the preceding four years, the stockholders had minimized profit-taking and had plowed an impressive $11 million in "excess" earnings back into the property. These robust earnings more than bore out Hill's predictions about the Manitoba's earning potential. Now they floated a $50 million consolidated bond issue, with $19.4 million going to retirement of the old bonds, $20 million to new construction, and $10.6 million to profits. The last sum, naturally enough, aroused considerable comment.

Each stockholder was allowed to purchase $500 in these new bonds for each $1,000 owned in stock, at ten cents on the dollar. Hill and his partners rationalized this tidy insider profit-taking with the argument that it was only deferred income, since the owners had been acting as their "own banker" during the prior period of intensive building, at costs of $12,000 per mile and higher. Hill characterized it as "wise and for the best interest of the company." Inevitably, however, critics called it a "bond grab"; and the old image of the associates as sharpers, dating back to the 1878 purchase, gained new life.

There was nothing intrinsically wrong with the practice of allowing the insiders, in such a tightly held and profitable road, to help themselves to deferred profits in such a manner. But Hill still bristled at the eyebrows that were once again raised in his direction. Writing thirty years later, at the time of his retirement, he commented to the Great Northern shareholders:

> The period from 1879 to 1883, when the railroad was still an experiment in the minds of most Eastern capitalists, was not a time to enlarge the volume of the securities or ask outside capital to bid for

them. . . . So another method was adopted. The Company diverted to these uses the money which might have been divided as profits among the stockholders. . . . The stockholders temporarily renounced their profits in order to leave their money in the enterprise. But it remained their money, and the title to it was indisputable. . . . To the stockholder the only difference was they received a portion of the legitimate earnings of the Company in the shape of bonds instead of cash, and were deprived of the personal use of it during the time it had been used by the Company. . . . The difference to the public was not a penny either way.

With such solid fiscal support abetted by land grants, with such capable management, and with such a rich heartland to embrace, the Saint Paul, Minneapolis, and Manitoba spread its trunk and branch lines like a robust plant during the years 1879–86. Unlike its larger rival, the NP, it faced little temptation either to place speculation ahead of solid building or to build far ahead of settlement and markets. Even more than Hill had predicted, the Manitoba proved to be a remarkably productive profit maker. In the gently rolling hills of west-central Minnesota and across the nearly flat bottomlands of the Red, where rails swept from one far horizon to another, each capped by a cathedral-like grain elevator, fertile soils and a densely packed agrarian population fed ample harvests into a highly cost-effective system of well-ballasted, well-built, and constantly improved rails and terminal facilities.

Over nine hundred miles of new track were spiked into place between 1879 and 1883. This trackage generally followed the basic original matrix of the railroad on a southeast-northwest axis; but tendrils also reached down from the Twin Cities toward the rich farmlands of southwestern Minnesota, into the domain of the Chicago and Northwestern. Similarly, a long and highly significant taproot also pushed west across the Red River valley, funded by nearly $6 million in "Dakota Extension" bonds, toward Devils Lake in Dakota Territory, to the great consternation of the NP. A "West Side Line" now paralleled the prime tracks of the road, which lay along the east bank of the Mississippi, serving the boomtown of Minneapolis and hopefully keeping it securely in the Manitoba fold.

Jim Hill worked incessantly at improving every aspect of the railroad's structure and operation. He traveled back and forth along the line in his business car, looking for dips and bumps and spying out curves that could be straightened and grades that could be lessened. More than any other railroad leader of the day, he had an engineer's passion for minimizing curvature and grades, knowing that these were the keys to the lower rates that would vanquish any competition. As employee John Stevens recalled, "It was entirely against Mr. Hill's principles to build any 1 percent lines other than in semi-mountainous country."

Hill spent hours determining where best to invest—and when—in steel trestles to replace wooden ones and masonry culverts to replace earlier wooden ones. He stopped often to talk to the gangs of track layers and the graders carving at the earth with their horse-drawn blades. Soon, he had all locomotives using coal for fuel and then set about acquiring larger and more powerful ones that could pull equally enlarged rolling stock. Beginning with the main trunk lines, his crews pulled out the old iron rails, sometimes relocating them to the less-traveled spurs, and replaced them with superior highly tempered steel rails.

The Manitoba also invested heavily in terminals and other facilities in its Twin Cities bases of operations. In 1880, it opened its new four-story office complex on Wacouta and Fourth Streets in Saint Paul. And then, only eight years later, the expanding corporation moved into a new, five-story Richardsonian Romanesque building on present-day Wall and Kellogg Streets. Meanwhile, in 1882, the Manitoba opened its massive Jackson Street shops complex, built at the cost of nearly $500,000 and outfitted with the most modern machinery for maintenance and repair.

With Hill serving as vice-president, the seven railroads serving the city formed the Saint Paul Union Depot, opening a $200,000 station and train facility on Sibley Street in 1881. Also in 1881, five area carriers created the Minnesota Transfer Company, which built heavy trackage transfer operations between the two converging cities. It was considered one of the best of its kind in the nation.

In Minneapolis, where the Manitoba had severe public relations problems born of perceived neglect, the road now had to face the direct competition of the NP, which finally completed its own line into the city in 1885. The Manitoba constructed a handsome new station on Hennepin Avenue, which it agreed to share with rival roads, including the NP, and developed a two-track (soon four-track) artery system between the milling city and Saint Paul; this system carried eighty passenger trains daily, as well as freight.

This subsidiary Minneapolis Union Railway spanned the Mississippi near the Falls of Saint Anthony by way of a beautiful, curved, granite bridge that opened to dual-track traffic in 1884. Obstructed by other structures and seldom seen today, it was for many years as much the signature edifice of the Twin Cities as the Golden Gate Bridge later was for San Francisco. Reaching across the river on a twenty-three-hundred-foot causeway supported by classical arches, the bridge took ten minutes off the intercity commute for Twin City residents. The *Railroad Gazette* called it "one of the greatest specimens of engineering skill in the country." Seldom paying much heed to amenities, Jim Hill did love his bridge and also the swank Hotel LaFayette, which he erected on the shores of Lake Minnetonka in 1882 to cater to the wealthy tourists his railroad carried to the location.

By 1880, the Manitoba had begun to place greater emphasis on the construction of branch lines. And after 1883, the building of these far outpaced main-line construction, which had dwindled to only a few miles per year. In characteristically tough-minded fashion, Jim Hill faced the hard issues of when, where, and whether to build branches. That is, he made such decisions based on traffic potential and the danger posed by encroaching competitor lines. He did not usually indulge in the common practice of extorting subsidies from towns hungry for service, nor did he normally bypass established towns out of spite. Such actions, after all, simply left him vulnerable to inroads by other carriers. On the other hand, this fierce competitor did not succumb to threats. He knew that the best defense against invading roads that were looking for budding branches to gobble up was a well-built system that could outcompete any interloper with rock-bottom rates.

The Manitoba followed a general policy of relying on small and separate companies to construct its branch lines. It usually invested in the stocks and bonds of these little area lines and in turn leased and operated them directly. Such branches might, on occasion, link major cities in the heart of the railroad's empire, like the Minneapolis and Saint Cloud. More often, they reached out to the less populous hinterland.

As the NP, Manitoba, and Soo lines spread their rail networks westward across the Red River valley, they pioneered the building of communities on the northern plains. More than its two rivals combined, as historian Thomas Harvey has revealed, the Manitoba built "proprietary," or company-established towns, mainly along its main lines. This allowed the railroad, of course, to profit directly from real estate development; but Hill and his associates also found that this policy had severe disadvantages. As Ralph Budd summarized years later in a letter to Hill's son Louis: "Our townsites have nearly all made us quite a lot of money up to the time tracks reach them and, usually, for a very short period after that date. After that period we have generally quite a lot of land on hand and sales practically cease, while taxes, office expense, and other items continue and our profits gradually are dissipated."

Most towns and townsites, naturally, lay away from the main lines, and they all pined for rail connections. Some, like the town of Malung, Minnesota, simply beckoned with offers of free access. Others, like the Warroad Townsite Company, promised 110 acres free for a spur in from Thief River Falls. In building to these locales, the Manitoba drew on its experience and dealt more with "subsidiary agents" or "affiliated proprietors" to manage affairs, thus exercising less authority in these settings and allowing allied entrepreneurs to share in both the profits and the risks. Private, unaffiliated developers, of course, also built up plausible townsites to entice the road.

The best example of Manitoba subsidiary agents was the Moorhead, Minnesota, team of Solomon Comstock and Almond

White, who built nine branch-line towns before constructing the Minnesota and Dakota Northern, along which they developed five more. They received no money from the railroad but worked closely with it. Receiving advance information from the Manitoba about its construction plans, they in turn conveyed free trackage, depot, and yard sites to the road on its arrival.

The new railroad towns were monotonously alike, long on utility and short on amenities and esthetics. Most bore the standard, rectangular-grid design, with the rails bisecting the community, often into "right side" and "wrong side" districts. Along the Manitoba, another style developed in the early 1880s. This featured a "T" design in which the town abutted rather than straddled the tracks, with the main thoroughfare running into the railroad at a right angle. Only an occasional exception, such as Saint Vincent, with its curved roadway, deviated much from these patterns. Speculative and optimistic, the plains towns sprouted up like mushrooms. Many of them would eventually shrivel, but most are still there today.

One of James J. Hill's favorite themes, voiced repeatedly in the years to come, stressed the community of interest, the mutual interdependence, between the railroads and the regions they served. The two must, he reasoned, be rich or be poor together; and any regional carrier, even one with a de facto monopoly, would only harm itself if it gouged consumers with excessive rates. Although this assertion, as we shall see, was highly debatable, it was most certainly true that the railroads promoted settlement, economic growth, and community building in many different ways, for example, in the sales of its publicly granted lands to settlers. Selling off these prime farmlands presented little challenge, particularly during the flush times of the early 1880s. The NP had already sold most of its Red River valley lands; those held by the Manitoba, on the Minnesota side, were highly fertile, although plagued by problems of water drainage. Thus, even by the time the associates took over the road, it was already in the midst of a major land promotion. The Manitoba sold nearly 180,000 acres during the formative period between January 1878 and June 1879.

With his usual aggressiveness, Hill pressed the sales onward, at prices that in choice areas like Crookston, Minnesota, and Grand Forks, Dakota, reached $3.00 per acre. He well knew that the rising volume of freight that would come with settlement would far outweigh the value appreciation that would result from holding the properties. Between mid-1881 and mid-1882, the road sold over 203,343 more acres, for $1,108,312. To thwart speculators and to encourage rapid cultivation, as Joseph Thompson's study of the Great Northern reveals, the Manitoba pursued a policy of granting "rebates" of one-fourth or more of purchase prices if the lands were immediately put to the plow. It worked, and the average size of holdings on these lands dropped from 156 acres to 76 by mid-decade.

To promote sales, as well as the development of agriculture along his lines, Hill hired James Power as his land commissioner. Power, who had earlier held a similar post with the NP, would later go on to become the president of the North Dakota Agricultural College. Adopting a well-worn metaphor, Power's publications advertised the valley as the most blessed granary in the world, the "Nile of the North." Jim Hill joined personally and enthusiastically in these promotions. In a growing number of speeches and writings, he warned against relying on single-crop cultivation, pointing to the backwardness of the cotton South as the natural result of such vulnerability. The answer lay instead, he preached, in diversification, especially into beef and dairy cattle, so that drops in wheat prices and yields would not turn short-term crises into long-term failures.

Always a farmer at heart, Hill began in the 1880s the agricultural experiment farms that would become a preoccupation of his later life. At his seven-thousand-acre Northcote Farm, near the Canadian border, his workers imported and crossbred European cattle and other animals, and he began the practice not only of passing on his findings but of loaning or donating the resulting animals for breeding to agriculturalists located along his lines. He was a true Jeffersonian agrarian, and he especially hated the giant "bonanza" farms—specialized, commercial wheat operations—that the NP encouraged with sales of or stock exchanges for its Red River valley lands. Few of these appeared on Manitoba lands, since its policies encouraged smaller, family farms. And in any event, declining prices as the decade wore on soon brought an end to these premature efforts at big-time commercial agriculture.

In these early years, the Manitoba tended simply to follow the ambitious lead of the NP in recruiting settlers to its hinterland. It published its first gazetteer in 1882 and spread one hundred thousand copies across the United States, Canada, and northern Europe. Five years later, Hill dispatched a "special emigration agent" to Norway and Sweden, where land shortages and inheritance laws favoring the eldest son motivated rising numbers of younger sons and daughters to leave. They, along with numerous Germans and Anglo-Irish, responded by the tens of thousands. Long after his death, they would remember "Yim" or "Yem" Hill, fondly or less fondly, as the man who had recruited and located them. As Hill put it, "We are always anxious to help the people and get them into the country so as to build it up, to do anything we can to help them, even if it costs more than we get for it."

Under Hill's close management, the Manitoba made many efforts to serve its agricultural and other constituents. Some of this was simply good business, for instance Hill's drawing on his background in the fuel industry to stockpile wood and later coal at his depots. This practice allowed his grain cars to avoid "deadheading" empty on their return from the Twin Cities, and it provided a similar advantage to the farmer, who could now load his wagon with fuel when returning from the elevator. Good business as well as the cultivation of goodwill also prompted the Manitoba to carry seed grain free to farmers hit by drought and depression later in the decade and to utilize the U.S. diplomatic service to procure hearty spring wheat seed varieties from the Ukraine. Like other railroads, the Manitoba also cultivated goodwill by donating land to small towns for parks, schools, and churches, the last especially welcomed by newly arrived immigrants.

Yet, for all that, farmers naturally built up strong resentments against railroads that, more often than not, held them in a grip of monopoly. Although rail rates fell steadily during this age of deflation, producers felt that they did not fall as rapidly as they should. The lines never seemed to have adequate numbers of cars on hand to haul grain after harvests. Farmers focused their wrath on the grain storage elevators, many of which were owned by the railroad and most of which were woefully too small, with capacities of only five thousand to ten thousand bushels. The elevator interests routinely practiced "docking," or deducting several pounds per bushel of premium number-one hard red spring wheat for dirt and impurities. So far as the farmers were concerned, this was nothing but thievery.

Hill genuinely cared about quality rail service and about public opinion. Immediately in 1879, he dealt with the elevator capacity problem—which disadvantaged his railroad just as it did the farmers—by ordering that such facilities controlled by the Manitoba be enlarged to a minimum thirty-thousand-bushel capacity. Recognizing the potency as well as the justice of the docking issue, he supported the reformers in the Minnesota legislature, which enacted an 1885 law regulating grain grading and handling.

Still, popular unrest mounted. What railroad leaders feared most, of course, was that this would lead to government regulation. This issue, like most others, was not particularly an ideological one for James J. Hill but rather a practical one. He preferred the free-trade, Jeffersonian Democratic Party of the 1880s to the protectionist Republicans, but he consistently placed his political support where it would do him the most good, regardless of political preference.

He distrusted not only the antirailroad agrarian radicals—such as the Grangers in Minnesota and the "Grits" in western Canada—but politicians and legislators in general. Nonetheless, he welcomed and cooperated with the state legislature when it acted in his interest, for instance with legislation that forbade the granting of free rail passes to government officers or shipping rebates to pesky producers. If necessity required it, he would "contribute" to politicians who served him well, for instance by granting free or underpriced corporate stock to politicians like

Minnesota Congressman H. B. Strait for help rendered. Whether due to principle or perceptivity, however, he was never known to bribe politicians outright. When an agrarian "Grit" reformer in Canada stated that Hill had offered him a $20,000 bribe, Hill forced an immediate retraction from him.

Like other midwestern states, Minnesota had enacted "Granger laws" back in the early 1870s that attempted to set maximum rail rates, with mixed results. It now had a railroad commission that was struggling to regulate carriers, amid a mounting public clamor against perceived excessive rates and deficient service. Knowing the vulnerable position his road occupied, between the producers on the one side and the millers on the other, Hill essentially followed a "rule of reason" approach, as he always would. He knew that some measure of state, and soon federal, regulation was inevitable; so he attempted to fend off what he could and to divert the rest as much as possible in his favor. This was a sensible approach, but it would become more difficult in the future.

For all their importance, political strategies weighed far less heavily on Jim Hill's mind than did rail strategies. During the big boom of construction in the early and mid-1880s, as the regional roads of the Upper Midwest encroached on each other's territories and sought to force out the opposition, their encounters came to resemble those of opposing armies. This suited Hill's combative nature very well. He held the advantages of a wonderfully productive and naturally confined hinterland and a well-built road—slowly and carefully constructed—along with a firmly controlled base of operations in the commercial capital of his region.

Thus he had less reason to worry about episodic rate wars, such as the large one of 1884, or about freight pooling agreements, such as the "Omaha Pool" of the 1880s, than did the bitterly competing Granger Roads radiating westward from Chicago toward the Twin Cities, Omaha, and the Kansas City area. Simply put, he hated pools, and firmly in command of his own turf, he had little need to abide by them.

As the decade unfolded, and as these roads thrust their rails rapidly westward amid destructive rate wars, Jim Hill gauged his situation well. He now became one of the first men in the business to see the looming shadows of coming events and to act accordingly. Assessing the status of his prosperous regional railroad, he came to see it as one component in an evolving *national* transportation system. The day of prosperous, independent, regional roads must soon end; the future lay in integrated, continental systems that could move heavy tonnages rapidly and without interruption, at uniform and falling rates. Either the Manitoba would find its own way from sea to sea—building its own tracks to the Pacific or integrating existing roads into its own—or it would be absorbed, perhaps by the NP or by one of the Granger Roads linking it to Chicago, the key "gateway" or "break point" for commerce with the dominant Eastern-Atlantic region via eastern trunk lines like the New York Central or the Pennsylvania.

The NP, the traditional rival of the Manitoba, presented a lesser threat now than it had earlier. Villard's frenetic transcontinental building spree had left the NP severely overextended and in need of rebuilding much of its hastily constructed main line. And its vacillating management, which Hill continued to despise as a crew of mindless speculators, seemed unable to hold to a consistent policy.

The two roads still nominally adhered to their 1879 agreement to a north-south axis for the Manitoba and an east-west axis for the NP. But in fact, neither side considered the agreement worth much more than the paper on which it was written. President Frederick Billings of the NP had disavowed this part of the agreement and had thrust a spur northward along the west side of the Red Valley from Casselton, Dakota Territory, to meet an independent Canadian line building south from Winnipeg. At the same time, Hill's thrust westward to Devils Lake, Dakota— at the far rim of the Red River drainage—similarly unmasked his thoughts about building to the west.

The Manitoba's most dangerous competitor, at this time, was the Chicago, Milwaukee, and Saint Paul, which had earlier missed a chance to buy the road in its infancy. Naturally enough, the Milwaukee Road looked not only toward but beyond the Twin Cities, westward across the Red River valley, and longed to carry the valley's bounties of grain directly to its home base in Chicago. Hill was able, however, to checkmate the Milwaukee. He kept its primary westward arm, the Hastings and Dakota, deflected well to the south of the Twin Cities, holding a careful watch over budding local lines that the opposition might acquire.

When the Milwaukee sought directly to invade the valley with another subsidiary, the Fargo and Southwestern, Hill proved able to blunt their thrust by the simple expedient of forcing rates below what the opposition could bear, bolstered by his own well-built road, which could haul high tonnages more cheaply. Then again, the Milwaukee could not link downstream to the CP, since the CP was controlled by Manitoba investors. Once again, the advantage of a tightly controlled regional railroad against competitively besieged, trunk-line invaders became obvious. As for the war between Hill and the Milwaukee, it would flare intermittently for all the years of his life, almost always with Hill coming out on top.

Obviously, in his search for an allied line to Chicago, which he had to find in order to build the through-routes and through-rates he envisioned, Jim Hill could not turn to the hostile Milwaukee. Nor did the more friendly but also expansion-minded Chicago and Northwestern fit the bill. Its center of activity focused well to the south of Manitoba territory. Rather, the ideal community of interest for the Manitoba seemed to lie with the robust Chicago, Burlington, and Quincy, and the resulting marriage would prove to be both profitable and enduring.

The Burlington Road, or the "Q," as Hill and others sometimes called it, was expertly and conservatively financed and controlled by a group of Bostonians led by the venerable John Murray Forbes. Its highly regarded president, Charles E. Perkins, traveled over the Manitoba's route with Hill in 1883. Afterward, he penned a handsome appraisal: the Manitoba seemed "probably the snuggest and best of the properties lying west of St. Paul . . . every mile of it in the best kind of a wheat country." Forbes also came out to assess the property and admired it.

So in August 1885, Kennedy arranged the sale of twenty thousand shares of Manitoba stock to the firm of Lee, Higginson, and Company, as agents for the Bostonians. The four associates—Hill, Kennedy, Smith, and Stephen—put up the stock for sale; soon after, Hill and Kennedy made similar purchases of Burlington stock. Marshall Field, who had never been an active board member, allowed Hill to replace him with a young scion of the Bostonians, Henry D. Minot. Thus, a fruitful and portentous alliance was born.

In 1886, the "Q" built its Burlington and Northern subsidiary, a high-quality, doubled-tracked road capable of carrying heavy tonnages, into Saint Paul. Hill invested $500,000 in the line and gave it favorable lease rights to his Saint Paul freight and depot facilities and access to Minneapolis over Manitoba tracks. Although the Burlington and Northern failed to record profits in the face of fierce competition, it did augur a new era both for its parent railroad and for the Manitoba. As Kennedy noted, the Manitoba's "jealous neighbors" must "be careful," for "they must know the inevitable consequences should they provoke a conflict."

The Burlington affiliation brought with it another asset, one of mixed blessings: Henry D. Minot. Haughty, brilliant, aloof, and acerbic, Minot was Forbes's nephew, and he burned for glory in the romantic world of railroading. Complying with the wishes of the Bostonians, Hill not only took on Minot as a director but also welcomed him to an executive assistant position in Saint Paul. Since poor Alan Manvel had by now, in 1886, been driven to the verge of distraction by overwork and the frustrations of working for his boss, Hill furloughed him to a vacation in Europe. Manvel would soon move on to the presidency of the Atchison, Topeka, and Santa Fe Railroad and was replaced as general manager of the Manitoba by the equally unspectacular E. L. Mohler. Minot blew into this situation like a tornado and vastly impressed Hill with his strategic vision and drive. The boss quickly gave him one major assignment after another in the thrusts now beginning to the south, west, and east.

Unfortunately, the young Minot was also a thoroughly nasty

individual, who indulged constantly in backbiting and in setting one individual against another. He especially delighted in belittling Hill's closest associate, old John Kennedy, whose senior vice-presidency he coveted. Finally, Kennedy lashed back in a hot letter to Hill: "He is an absolute failure . . . and none of us here can understand why it is that you do not get rid of him as we all agreed it was best to do last December. . . . He has been a fraud from the beginning and an intolerable nuisance."

Curiously, however, Jim Hill, who always had so much difficulty passing on authority to his subordinates, clung loyally to this one; Hill was impressed by his strategic brilliance and probably smitten with his obsequiousness. Minot might well have become Hill's successor, but he did not. Only four years later, in 1890, he died suddenly in Pennsylvania when an oncoming locomotive, sent down the wrong track by a wrongly thrown switch, smashed into his private car, coupled to the rear of a parked train.

Minot's brief time with the Manitoba coincided with its period of remarkable expansion that began in 1886, and he played a prominent role in it as Hill's right-hand man. Even with the favorable access to Chicago provided by the Burlington alliance, James J. Hill still looked fondly north and east toward Lake Superior and the highly competitive access it could offer to eastern markets via the Great Lakes and Buffalo, at the eastern extremity. Here beckoned a shipping route that, during the warmer seasons of the year, offered solid competition to the Chicago linkage. But it also required major investments: heavy-freight trackage north-northeast to Duluth, good storage and dockage facilities there, and of course, big ships to traverse the Great Lakes.

Before 1886, the Manitoba had relied on the less than dependable Saint Paul and Duluth line, on whose board Hill sat, for access to Lake Superior. Now, Hill precipitously broke with that line, much to its consternation, in favor of a new Manitoba subsidiary, the Eastern Railway of Minnesota. This road was organized in 1887 and was rapidly constructed through the sixty-eight miles of dense forest lying between Hinckley and Duluth, employing three thousand workers at the height of building. It opened service in the fall of 1888. Hill installed Minot as president of the Eastern Railway, a move that eased the strains the young man was causing in the Manitoba organization, and once again Minot did a first-rate job.

Meanwhile, Hill focused a great deal of his attention on pressuring the U.S. Army Corps of Engineers to improve harbor facilities at Duluth-Superior and on the NP to structure its bridge facilities there so as to allow large steel freight vessels to pass under them. Ever the geopolitical strategist, he also became an advocate of what would prove to become a long-term issue: widening and improving the narrows at Sault Sainte Marie, joining Lakes Superior and Huron, so that the big ships that were the keys to his strategy could navigate them.

Taking the advice of influential Ohio steamship manufacturer and political sage Mark Hanna, who would remain his friend for life, Jim Hill determined to construct six massive cargo ships for his newly created Northern Steamship Line. The giant steamers, over three hundred feet long and with tonnage capacities of twenty-seven hundred, were constructed by Hanna's Globe Iron Works at Cleveland. Each vessel carried "Northern" as its first name, for instance *Northern Light*. And each embodied the same philosophy of massive tonnages and low rates that Hill and others were applying to rail transport.

Later, in 1892, Northern Steamship had Globe Iron Works build two great passenger ships, the *North West* and the *Northland*, the only vessels of their kind on the lakes. These sumptuous ships provided Hill's rail lines with a one-thousand-mile connection across the Great Lakes and offered staterooms with private baths and electric lighting, amenities equivalent to those of topline luxury hotels of the day. Ohio Governor and future President William McKinley declared the *North West* to be "a veritable floating palace."

Another Hill-Manitoba subsidiary firm, the Great Northern Elevator Company, provided large grain storage and transshipment facilities at Lakeside in West Superior, at the very westernmost point of Lake Superior, along the Minnesota-Wisconsin border. With Hill arranging good dock facilities at West Superior, and Kennedy equally good ones at Buffalo, the Manitoba had by 1888 an excellent and cost-efficient lake transport system in operation, specializing in hauling grain eastward and coal westward.

As Julius Grodinsky has noted, Jim Hill's big Great Lakes freighters abruptly changed the transportation situation in the Upper Midwest. They vastly surpassed the tonnage profits of their smaller predecessors, and they competed very favorably, during the nonwinter months, with the Granger Roads that extended the four hundred miles from southern Minnesota to Chicago. Even Perkins, of the friendly Burlington Road, fretted about how to compete with "the tendency of grain to go to Saint Paul and Duluth."

As he would again and again later, Hill gloried in the role of rate-slasher and disrupter of pooling agreements. With his well-financed and profitable railroad and his alternate outlets via the Great Lakes eastward, he could fashion through rates—from the Atlantic to the northern plains—that could undercut rates via Chicago. Thus in 1890, as he refused to attend a rate parley in New York, he stated: "It is only 150 miles from Duluth to St. Paul, while it is 400 between Chicago and St. Paul, which is 250 miles in our favor. Why shouldn't we carry freight cheaper?"

The mid-1880s saw a similar expansion of the Saint Paul, Minneapolis, and Manitoba system into the inviting farmlands of southwestern Minnesota and beyond, into the easternmost region of what in 1889 would become the state of South Dakota. This was territory claimed by the Granger Roads, but that did not trouble the aggressive Hill. He clearly saw that his railroad, which had been built on a southeast-to-northwest plane from the Twin Cities to Grand Forks and Devils Lake in Dakota, might just as well also lay down crisscrossing, southwest-to-northeast lines to carry grain from these rich farmlands lying west and south either to the Twin Cities or on north to Duluth and the Great Lakes.

During the period 1886–88, a phalanx of such southwestern branch lines probed out to and beyond the border of Minnesota with southern Dakota. Urged especially by Minot, the southernmost of these, the Willmar and Sioux Falls, reached to the latter community, a booming burg of seventy-five hundred. Just to the north, the Duluth, Watertown, and Pacific probed even farther into Dakota, to Huron on the James River. And still farther north, another line extended westward from Breckenridge to Aberdeen and Rutland, in the northeastern quadrant of present-day South Dakota. These were grain-belt roads, and they served as a great net, thrown out to bring in the traffic flowing eastward from south of the NP line through Bismarck, Dakota. They ate heavily into the traffic of the Burlington, the Milwaukee, and the Chicago and Northwestern railroads.

Due south, Hill projected a long and unique tendril all the way into central Iowa in the form of the Mason City and Fort Dodge Railroad. The Manitoba had operated central Iowa coal mines for several years before divesting itself of them in 1885. But, still eyeing his investment in coal lands in adjacent Webster County, Hill purchased this narrow-gauge line the following year and seemed intent on integrating it into a solid line all the way north to the Twin Cities.

But instead, as the research of H. Roger Grant reveals, he let the enterprise lapse, in part because better sources of coal were now becoming available both from the east via the Great Lakes and from Montana to the west. The directors of the rival Milwaukee Road very much wanted this line, but of course Hill would not let it go to them. Instead, he held it until 1901, when he sold it to the friendly Chicago Great Western, which was managed by his Saint Paul neighbor A. B. Stickney, for $1.4 million, together with the Webster County Coal and Land Company for another $1.2 million. The Mason City Railroad had not been a particularly successful venture; and its neglect and then demise symbolized the extent to which the Manitoba's future lay more to the east and west than to the north and south.

Thus, the critical period 1886–88 marked a point of major departure for the Saint Paul, Minneapolis, and Manitoba. The Manitoba had, on the one hand, emerged as a mature, powerful, and profitable regional railroad. Its main lines and branch lines crisscrossed the state of Minnesota in all but the remote, forested, and lake-strewn northeastern quadrant. Branch lines extended into the humid regions of neighboring Dakota Territory out to the ninety-eighth meridian, where the dry lands begin; the northernmost of these, to Devils Lake, was about to move on west as the main line of a transcontinental railroad. The Duluth facilities and fleet of steamships gave the Manitoba ready access to New York, and its Burlington alliance offered excellent trackage to the key hub of Chicago. Few regional railroads could match it either for solidity of capitalization and infrastructure or for excellence of management.

On the other hand, the Manitoba now stood on the threshold of its dramatic westward expansion and of its emergence as a transcontinental carrier of national importance. Jim Hill's closest confidants, such as directors D. Willis James and Samuel Thorne, and even John Kennedy, worried that the railroad was already dangerously overcommitted financially as a result of these regional extensions. Outwardly, at least, he agreed with them. But inwardly, his every instinct and prescient thought told him that the moment of decision was at hand. Caught in the new wave of prosperity and rail building, the Manitoba must either lay tracks to the Pacific or become a link in someone else's system. Rising to this challenge, he would take his place in the national and international firmament.

CHAPTER 4

Westward: The Great Northern

THE great adventure of James J. Hill's life came during his prime years, 1886–93, with the epic westward construction of his midwestern railroad to the Pacific. The Saint Paul, Minneapolis, and Manitoba became the Great Northern Railway, a transcontinental—in fact, one of best constructed and most profitable of the world's major railroads. This massive effort drove Hill to the limits of his very considerable endurance. But in turn, it also drew him from the ranks of regional influence to the forefront of national and international stature and power. By the time of the completion of his railroad, he would have, indeed, become the single most powerful individual in the northwestern United States.

Jim Hill was in the prime of life in 1886. Approaching his fiftieth birthday, he typified the life experience of most people in that the traits of his youth now became more pronounced with middle age. The rock-hard, short, and stocky body of younger days had given way to a spreading girth that resulted from long hours at the desk, lack of exercise, and an unrestrained diet. The receding hairline of young manhood had long since become a bald pate, which he often graced with a western homburg hat. His beard, earlier clipped and dark, was now full, bushy, and flecked with gray. In fact, the unkempt beard and hairline, the penguin-like profile, and the homburg hat became his trademark.

But for all the signs of middle age, the fires of intensity, determination, and ambition burned within him hotter than ever, now that he had savored the headiness of power and wealth. The long hours at the office continued, and once at home, he often sat up late into the night writing long letters to associates, letters that are today collected in the Saint Paul research library bearing his name. He complained frequently of fatigue and, never a sound sleeper, lay awake through much of the night. The aches of neuralgia afflicted him more and more; and on an almost predictable basis, no doubt as a partial result of stress, he was forced to stay in bed for days at a time with cold or flu congestion symptoms.

His near-manic preoccupation with his business gripped him like a demon. Thus he could agree with the admonition of George Stephen in 1881 to "take more leisure." Stephen added, "It is simply impossible you can, without great risk, go on working as you have been these last 3 years; were you made of 'steel' you could not stand it for long." In 1887, he heard from his closest confidant, John S. Kennedy, who wrote, "You and I have got all we need and a great deal more besides, then what is the use of toiling and laboring night and day to increase it?" This sound advice failed to change Hill's behavior, though, and he allowed very little time for recreation, even for the hunting and fishing trips that had always meant much to him. The reason why lay not only in his work obsession and love of the enterprise but also in his love of acquiring wealth, for Jim Hill enjoyed the spending as well as the making of money. He verged closer to being a spendthrift than a miser.

Hill doted on his wife and children, despite the parsimony of time spent with them, and he always lavished favors on them. Everyone in the Twin Cities knew, or knew of, the growing Hill clan. And all knew of the family's closeness and knew that Jim relished the role of the stern but loving paterfamilias, who supervised every detail of the children's upbringing. With the birth in 1885 of a third son, Walter—who would grow up to be more indulged and spoiled than his much older brothers—the brood rounded out at nine living children: Mary Frances ("Mamie"), James Norman, Louis, Clara, Charlotte, Ruth, Rachel, Gertrude, and finally, Walter.

The physical and emotional stress of delivering and tending to ten children, including little Katy, who died in infancy, took a predictably heavy toll on James's stoic and good-hearted wife. Like her husband, Mary struggled with being overweight, but her most alarming problem was the endemic bronchial congestion then referred to as "consumption." This condition, which was eventually diagnosed as tuberculosis, became so severe by the mid-1880s that she spent several winters in the south to secure relief. Often accompanied by their friends and neighbors the Uphams, Jim would journey down in his private car, the *Manitoba,* spend some time with her, and then bring her home.

She continued her role as wife just as she had begun it, as an intensely Catholic, subservient, and traditional woman. She seemed perfectly content bowing to her husband's wishes, and she never openly challenged him. Even as Jim shed what little Catholic interest he had earlier demonstrated, now seldom attending mass with his family, Mary dwelt more than ever on the proper religious upbringing of her children. Her special confidant, Father Caillet, advised her closely on all matters religious and familial. Although surrounded by servants, she did her own shopping every day, carefully allotting princely sums for everything from meats, sweets, and wines to the large variety of newspapers and magazines that always graced their homes. Whereas her husband was volatile, impetuous, and self-centered, Mary was calm and supportive. She made Jim Hill the perfect wife. He knew it and very often said so.

The tightly clustered procession of children were moving rapidly toward maturity. Some people described Mamie, the eldest, as "pouty"; she had a dark complexion and, like her sisters, was understatedly pretty. She was married in 1888 to Samuel Hill, a debonair attorney who was no relation. Jim gave them a handsome wedding gift of one thousand shares of Manitoba stock, which would provide them a satisfactory lifetime income. Sam Hill was a worldly fellow, and they became an urbane and free-spending couple, whose marriage would eventually become alienated. But for now, within a year, they had provided her proud parents with their first grandchild, yet another Mary.

Jim Hill paid special heed to the raising of his two older boys. Sparing in the time he spent with them, he lavished his attention instead on their education. The Hills felt that the Saint Paul public schools were too Protestant and that the Catholic schools were inadequate. So Jimmie and Louie were tutored at home, under the watchful eye of a father who dealt mercilessly with the teachers when he disagreed with them. Then the boys were sent off to Philips Exeter Academy in New Hampshire.

The two sons both went to Yale. Partly as a result of their sporadic preparation, each had troubles there, but they eventually did graduate. Observers often commented that the two sons failed to blossom because their father could never wean them—or anyone else, for that matter—from his own close control. James Jr. replaced Henry Minot at the head of the Eastern Railway of Minnesota and indeed demonstrated ability in so doing; Louis soon joined him there. Louis then served his father as special assistant; as his abilities increasingly surfaced, he became the apple of Jim Hill's eye.

The five younger Hill girls, who were frequently described as stairsteps, were never accorded such aspirations. One after the other, they attended the diocesan convent schools in Saint Paul and then went east to proper finishing schools, always under the watchful eye of their mother and always under the aegis of Catholicism. The Hills raised their children in good Victorian fashion, the girls sheltered and educated to be proper ladies and the boys taught to follow in their father's footsteps. But the boys also had their constraints. Jimmie and Louie had to learn to go it on their own, and thus for their first years out of college, they got only modest monthly allowances. They did not receive their equivalences of Mamie's $100,000 bequest until 1898.

Perhaps as a partial result of his own besieged youth, Jim Hill focused nearly all his private life on his family. By the mid-1880s, the burgeoning growth of the Manitoba made it necessary to keep corporate offices in New York City, at 63 William Street. On his numerous trips there, approximately six per year, he unfailingly had his assistant daily check on his home. Wisely, he purchased a handsome farm northwest of Saint Paul; complete with a sizable lake and woodlands, it was called North Oaks. Here he both raised his prized herds of cattle for experimental breeding and retreated in the summer for time with his family. The Hills maintained stables at their home; and the rides to and from North Oaks, as well as the leisurely time spent there, afforded him welcome solace.

Meanwhile, the family home on Ninth and Canada in "Lowertown" had become inadequate, either to house a growing family in proper style or to signify the status of its fast-rising owner. So Hill set out to build one that would, simply put, outshine all others. For a site, he chose beautiful Summit Avenue on the western bluffs of Saint Paul, with a rear perspective that looked down on the winding Mississippi and a frontal vantage that spanned the city. This street still provides the visitor one of the best vistas of opulent life in the Victorian Era. For the architecture, he selected the prestigious Peabody and Stearns firm of Boston. It, in turn, adopted the "Richardsonian Romanesque" style, featuring massive, carved wooden arches, great doors and hallways, an exterior of red stone quarried in Massachusetts, and imposing brick interior walls that—along with the protective bars over the windows—gave the huge home the forbidding appearance of a castle or fortress.

Built at a cost of $930,000, and requiring three years and the efforts of more than four hundred workmen to construct, the Hill mansion was truly grand in every aspect—"the most important and impressive house ever built in Saint Paul," in the words of historian Robert Frame. It contained thirty-six thousand square feet, thirteen bathrooms with modern plumbing, a large art gallery complete with a pipe organ, $132,532 in "new furnishings," a grand hallway with huge doors, and an exquisite dining room finished in mahogany and leather. It was the first fully electrified home in the city. The lower floor housed a giant boiler room and a laundry facility and quarters for ten to fourteen servants.

Massive, looming, even forbidding, the mansion seemed to embody Jim Hill himself. He loved it, and he loved the evening walks with Mary past the neighboring home of son Louis and past his friends' homes that lined handsome Summit Avenue. The Hill mansion still stands today and is in fact one of the most popular tourist sites in Saint Paul. When the family moved into the house in 1891, Jim stunned everyone by having the old place razed to the ground. Evidently, he could simply not stand to see it placed in other hands or neglected. And of course, he did not need the money he had invested in it!

Even when ensconced in their new home, the Hills maintained

The James J. Hill home on Summit Avenue, Saint Paul, 1905. Courtesy of Minnesota Historical Society.

a quite modest social life. Entertainment was low-key and often focused on Catholic priests, nuns, and dignitaries. But when their circle of close family friends did come over, Jim loved to play the role of host and center of attention. Favorite activities consisted of picnics and family games on the lawn during the afternoons and formal meals in the evenings, after which the males enjoyed retreating to the den for brandy and cigars, and the women gathered in their own retreat. In other words, their world typified the ideal of Gilded Age gentility.

Jim Hill made one notable exception to his reclusive home life, and that was his art collection. Even before moving to 240 Summit Avenue, he had taken up the pastime, typical of refined Victorian men of wealth, of collecting art, initially that of local artists but soon the work also of first-rate Europeans. He genuinely loved his art collection, studied his favorites and his investments carefully, and did not aggregate the collection merely for conspicuous display. By this time, it included major works by such prominent figures as Camille Corot, Henri Rousseau, Jean-François Millet, and Eugène Delacroix. He loved to show and share it. Hill had added a gallery to the front of the old home, and now the new one featured a large and beautiful gallery with a separate entrance for public showings. He gloried in these public art exhibits and soon took up the practice of loaning and occasionally even donating his pieces throughout Minnesota.

The Hills enjoyed and demonstrated their rapidly rising wealth and status in other ways too, ways that typified the age. For years, one of James's few self-indulgences had been the treks to Canada's Saint John River to join Stephen, Kennedy, and the clan in the joys of "killing" the renowned, fighting Atlantic salmon. Now, in 1888, he ponied up $3,750 plus $350 per annum to join an exclusive gentlemen's fishing association on the Restigouche River in New Brunswick.

Hill also bought into the crème de la crème Jekyll Island resort off the Georgia coast and into North Carolina's similarly exclusive Currituck Shooting Club for gentlemen duck hunters. Soon, he even joined that ultimate paragon of upper-class camaraderie, the New York Metropolitan Club. Now, he was hobnobbing with

Rockefellers and Morgans. But his ferocious work ethic, combined with his careful marshaling of spare evening and weekend hours for the family, left little time to enjoy these hard-won social niceties.

Again like most of their nouveau riche peers, the Hills demonstrated their newly won status through the typical forms of charity that predated the modern federal income tax. These tended to be religious in nature, and James made it a practice to balance his donations between Catholic and Protestant organizations. He gave freely to the quality denominational colleges—such as Carleton in Northfield—that then as now abounded in Minnesota; but he steadfastly refused to support public educational institutions, even the fine state university then evolving in his home state.

His favorite project became the Saint Paul Seminary, for which his friend Catholic Archbishop John Ireland donated the land but for which Hill eventually came up with $500,000 for design and construction. The great Minnesota architect Cass Gilbert designed the seminary, but Hill and his subordinates planned and oversaw its construction in elaborate detail. When it was dedicated in 1895, Hill told the crowd, with obvious sincerity and emotion, that although he was not a Catholic, he did it for his "Roman Catholic wife, of whom it may be said, 'Blessed are the pure in heart for they shall see God.'"

It was, indeed, a wonderful life, the sort of wonderful life to which almost all Americans aspired but which very few came near realizing. But the fact remained that, for Jim Hill as for such other captains of industry and finance as J. P. Morgan or Collis Huntington, there seemed little time to enjoy it. As he embarked on his life's great adventure, the extension of his railroad west to the Pacific, he found that he must bear even greater burdens of work and responsibility than those to which he had become accustomed. His mettle would now be tested as it had never been tested before.

The westward thrust of the Saint Paul, Minneapolis, and Manitoba Railway began in 1886 from its westernmost railhead, at

Devils Lake, in the northeastern quadrant of giant Dakota Territory. As North Dakota historian Elwyn Robinson comments, Jim Hill had become "a central figure in the opening of North Dakota" beginning six years earlier, in the spring of 1880, when the Manitoba first forged across the Red River at Grand Forks. During the next several years, he had focused his effort on building his rail network throughout the western drainage of the Red, which forms the northeastern portion of what would become the state of North Dakota in 1889.

The Manitoba rapidly built a highly efficient gridwork of rails across the flat western floor of the Red River valley. Two main lines ran north and south: one along the river from Fargo down to Grand Forks and on to Neche on the Canadian border, and another farther west from Wahpeton, opposite Breckenridge, Minnesota, north-northwest through Casselton, Mayville, and eventually to Park River and Langdon. A main east-west line ran out of Wahpeton, and by 1883 another extended from Grand Forks out to Devils Lake, on the rim of the valley itself. It was this northernmost track that would become the highway to the West. These lines, like their earlier counterparts east of the Red, were a railroad man's dream: flat and easy to grade, they served a big and bountiful hinterland and hauled massive tonnages of grain efficiently, for high profits at low rates. They would form the rich root structure for the trunk that would now grow westward.

As the Manitoba forged westward, anxiety mounted apace in several quarters. When the road reached the strategic north shore of Devils Lake in the summer of 1883, Hill once again demonstrated his dexterity in outfoxing townsite speculators. Although he continued to maintain that the railroad did not invest in townsites, which was true enough, Hill sometimes did so personally, in collaboration with friends and company associates. This now occurred with the town of Devils Lake, which was platted by a syndicate that he joined. As a result, a cluster of other budding townsites in the area abruptly withered, including one called Harrisburgh, whose promoters numbered his former steamboating partner Alexander Griggs. At neighboring Cando, on the other hand, the insiders chose to stand aside and allowed local folks to cash in with their own development.

The next thrust westward, and a highly significant one at that, came in 1886, when the Manitoba laid over 120 miles of track from Devils Lake all the way west to the railhead town of Minot on the Mouse or Souris tributary of the Assiniboine River. Two thousand graders, most of them Scandinavian farmers from the area, labored through that summer along the route under Hill's favorite contractor, D. C. ("The Dean") Shepard; and experienced Irishmen "ironed" the line behind them.

Named after Hill's frenetic and visionary second vice-president, Minot sprang up by the end of the year as a classic railroad boomtown, located in an oasis setting along irrigable bottomlands flanked by benches that became increasingly dry as the road moved west. Within five weeks of its founding, Minot boasted one thousand inhabitants. The boomtown housed twelve saloons and five hotels, flanked by an ugly sweep of shanties and tents, and "Reverend Wirt" held Sunday school classes in the Hope brothers' hardware store. This remote railhead lay far beyond the Red River drainage, north and west of Bismarck; the latter town, on the bend of the Missouri River, served as the hub for the NP and was about to become the capital of a new state.

The NP, spanning west from Fargo through Bismarck in the southern portion of present-day North Dakota, had been granted 24 percent of the land mass of the future state—nearly eleven million acres. But, overextended and still recovering from Henry Villard's reckless expenditures, the NP had grave trouble competing with Hill and the Manitoba, which was advancing carefully and methodically, securing its hinterland with branch lines as it progressed. By 1888, the Manitoba had constructed nearly 1,000 miles of North Dakota track, compared with only 814 miles for the NP, which had invested so heavily in the transcontinental thrust and which was constrained by its charter in the building of spurs. The efficient network of Manitoba trunk and stub lines easily outperformed the hastily built NP system, gathering up the larger share of northern Dakota's spring wheat harvest and funneling it into the Twin Cities rather than

Duluth. Eastern Dakota, in short, had become as much an economic hinterland of Saint Paul–Minneapolis as had Minnesota itself.

This Manitoba consolidation of the Minnesota–Red River valley heartland, of course, threatened the NP considerably. But even more threatening was the thrust of the Manitoba railhead past the geographic midpoint of the territory, a move that seemed to pose the impossible: the growth of this once-small regional road into a full-blown transcontinental. As it now stood, Hill had already shredded the tenuous agreement that the Manitoba would work mainly a north-south axis and the NP an east-west axis.

In 1882, the two railroads had attempted an accord on Dakota branch lines. The NP sold its road paralleling the Manitoba's Casselton-Mayville line and in turn bought from its competitor the westward extension out of Wahpeton as well as the key trackage from Sauk Rapids into Saint Paul. Nevertheless, the rivalry barely abated. By 1887 the NP had a line all the way to Winnipeg, paralleling the Manitoba's tracks along the Red, and Hill ranted once more at NP executives he considered insanely ambitious and impervious to their own best interests.

These two northern railroads, along with three others—the Minneapolis, Saint Paul, and Sault Sainte Marie (the Soo Line), the Chicago and Northwestern, and the Chicago, Milwaukee, and Saint Paul—catalyzed the "Dakota Boom" that surged as the Panic of 1873 abated in about 1878 and that lasted until 1886. Future North Dakota had a mere 200 miles of track in 1876, the NP line from Fargo to Bismarck on the south-flowing Missouri River, which bisected Dakota Territory. By 1890 the new state of North Dakota had nearly 2,100 rail miles: 110 miles per 10,000 people.

The Dakota Boom crested in 1882, during which year forty-two thousand immigrants came to the Red River valley. The promotion-immigration bureaus of the NP, the Manitoba, and the other railroads brought a tidal wave of settlers to the region. By 1890 the valley was settled and no longer in any sense a frontier, and a thin wave of white habitation lapped into the Drift

Prairie, beyond to the west. In the first state census of North Dakota (1890), fully 43 percent of the population was foreign-born. Most of these were northern Europeans: Scandinavians, especially Norwegians, and also Germans, German-Russians, and British Islanders. In effect, the midwestern-agrarian-Scandinavian culture of Minnesota was extending westward into the neighboring Dakotas.

The Dakota Boom came to a halt in 1886. A cycle of drought began that year and intensified in the next; the price of wheat, bombarded by overproduction, fell to fifty-two cents per bushel; and a recession struck the national economy. In any event, the best humid farmlands of eastern Dakota Territory had by now been taken. Nearly half of the North Dakota farms and ranches fell into mortgage, and the flood of migration turned into a trickle outward. For the railroads, of course, this meant lost revenues and a stall in construction. But the healthy Manitoba, with its Minnesota–North Dakota base now constructed and secure, remained poised to move on as planned.

The construction of the Devils Lake–Minot line truly made 1886 the year of decision for the Manitoba and its managers. Would this remote western railhead prove to be only the over-extended terminus of a midwestern regional carrier? Or would it become the staging point for a major, highly expensive thrust westward? Any informed observer could plainly see that the latter option was Hill's clear intent. Otherwise, he would not have built far beyond Devils Lake. But still, the obstacles in his path seemed almost insurmountable.

Now well beyond the one hundredth meridian, the frontiering Manitoba had crossed the "rainfall line," approximately nineteen inches per year, which runs through the east-central Dakotas. The prime, humid farmlands of the Midwest now clearly lay behind. Ahead lay the upward sloping and increasingly arid lands of the Missouri Plateau, the cleft and wind-swept western Great Plains. This seemingly desolate region was populated only by small numbers of Indians, who had recently been forced onto remote reservations, and by an even smaller populace of scattered, open-range cattle and sheep ranchers.

There was little business for a railroad in this vast, 400-mile stretch of inhospitable, rolling plains between Minot and the Montana mining towns in the Rocky Mountains and seemingly little hope for future agricultural settlement. And beyond these remote communities lay even more formidable obstacles: the 250-mile-wide swath of the crosscutting peaks and valleys of the northern Rockies, the arid expanse of the Columbia Basin in central Washington, and finally, in western Washington, the broad shoulders and soaring summits of the Cascade Range, which loomed over the waters of the Pacific in Puget Sound. These areas totaled 1,000 air miles of easily crossed plains and hard-to-cross mountains, almost all wilderness.

The route west from Minot posed a major question. Due west lay the confluence of the Missouri and Yellowstone Rivers, just east of the Dakota-Montana boundary. It made little sense to follow the meandering southern Montana route up the Yellowstone River and then down the even more shifting, west-flowing Clark Fork of the Columbia through the Rockies. This would mean paralleling the federally subsidized NP. Rather, the obvious route lay more directly west, staying north of the Missouri, which here ran from west to east, along the Dakota-Montana "Highline," passing through the relatively level valley of the Milk River, the major northern tributary of the Missouri. This was the route mapped by the mid-1850s expedition of Isaac Stevens and traversed by the so-called Minnesota-Montana Road to the gold camps in the 1860s.

This route was more direct and level than the southern course of the NP and required less bridging, curvature, and grading. But it had two major drawbacks. Two large Indian reservations covered its entire length to the peaks of the Rockies: the Fort Berthold Reserve in Dakota and the Blackfeet Reserve—actually a continuum of reservations for several tribes—in Montana. Equally worrisome, in the entire northern Montana expanse of the Rocky Mountain front, which lay farther beyond, no feasible pass had yet been identified.

These pitfalls did not deter the hard-charging Jim Hill, who, well before 1886, saw ever more compelling reasons to forge ahead rapidly. As noted previously, he was one of the first to comprehend that the day of independent regional roads was coming to an end, that only transcontinental systems offering low through-rates would survive as independent systems. Regional roads, even prosperous ones like the Manitoba, would be swallowed up by the transregional railroads.

He also saw that now was the time to build. The United States had entered a long period of deflation and concomitant low interest rates, which meant that he could build and capitalize his road at lower cost than could his on-the-ground competitors. And out in southwestern Montana, the hottest industrial mining boom on earth, centered at Butte and Anaconda, offered a tempting target. Conversely, if the Manitoba waited too long, its Highline corridor through the high plains and northern Rockies might be preempted, by spurs of either the NP or the CP or both.

As Hill saw it, the move west should be made in two long leaps. First, a "Montana Extension" should build in one hectic season from Minot all the way to some strategic spot in north-central Montana; from there a long spur could reach southwest to Helena and Butte in the mountains, in the process linking to the tracks of both the NP and the Union Pacific (UP). Then, at some appropriate time in the future, his railroad could extend on across the Rockies to the Pacific. Some members of his board of directors, particularly such hardheaded financial types as Samuel Thorne and D. Willis James, were skeptical of taking on such an enormous construction debt. But Stephen, Donald Smith, and Kennedy once again hung with Hill, and he would soon have the group in tow, as he usually did. Well before the big move of 1886–87, though, Hill had already begun to involve himself deeply in far-off Montana Territory.

Paris Gibson, a New England Yankee and an old friend of Hill's who had gone broke as a Minneapolis miller in the 1873 Panic, had since moved on to the Fort Benton area of north-central Montana. A dreamer as well as a future U.S. senator, Gibson became enamored of the nearby and beautiful Great Falls of the Missouri River as a future townsite. Attracted especially to its waterpower potential, he believed, as Richard Roeder has written, that a town located there could become a model community, a "New Minneapolis."

Gibson bombarded his old friend with his ideas and even proposed naming the townsite Hilltown, a suggestion that Hill had the wisdom to decline. Intrigued, Hill came out for a visit in 1884, complete with camping trips and songs around the campfire. Soon after, he wrote a friend: "I do not recall another spot where I have ever seen so many natural advantages. . . . I see no reason why it is not the cheapest and best place in Montana to reduce the ores of that whole country." Collaborating with Gibson, he soon sank major investments into the Great Falls Water Power and Townsite Company and parceled out shares to Kennedy and other close friends. The group also bought into the rich coal deposits immediately to the east at Sand Coulee and Stockett, coal that would figure largely in the future of the railroad.

Jim Hill's primary "corporate point man" in Montana, to borrow historian William Lang's apt phrase, was not Gibson, however, but rather C. A. Broadwater, of the territorial capital of Helena. "Broad" had made his money in wagon freighting and banking and in supplying military posts. His main rival, the ruthless Sam Hauser, was at this time the most potent political broker in Montana and had just shouldered Broadwater out of the affairs of the NP, which crossed the Continental Divide just west of Helena.

So Broadwater shifted naturally toward a Hill alliance. "Broad" joined Gibson in hosting the rail magnate on his 1884 visit, persuaded him to buy into the rich Red Mountain gold deposits near Rimini, west of Helena, and took him south to see the frenetically booming silver- and copper-mining city of Butte. On his return, Hill wrote Broadwater: "I cannot forget the many beautiful scenes of the few days spent with you in Montana, and I am more than ever impressed with the future of your territory. I do not recall another spot where I have ever seen so many natural advantages to build up a city as at Great Falls."

A unified Montana empire quickly emerged in the minds of Hill, Broadwater, and Gibson. By building a north-south railroad linking Great Falls to Helena, and soon after to Butte, they could ship copper concentrate in huge volumes north to Great Falls for smelting and then on eastward, and they could freight coal from the Great Falls area on return trips south for consumption in Butte. A fifteen-mile stub west from Helena would develop the Red Mountain complex. This Montana Central Railroad, under Broadwater's direction, would, in turn, link to the west-building Manitoba at Great Falls.

The Montana Central Railroad Company was chartered in January 1886, issuing $5 million in stock and, later in 1887, $10 million in bonds. Although it bore no evident relationship to either Hill or the Manitoba, few could mistake its real identity. E. J. Dodge, whom Hill hired away from the NP, served as chief engineer under Broadwater and quickly preempted the key points along the ninety-mile route between Helena and Great Falls, particularly the rugged but strategic Prickly Pear Canyon.

The grading of this line proceeded rapidly toward completion throughout 1886, even as trackage out in Dakota fell into place en route to Minot. Broadwater, meanwhile, bought up depot and facility sites in Helena and smelter locations east of the city. And grizzled old Major A. B. Rogers ventured back into the field, this time into the sixty-mile clump of tortuous mountains south of Helena en route to Butte. Here he found a workable crossing of the divide, "at a grade not exceeding 116 feet per mile."

The NP, of course, watched all of this activity with mounting anxiety. Just as Broadwater warned Hill to hurry before the NP could block or contest his route, Hauser pleaded with NP officials to move fast from the east-west trunk line through Helena, building spurs laterally into the north-south corridor between Great Falls and Butte. In New York, Alan Manvel casually lied to NP executives T. F. Oakes and Robert Harris, assuring them that the Montana Central was a purely stand-alone enterprise.

Former Montana congressman and current Hill agent Martin Maginnis similarly assured them that "the Montana Central was started as a purely local enterprise," that Hill's interest in it "was limited," and that "only wantonly aggressive acts on their part would cause any one to push it out for Eastern connections." They knew better and fulminated that the Manitoba had no right to be west of Devils Lake. But the NP once again found itself

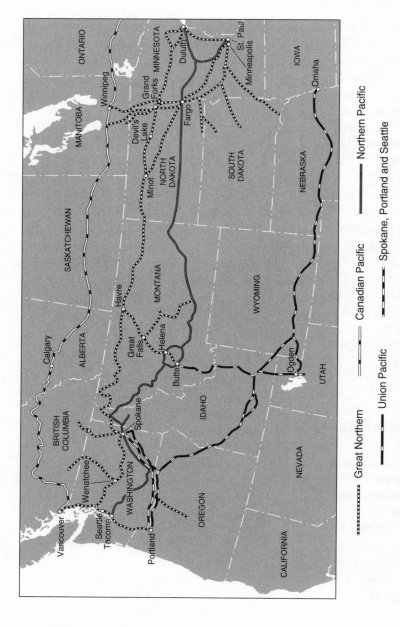

The primary lines of the Great Northern Railway, along with the trunk lines of the Canadian Pacific, the Northern Pacific, and the Union Pacific Railroads.

boxed in: as usual, the creditors were at its door, and Hill's men controlled the key passageways along both the main line and the Rimini extension.

The NP still attempted to block the Montana Central, but to no avail. On the Rimini line, NP survey crews actually obstructed the progress of construction until Broadwater forced them out by court injunction. And now, belatedly, NP executives finally heeded Hauser's advice and began plotting a rival line between Helena and Butte. When Hill sought a standard twenty-dollar-per-ton rate to haul his rails to Montana, the NP demanded thirty-five dollars, which prompted him to delay "ironing" the Montana Central until the next year, when the Manitoba could carry the rails west itself.

In the end, the established transcontinental could not stop its rival intruder; and eventually, an edgy truce set in, after the Montana Central sold its Rimini line to the NP, and the NP decided to abandon its Helena line to Butte in favor of an access route to the mining city directly from the east. Hill told a wildly cheering Helena crowd in September that they would have their second railroad within a year, but the NP remained angry until the end. It even laid tracks across the Montana Central right-of-way and removed them only at the last minute before a final confrontation.

In the meantime, Hill and his cohorts faced a far more serious problem in securing federal approval to build through the long corridor of reservation lands north of the Missouri. The smaller Fort Berthold Reserve in northwestern Dakota housed Hidatsas, Arikaras, Mandans, and Gros Ventres of the Prairie. On the much larger Blackfeet Reserve, stretching all along the three hundred miles of the Milk and Marias Valleys, dwelt Assiniboines, Sioux, Gros Ventres, and farthest west, the large contingent of Blackfeet. To press his case in Washington, Hill assembled a powerful force of lobbyists that included his old friend Minnesota Congressman Knute Nelson, former Montana Congressman Martin Maginnis, current Montana Congressman Joseph Toole, fellow railroad man Congressman William Scott of Pennsylvania, and New York politico William Smith, who was a close friend of

President Grover Cleveland's and who would soon serve as comptroller of the Manitoba.

This powerful and influential team advanced on several fronts at once. In April 1886, they drafted right-of-way bills that Congressman Nelson and Massachusetts Senator Henry Dawes, who was ironically about to become known as the nation's supreme champion of reform as chairman of the Senate Committee on Indian Affairs, introduced concurrently in the House of Representatives and the Senate. Lobbyist Maginnis came forth with another bill that would move the tribes of northern Montana to other reservations, an appalling idea that would have drastically increased the evil practice of placing traditional enemy tribes on the same turf. And Congressman Toole sponsored yet another proposal that would shrink the size of the northern Montana reserve. Peculiarly enough, Indian Commissioner J. D. C. Atkins recommended both of these latter measures to Interior Secretary Lucius Q. C. Lamar.

The effort to relocate the tribes would not succeed, but the campaign to shrink the reservations and open the ceded lands to white settlement would. The Manitoba forces stated their arguments to members both of Congress and of a special federal contingent that was negotiating with the northwestern tribes to cede these lands. Indians and whites alike, they reasoned, were victims of high rates charged by their monopolistic rivals. The Indians had far more land than they could ever need.

And, they argued, more horrific yet, these large, unpopulated reserves lay along an unpoliced border, which made the areas havens for roughnecks, murderers, rustlers, and thieves, who stole from one side of the boundary and fenced their gains on the other. As everyone knew in 1886, the concerns of Indians meant little in such cases; Indians were passing out of the consciousness of white Americans, into neglect and romantic fantasy. Congressional and presidential approval normally came quickly. But, as Hill fussed and fumed, the key right-of-way bill ground slowly through both houses of Congress and did not emerge favorably until late June.

As the right-of-way bill went to President Cleveland for his signature, Jim Hill had every reason to feel confident. Cleveland had approved numerous other railroad access requests to Indian lands, as had his predecessors. And Hill, a free-trade, conservative Democrat, was an admirer and supporter of the president. Rumor had it, though, that trouble was brewing; and the rumors proved true when, on July 7, Cleveland vetoed the Manitoba access measure. Cleveland rubbed salt in the wound by referring in his veto message to a "class of corporations carrying with them individuals not known for any scrupulous regard for the interest of the Indians." The president went on to explain his reasons. The Indians themselves had not been consulted, although he conceded that he had signed previous bills that had the same problem; the white population in the area was very sparse; and the bill could lead to speculation in the opened lands, even though its wording clearly stated that the easements could not be sold or transferred to other parties.

The Manitoba associates, predictably, howled in outrage. Hill claimed that Cleveland's logic was "ridiculous, and against the acts and actions of Congress for the past forty years." After all, he reasoned, the bill had been "originated by the People of Montana in an effort to secure relief from very oppressive railway charges." Congressman Scott agreed: "The only wonder to me is he does not make more mistakes than he does." Paris Gibson wisecracked, "Cleveland may be qualified for sheriff or Mayor of Buffalo, but beyond that, he is not safe." Perhaps Congressman Nelson best expressed, however, their true feeling of fear: "On the whole we are in the hands of the Philistines. A Democratic administration is not as kind to our Northwest as were our Republican administrations. We are evidently regarded of no consequence."

They had good reason to fear—not the irreversible prohibition of access through the reservations, since any such decision would have been unprecedented, but rather a long delay, which could force them to miss the 1887 construction season and thus to suffer millions in lost revenues. Almost everyone reckoned that Cleveland's real concerns had little to do with the welfare of the Indians and much to do with pressure from competing roads, particularly the NP and the UP. So the Manitoba team set out once again to roll the rock up the hill, redoubling its efforts. Senator Dawes, an unabashed admirer of Hill's, again lent his full support. And Jim Hill himself directly solicited the president, through the good offices of their mutual friend Postmaster General William Vilas. Vilas was soon reporting back that the vacillating president had seen the light.

When Congress reconvened in December 1886, Congressman Toole introduced a new bill providing a 150-foot easement not only through the Highline reservation lands but also through the three military reserves amid them—Forts Berthold and Buford in Dakota and Fort Assiniboine in Montana. This bill rapidly cleared the Congress, and to no one's surprise, President Cleveland quietly signed it on February 7, 1887, thus tacitly admitting his earlier error and quietly walking away.

During these same months of late 1886 and early 1887, the federal Northwest Commission also negotiated massive cessions of reservation lands north of the Missouri, cessions that Congress ratified over the next few years. In return for just over $5 million, the Indians deeded nearly twenty million acres, fully recognized the railroad right-of-way, and moved to four smaller reservations and agencies: Fort Berthold in North Dakota and Fort Peck, Fort Belknap, and the Blackfeet Reserve in Montana. It all happened rapidly and with very little public notice; but in truth, an imperial domain north of the Missouri had now been removed from Indian hands and opened for white invasion. As historian Frederick Hoxie put it, the Manitoba had become the most Indian-subsidized railroad in America. Although Jim Hill's road directly received only a part of this once vast kingdom—for easements—the opening of the reserves for white agricultural settlement would provide a midroute hinterland for the Manitoba to promote and develop.

If the final victory of February 1887 seemed anticlimactic, it was because of the frenzied buildup for the looming construction season. Hill had written Kennedy the previous October: "We must build 733 miles road next summer in eight months, from present end of track to Montana to insure our position of advantage. This has all to be done from one end and is more track than has ever been laid in ten months elsewhere; over twice this year's work, which has been carried on at four places, and will take hundred million feet timber and ties." To the dubious D. Willis James, he commented, "I feel sure that the future of the company depends on our work during the coming year."

Indeed, it did. Both Hill and Kennedy struggled mightily to secure bonding for the Montana Extension and for the Montana Central Railroad. This was not easy in the climate of the late 1880s, as a myriad of rail companies around the country and around the world competed for investors. They succeeded, but only by attracting bluebloods like the stately and highly respected Jacob Schiff, at New York's Kuhn, Loeb, and Company, who could market the bonds in Europe but who extracted in return a voice in the Manitoba's financial future. The aging Kennedy felt the strain sufficiently that he retired from his vice-presidency before the year was out to nurture his health, turning over the reins of his New York firm to his nephew J. Kennedy Tod.

Once the Manitoba's engines had finished hauling the 1886 crop to market, they converged on the movement of vast tonnages of construction materials westward to the end of the rails at Minot. Steel rails came from a host of American and European mills; Hill continued to favor the heavy-gauge imports from the Krupp works in Germany. Huge ladings of lumber for trestles and other construction also included three million ties; feed for horse teams to pull the grading equipment added up to six hundred thousand bushels of oats. Meanwhile, locators and surveyors laid out the route from Minot to the townsite of Havre on the Milk River in north-central Montana; from here the route turned southwest down to the Missouri and along the west bank of the river to Great Falls. Here, the grading of the Montana Central north from Helena was nearly completed. The total distance, from Minot to Helena, was over 640 miles. To build the whole line in one season, entirely from one end, would dwarf any previous rail construction effort ever attempted anywhere.

With the coming of the late spring on the Great Plains in 1887,

Shepard's seasoned construction army moved west out of Minot in highly disciplined units. Ahead of them lay open country, where grading and hauling would be easy. The grading crews—eight thousand men and sixty-six hundred horses hitched in yokes of two—headed out first. During the early months, they graded one hundred miles per four weeks, scalloping the roadbed two to three feet above the prairie floor so that prevailing winds would help to remove the snow.

They moved 9.7 million cubic feet of earth and over 32,000 cubic yards of rock. By the autumn, the grading crews were preparing several miles per day. Next came the tracklayers, heavily Irish and loudly raucous. Including timber workers, they numbered 650 men and nearly the same number of horses. On one day, August 8, they laid down eight miles of track, which the spikers, following closely behind, fastened into position. Shepard's work force was expertly led and provisioned, right down to the triple-decked dormitory cars in which they lived. Charles Dudley Warner, Mark Twain's coauthor of the epoch-naming *The Gilded Age,* reckoned that the vast panorama of these tracks, spread across the endless prairie floor, constituted "one of the most striking achievements of civilization."

Jim Hill, driving himself incessantly, moved back and forth across the completed track in his executive car and then beyond by wagon, supervising every detail. He had not pressed himself this hard since the original construction drive of 1878. When the tracks reached Great Falls in mid-October, he did not even allow his men to pause for the festivities that Gibson wanted to stage; instead he pressed directly on, reaching his destination of Helena by the end of the construction season in mid-November. Terribly fatigued and racked by neuralgia and lung congestion, he could still take great satisfaction in what had been accomplished: "It was a long and hard summer's work."

The Manitoba had, in one hectic season, entered a wholly new geographic province—the cleft, northwesternmost Great Plains and the creviced foothills and high valleys of the Rocky Mountains. The road now performed the classic function of a frontier railroad, "opening" and integrating the new region into the

Construction crews on the Montana Extension. Courtesy of Montana Historical Society, Helena.

national economy. Centrally located on the plains, in a handsome setting that artist Charley Russell was then making known, Great Falls served as the regional hub of the road; by 1888, its population was already two thousand, and by 1900, the total would grow to nearly fifteen thousand.

The spur line east to Sand Coulee now brought in large tonnages of good coal, and this coal quickly supplanted Hill's earlier source in Iowa; as noted earlier, he proceeded to divest himself of the Iowa source. Within a year, the Montana mines supplied over 40 percent of the coal burned by the railroad. Helena meant less to the Manitoba, since it was already a main-line town on the NP. But sixty hard miles to the southwest, across the Continental Divide, the great copper- and silver-mining center of Butte beckoned.

The Montana Central extended its tracks through the tortuous mountains from Helena to Butte and arrived there in mid-1888. It

thereby shattered the fragile "gentlemen's agreement" that the
NP had struck several years earlier with the UP, which had extended its Utah and Northern spur line up to the mining city
from northern Utah. Simply stated, the NP had agreed to stay
out of Butte, except via a minor stub line from the west, and the
UP had agreed not to proceed north to the gold- and silver-
mining center of Helena, in a classic case of short-circuiting
the supposedly free-market economy of the nineteenth-century
frontier. The sequestering of the big Butte market was duck soup
for the aggressive Hill and allowed him to play the role that
would make him a legend: forcing competitiveness on a rigged
market.

Butte's mine owners had chafed, of course, at the artificially
high rates thus forced on them, and Jim Hill masterfully played
on their resentment. In 1886 he had written to Marcus Daly, of
the giant Anaconda silver-copper consortium, which was fast
becoming the world's largest mining operation: "When our lines
are completed through to your place, we hope to be able to
furnish you all the transportation you want, at rates as will enable
you to largely increase your business. What we want over our low
grades is heavy tonnage, and the heavier it is *the lower we can
make the rates*" (his emphasis).

Copper matte from Montana smelters and then blister copper
from its refineries gave Hill what he most wanted: heavy tonnages at bargain rates over efficient tracks. Whereas the UP had
been charging seventeen dollars per ton to carry smelted copper
matte to Omaha, the Manitoba now charged ten dollars per ton
to freight it to Chicago via the Burlington. Hill also brought in
Sand Coulee coal to Butte for half the rate that had prevailed in
the local market. Thus was born a long and happy marriage between the fast-growing Anaconda and the Hill railroads.

Not incidentally, the Butte connection also gave the Manitoba
another plus. Hitherto, it could send passengers and freight on to
the West Coast only via its linkages to the hostile NP. Now, by
joining to the Utah and Northern spur of the UP at Butte, it
could also forward bookings via the UP to Ogden, Utah, and
then via the Central Pacific to San Francisco Bay. Thus, the

farther west the Manitoba moved, the more it opened new options for the future. This UP connection was such a circuitous route to the Pacific, however, that its value was limited.

Hill immediately struck up an intense interest and involvement in the lucrative Montana mining industry. He became a close ally of Daly and a dedicated foe of Daly's archrival, mining baron William A. Clark. When two new and profitable Butte firms, the Boston and Montana Company and the Butte and Boston Company, came looking for the right location for a water-rich smelter site along a railroad, their search came down to a choice between Helena on the NP and the more distant Great Falls on the Montana Central–Manitoba. Ever the hardheaded, even amoral pragmatist, Hill closed the deal by quietly making the imperious master of the two consolidated companies, Leonard Lewisohn of New York, an offer he could not refuse. Hill simply slipped Lewisohn fifteen hundred shares of the Great Falls Townsite Company, and Lewisohn's decision immediately followed suit, regardless of the interests of his stockholders.

From mid-1885 through 1889, the year when North and South Dakota, Washington, and Montana gained statehood, James J. Hill and his allies consolidated their rapidly built Dakota and Montana lines and weighed their options farther west. They faced essentially an either-or strategic choice: either purchase the NP, if possible, or build their own trackage to the coast. The former choice offered the alluring advantages of eliminating a dangerous rival, whose shaky finances continued to cause it to behave erratically and thus to cause them trouble, as well as the bonus of securing the NP's lucrative land grant, most of which the NP still held. Hill actually embraced this option for a time, writing Stephen in the spring of 1889: "The more I think of it the more I am convinced that the thing for us to do is to 'take the bull by the horns' and get control of the Northern Pacific, and by one stroke settle all questions at once. This will cost less money and will bring the best results in the least time. . . . A starving man will usually get bread if it is to be had, and a starving railway will not maintain rates."

There were, however, strong arguments to the contrary. Increasingly disenchanted with the governmentally intertwined CP, and with attacks from prairie populists critical of the CP, Hill's old associates Stephen and Smith now refocused their efforts toward the Manitoba. Stephen argued strongly, and convincingly, that he could raise the funding necessary to build their own Pacific Extension; Hill was soon nodding agreement that a more northern and direct route could be made better, shorter, and with lower grades and easier curvature than that of the NP. Not all agreed. Directors James and Thorne, conservative financiers, angrily left the board, complaining that the railroad was plunging too recklessly into debt and that Hill simply went his own way, communicating with them too little. Nonetheless, with Hill and Stephen in agreement, the die was cast.

First, however, the construction of all these new lines, in Minnesota, Dakota, and now Montana, called for a major reorganization of the properties—an overarching corporation that could both hold and operate the disparate lines in a cohesive manner. Years before, Hill had had the foresight to secure the title of a railroad incorporated back in the 1850s, the Minneapolis and Saint Cloud. The charter of this old line was notably broad and expansive, and he had used it for previous projects.

Now, in September 1889, the Minneapolis and Saint Cloud gained a new name: the Great Northern Railway. The grandiose title of Great Northern had intrigued Jim Hill for years, in part because of a highly regarded line by that name in Great Britain and in part because he liked its grand sound. He had earlier applied it, in fact, to one of his giant grain elevators on Lake Superior. He was determined to use it now, and he argued down Stephen, who would have preferred keeping alive the identity of the old road with the merged title of "the Manitoba and Great Northern."

Meeting in New York on September 16, 1889, the directors of the Manitoba created the Great Northern Railway, with a $40 million stock issue, half of the stock preferred and half common. For now, only the preferred stock was issued. Most of the Manitoba faithful quickly converted their shares to the Great North-

ern (GN) at $50 per share, drawn by their faith in the manage-
ment and a highly secure 6 percent annual dividend and also by
the fact that the $50 investment bought a full $100 share, the
other half covered by the assets brought into the GN with the
Manitoba.

The new corporation assumed the obligations of the Saint
Paul, Minneapolis, and Manitoba, including $8 million in bonds,
and took over $22 million in its assets. In effect, the GN took a
999-year lease on the Manitoba and its affiliates, an arrangement
that allowed all of the existing rights and relationships of the
railroad to remain in place. The lease took effect at the end of
January 1890. In return, the Manitoba, with its well-established
credit and contract arrangements, would build the Pacific Extension for its parent company.

The favorable terms extended to Manitoba shareholders, and
their large switchover to the GN reawakened public concerns
about the insiders' control of the road and fueled rumors that it
remained secretly tied to the CP. An investor in Manitoba stock,
Frank Hollins, filed an unsuccessful lawsuit arguing that those
Manitoba investors who failed to invest in GN would be treated
unfairly. But obviously, few of them shared his concerns, since
over $16 million of the $20 million in GN stock fell immediately
into the eager hands of the old Saint Paul, Minneapolis, and
Manitoba shareholders. J. J. Moore, of the elite firm of Moore
and Schley, New York bankers, reflected Wall Street sentiment
when he wrote to Hill, "The Street and the stockholders seem to
take this matter kindly."

As the new railroad, destined to become one of the world's
greatest, took shape during the next several months, the rising
dominance of James J. Hill became readily apparent. On the new
nine-member board, J. S. Kennedy was replaced by his nephew
and banking successor J. Kennedy Tod. Stephen and Smith were
still there; but Smith was aging, and Stephen would soon step
down to savor the glories of his wealth and English peerage.

Among the new directors, two bore special significance. Mary's
husband, Samuel Hill, had the credentials to serve, but he also
stood in the shadow of his domineering father-in-law. William P.

Clough, an able administrator whom Hill had lured away from the NP, would soon advance to the senior vice-presidency of the organization. He and two other new directors, Edward Sawyer and M. D. Grover, came from the ranks of the corporate structure itself. The GN, in sum, would be a Hill operation, pure and simple.

In the meantime, planning and preparation for the great thrust across the Rockies and the Pacific Northwest to the sea continued apace. Out on the coast, both Clough and Henry Minot, who would not survive the year 1890, studied the prospects for the best port facilities and reported back to Hill. Shrewdly, Minot downplayed Portland, which was already the terminus of the UP, and Tacoma, the port of the NP. Rather, he favored the ambitious little city of Seattle, which was located north of Tacoma on Puget Sound and well to the south of the CP's port of Vancouver on the Strait of Georgia and was beautifully situated with a deep-water harbor flanked by adjacent freshwater lakes where ships could dock and be scoured of marine growths. Minot wrote Hill in May 1890 that Seattle, in his opinion, could be worth an extra $1.2 to $1.5 million annually to the GN beyond what the competing port cities could generate.

Jim Hill now focused nearly his entire attention on organizing the Pacific Extension. With the departure of the harried Manvel to the presidency of the Atchison, Topeka, and Santa Fe, Hill found himself hard-pressed to find a first-rate replacement as general manager. His reputation as a tyrannical taskmaster and poor delegator was by now too well known. So he simply moved the dutiful and methodical E. L. Mohler into the position, with fast-rising William Clough as vice-president.

Elbridge Beckler, whom Hill had earlier hired as chief engineer of the Montana Central, now advanced to that same position for the Pacific Extension. Beckler brought with him invaluable experience in mountain construction, gained earlier with the CP and the NP, and he was capable, but he also would soon find how difficult a taskmaster Jim Hill could be. Once again, Shepard would serve as chief contractor, now joined by his son-in-law in the firm of Shepard, Siems, and Company with a host of subcontractors, many of them local, under his tutelage. Shepard's initial contract covered construction for the trackage across the remaining stretch of plains to the summit of the Rockies, whichever summit might be chosen.

Beckler soon had men in the field searching out four prospective crossings of the interlocking Rocky Mountain chains, from Butte in the south to a projection directly west of Havre in the north. This choice was of critical importance, for as Hill repeated and repeated, the wrong selection not only would prove costly but also might leave potential competitors free to seize the better route later. In any case, it made little sense to parallel the NP route west from the Helena-Butte sector, along the winding Clark Fork of the Columbia. And Beckler's men had no luck finding a good central pass anywhere near due west of the railroad's prospective main city of Great Falls.

Hill's main hope all along had been to find an easy pass over the Continental Divide more or less due west from Havre on the Milk River. This would afford a more direct route to the Pacific, in contrast to the circuitous path of the NP through southern Montana. He and others had heard of a legendary "Lost Marias Pass" that supposedly lay somewhere above, and west of, the headwaters of the Marias, a large northwest fork of the Missouri. The mid-1850s railroad survey led by Isaac Stevens had also heard reports of such a pass; and although those explorers never found it, they thought they had seen where it lay, and they recorded its presence. To attempt its rediscovery, Hill and Beckler turned to a man who would prove to be one of the ablest in the entire history of railroading.

John F. Stevens, a New Englander in his mid-thirties, was an anomaly in the Hill organization. He was a college-trained engineer whom James Hill respected rather than deprecated, as he frequently did such non-"practical" types. It is easy to understand why, for Stevens personified the beau ideal of Victorian manhood. Ramrod-straight, ruggedly handsome, and self-confident, he specialized in "location" and basic construction. In other words, he was part-explorer and loved the wilderness, and he had a solid background in such work with the CP, the Soo

Line, and other roads. In early December 1889, Stevens set out
westward from Fort Assiniboine near Havre; at the Blackfeet
Agency, in the foothills of the towering northern Rockies, he
finally prevailed on a lone Kalispel Indian to head into the mountains with him, in the face of severe cold and storms.

Trundling on snowshoes they had just made, Stevens and his
companion climbed to the Marias headwaters in deep snow on
the night of December 11. When the thoroughly frightened Indian refused to go farther, Stevens left him behind by a fire and
went on alone toward the towering peaks. Suddenly, Stevens
realized that he was astride an especially advantageous pass. Unable to build a fire, he stomped around through the night in
minus-forty-degree cold, both to stay alive and to be sure that
the western end of the passage really did lay across the divide.
Then he returned to rejuvenate his nearly frozen friend and proceeded back to the railhead. The news he brought was glorious
indeed.

Marias Pass, along the southern border of today's Glacier National Park, lies at only 5,214 feet elevation, the lowest crossing of
the northern Rockies. The approach from the east is remarkably
gentle, and no summit tunnel would be required, although the
westside descent into the precipitous canyons of the Middle Fork
of the Flathead River was steeper and would require elaborate
snowsheds to avoid dangerously heavy accumulations.

Hill rejoiced in Stevens's discovery. Now, the aborning GN
could cross the main chain of the Rocky Mountain cordillera on
a direct line from Grand Forks to Minot to Havre to Marias Pass.
The resulting avoidance of grades and curvature spelled out once
again the torah of his credo: a highly efficient, low-cost line that
could, better than any competitor, carry long-distance cargoes of
heavy tonnages.

To his old friend Paris Gibson, however, the news proved less
happy, for the main line would pass far to the north of his city.
Hill wrote him in late December 1889, "It would be folly to make
a detour as far south as Great Falls and turn around and go
north, using two sides of a triangle when one of them could be
saved." Gibson and his Great Falls compatriots were crestfallen,

but the good citizens of the smaller city of Havre were delighted. This little city, nestled less than thirty miles below the boundary, would now be the takeoff point for the Pacific Extension. And its future as a rail hub seemed doubly secure because its founding father, Broadwater associate Simon Pepin, had persuaded Hill to locate his area locomotive shops there as well.

The route across four hundred tortuous miles of mountains, valleys, and canyons, lying along a northwest-southeast axis, now became clear in the mind of James J. Hill. On the one hand, the far-north route through Marias Pass would miss the one truly valuable point in northern Idaho, the booming Coeur d'Alene silver- and lead-mining district, already served by the NP. More important, though, as Hill wrote Stephen in early 1890, this route to Spokane Falls, the emerging key rail center on the west slope of the northern Rockies, was two hundred miles shorter and had better grades than the route of the competition. Construction would, of course, be slower, harder, and far more expensive than the fast and easy plains crossings of 1886 and 1887 but not greatly harder than the crossing by the Montana Central. Rails and other materials would have to be carried farther; and as in 1887, most Manitoba-GN cars could not be fully utilized until after the late harvest season.

During the 1890 and 1891 construction seasons, Shepard's veteran crews made the easy ascent and the difficult descent of Marias Pass, emerging on the broad and beautiful floor of the valley lying north of giant Flathead Lake. Here, new rail towns emerged in the forms of Columbia Falls and Whitefish, where the GN tracks flanked the lake of the same name. The soon-to-be-larger city of Kalispell, meanwhile, grew up directly to the south. Surveyors and graders then headed on northwest through narrowing and heavily wooded valleys toward the long bend of the large Kootenai River, where the towns of Eureka, Libby, and Troy, like those on the Flathead, would become lumber producers cultivated by the railroad.

Trying to manage an imperial railroad while building it west, Jim Hill worked night and day, ulcerating about expenditures and the agonizingly slow pace of construction. Workers in these remote mountain fastnesses proved hard to get and to keep. They lived in wretched little hamlets like McCartyville, well described as "a seething Sodom of wickedness." And they often had to labor on steep slopes and in defiles with hand tools and to move dirt in handcarts in terrain where even horses proved difficult to use and feed. The pace of building fell to merely a few miles per week, and the boss fretted and ailed as he saw his hope of completion by 1892 fading away.

Meanwhile, by the fall of 1890, tracklayers pressed steadily westward, laying rails over majestic trestles at Cut Bank, Two Medicine River, and along the upper Flathead River; drillers bored four tunnels, totaling sixteen hundred feet in depth, through the worst mountainous passages. And other construction crews worked, on more limited scales, building 60 miles of line in eastern Washington, north of Spokane, and a rugged 146-mile stretch from Pend Oreille Lake in the Idaho Panhandle eastward toward Yaak River in far northwestern Montana. It all seemed nearly unmanageable, but Hill could finally write at the close of 1891, "We are getting a first-rate line—better than I supposed was possible—through the broken country in the Rocky Mountain sections."

Finally, in the early months of 1892, the GN crews pushed westward down the beautiful Kootenai River across the narrow Idaho panhandle, building from both east and west through rough country, to Bonners Ferry. From here, they turned southwest into Washington. The narrow strip of northern Idaho represented only a land to cross, and this state would never figure largely in GN affairs. The widening bulge of the Idaho panhandle farther south would remain NP country. And below the tangle of mountains in the center of the state, the broad Snake River plain that was coming to house most of Idaho's population would be the domain of the Oregon Short Line of the UP.

The nearly twenty thousand inhabitants of Spokane, Washington, feared that the GN would bypass their city to the north, and Jim Hill skillfully played on their concerns. But in truth, he had to build there, for the city stood on a strategic, upland plain adjacent to fine waterpower sites on the Spokane River, and it

The Two Medicine Creek trestle, 1891. Courtesy of Montana Historical Society, Helena.

represented too big a prize to skirt. Ever since the arrival of the NP in 1881, Spokane had been growing rapidly, in the process turning into the rail hub of the interior Northwest, or the "Inland Empire," as it soon became known.

In a broader perspective, Spokane was evolving into a counterpart of El Paso in the Southwest or of Ogden, Utah—a rail crossroads midway between the Mississippi-Missouri navigable waterways and the far Pacific. Villard had called Spokane "the handsomest town-site" he had seen "since leaving the East." Ravaged by fires in 1889, the city had pluckily poured $5 million into rebuilding, with imposing stone buildings that embodied its self-confidence.

Spokane's rapid growth stemmed from its hegemony over a booming hinterland. Wheat regions to the south, particularly in the Palouse and Lower Snake River valleys, provided a prosperous and stable base. Directly to the east, the booming Coeur d'Alene mines poured their wealth into the city, which even developed its own mining stock exchange. Soon after, more money came in from mines to the north, in the remote fastnesses of southern British Columbia.

The NP had extended spurs south to the Snake River, and by 1889, the OR&N also had a line running northeast to Spokane from Wallula on the Columbia River. Daniel C. Corbin was the primary local railroad entrepreneur. He had extended a winding, jerry-built line into the Coeur d'Alene district in 1886 and later sold it to the NP. By now, he had the Spokane Falls and Northern built north to Colville and was extending it on to the Canadian mines, to the great annoyance of the CP. This road would soon also pass into the hands of the NP and eventually into those of Jim Hill.

Still, even as it burgeoned as the hub of the interior Northwest, Spokane, like other interior rail cities, seethed with anger and resentment about unfair freight rates. The NP, like other roads, charged higher rates to such landlocked cities than to coastal rivals farther west, where it faced seaborne competition. This was the notorious "long-and-short-haul" system, and it served well the plans of Jim Hill, who strode dramatically into

town in February 1892 and waxed eloquently to a large and fawning crowd of admirers.

He told them how it would really make more sense for the GN
to bypass their city via the valley of the Little Spokane to the
north but how by coming to Spokane, he could drastically lower
rates as he had done at Butte, how he would locate key shops and
yards there, and how their city could grow quickly to one hundred thousand in population. But there must be a trade-off. True
to his long-term practice, he would not ask the city for a subsidy
to build lines across its expensive real estate; in return, however,
the city must donate to him a right-of-way.

> Now, what we ask of Spokane is that from the time we come to the
> city limits it would give us the right of way, so that the building of the
> road shall not cost anything. . . . The right of way we ask you to
> furnish because our expense in establishing shops here would be a
> million dollars. That amount of money would cover the distance
> from the east to the west side of the city limits,—five miles. And for
> that reason I feel that we are not asking or imposing a condition
> improper when we ask you to furnish the right of way to build the
> Great Northern Railway. . . . I do not come here asking for bonuses
> and gifts. . . . It is only by the addition of an enormous expense that
> we shall come into this city.

As Hill requested, a select committee of Spokane citizens recommended, and the city determined, to give the GN its desired
free access through the heart of their community. These highly
valuable lands would remain an unsightly aspect of midtown
Spokane until the city landscaped them as part of its world's fair
in the 1970s. In return, Hill made Spokane a primary hub on the
GN and located a major engine renovation works at the area of
the city appropriately named "Hillyard." But he never gave the
citizens of Spokane the rate reductions he had promised.

Unlike Butte, where a shaky pooling agreement had kept rates
artificially high, Spokane presented a situation that truly was
naturally disadvantaged. Its main competitors—Portland, Seattle, and Tacoma—all had the edge in maritime trade that could
force the railroads to deal with them. Like the NP before him,
Hill accepted the logic of long-and-short-haul, in fact embraced
it, since he had his eye on reduced through-rates to Pacific ports

for cargoes bound for Asian markets. The market would dictate rates, and if isolated interior areas thus suffered, so be it. But this left a bitter residue of resentment in the interior Northwest, and he would soon find himself becoming its object of focus.

Looking westward from Spokane, Hill confronted a convoluted strategic situation, in which two overextended transcontinentals—the UP and the NP—were locked in ungainly conflict. With alarm and dread, the executives of both roads watched the approach of this powerful interloper, which, unlike them, had a strong hinterland and infrastructure and low interest rates supporting it. Charles Francis Adams, Jr., of the UP, wrote as early as 1887: "All our properties are in very bad shape. The Northern Pacific, no less than the Navigation Company and the Union Pacific, is heavily-overcapitalized. We have to pay more for money than the Manitoba, and we will have to hold our own in a struggle for existence against it."

In that same year, 1887, the UP had made itself a transcontinental by building its Oregon Short Line across southern Idaho and linking to the tracks of the OR&N in northeastern Oregon. The OR&N, heir to the monopolistic and unpopular Oregon Steam Navigation Company, provided the UP access to Portland along the strategic south bank of the mighty Columbia River. The NP also used these tracks to reach Portland, but it now had its own rails from Spokane to Pasco-Kennewick, at the confluence of the Snake and Columbia Rivers in south-central Washington, and on across Stampede Pass to Tacoma on Puget Sound.

With Villard and his coterie back in charge of the NP, the two transcontinentals tried a cooperative approach through a joint-lease arrangement of the OR&N, but this marriage of convenience inevitably failed, especially because the NP had another, better route to the Pacific, a route over which it could independently ship. A natural dividing line between the UP and the NP lay along the north-south boundary formed by the west-flowing lower Snake and Columbia Rivers—that is, along the southern Washington–northern Oregon boundary. But a state of war soon ensued, with the NP probing below the line, into the rich wheatlands of southeastern Washington, and with the UP moving above, using its line to Spokane and the Coeur d'Alene country. Villard finally pulled out of the joint-lease of the OR&N, leaving this line entirely to the UP, but the battle between the transcontinentals continued nonetheless.

One reason Villard backed away from the OR&N joint-lease was his fear of a natural alliance against him between the UP and the approaching GN. He had reason to worry. Adams had dropped by Saint Paul as early as 1890 to offer Jim Hill a twofold cooperation: free use for the GN of the OR&N-UP tracks from Spokane to the Pacific port of Portland; and joint construction of a line from Portland north to Puget Sound. It must have been a sweet moment for the Canadian farmboy-made-good, to have this scion of two U.S. presidents come to him seeking terms.

Out of this came not a formal accord but a temporary alliance of convenience between the UP and the GN. The UP-OR&N tracks through the beautiful Columbia Gorge afforded the GN the second of two UP passages to the Pacific, the first from Butte to San Francisco and now this better one from Spokane to Portland. The Columbia River route had one great advantage: it followed a water-level path through the narrow crevice in the towering Cascade Mountains, thus avoiding terrible and expensive grades.

On the other hand, it had the singular disadvantage of meandering southwest from Spokane, which meant longer mileage than a direct route west. Far more important, the port of Portland had severe disadvantages when compared with the superb, deep harbors on Puget Sound. Portland lay 120 miles upstream from the mouth of the great river, and from Portland to the ocean wandered only a ten- to twenty-foot natural channel, obstructed by islands and shifting sandbars. This channel would require constant dredging and improvement, and even at that, the port facilities left much to be desired. The Willamette River, whose confluence with the Columbia River formed the port site, rose and fell sharply with the seasons. Tidal ebbs and flows on the Columbia also presented problems, as did limited dockage and tight turning radii for large ships.

As for the idea of a jointly constructed line between Portland and the harbors north on Puget Sound, it was an idea so good that Adams would have liked to save it as a stand-alone UP venture. But the UP found itself badly overextended financially, due to the building of the Oregon Short Line and its skirmishing with the NP. It seemed more sensible to draw the GN into a partnership—a case, as Adams nicely put it, of "two cats with one mouse." Hill agreed to the idea, but after a series of intractable problems, he and Sidney Dillon, of the UP, eventually decided to scrap the venture. As railroad historian Maury Klein concluded, "In the race to dominate the Northwest, the Union Pacific dropped behind the Great Northern and the Northern Pacific." The UP would remain confined generally below the Snake-Columbia line.

For all these reasons, Jim Hill now proceeded to follow his original plan: to proceed due west from Spokane toward a Cascades crossing and on to Puget Sound. The Columbia River corridor and Portland, long-established queen city of the Northwest, would one day attract an important arm of the GN system. But the main line would run along the shorter but harder route to the north.

Two major decisions had to be made before building west from Spokane: the location of the appropriate pass across the Cascades, and the best port city to select as the GN's terminus. Out on Puget Sound in western Washington, the local populace had been agog since 1887, when it began to appear likely that the Manitoba would build all the way to the Pacific.

Rival cities to Tacoma, such as Seattle, Everett, and the Bellingham Bay town of Fairhaven, groused about neglect by the NP. Further complicating the situation, the UP was, as noted, making noises about building north to Tacoma, and so was the Southern Pacific, which already had a long line north from the San Francisco Bay area to Portland. But to the residents of western Washington, as to their compatriots in Spokane, Jim Hill loomed up on the horizon as their true savior. An area newspaper saluted him as "the greatest railroad builder the world has ever produced." The paper added, "He is also one of the greatest men intellectually."

Hill warmed to this wonderful opportunity and played on the pining Puget Sound cities like a virtuoso. He had, after all, an advantage that earlier transcontinental rail builders had lacked. Since they had built rapidly to secure their land grants, they had located their West Coast termini early in the process. In contrast, Hill had built his road slowly, developing its hinterlands as it went. Now, surveying his final link, he had the nice advantage of being able to play coy with established port cities that desperately wanted his proven railroad.

Adopting yet another of his homely metaphors, he began making public statements in which he likened the GN's western end to the "head of the rake." Envisioning the main line of the transcontinental as the handle of the rake, he described the north-south axis along the Sound as the head, which would sweep in the bounty of the region, with tines representing cities from Portland on the south to Vancouver, British Columbia, on the north. This, of course, allowed him to play one city against another; and in fact, early rumor had it that Fairhaven—one of three burgs that would fold into modern Bellingham, midway between Seattle and Vancouver—would be the winner.

This was more than a little disingenuous. Of course, the GN had to choose one city for its primary Pacific dock facilities. More to the point, by 1890 it had already secretly chosen Seattle. When the NP had selected Tacoma as its port twenty years earlier, it had discounted Seattle, which lay farther north and thus closer to the ocean via the Strait of Juan de Fuca. The NP leaders knew that Seattle had a fine harbor in Elliott Bay and the advantage of freshwater lakes contiguous to it, where barnacles and other marine growths could be easily removed. But they saw the steep hills of the site as a major drawback, since these would necessitate expensive grading for roadways, yards, and dockage.

A virulent hatred for the NP arose in Seattle with the passing years, particularly as the city's population soared in the 1880s to thirty thousand and to forty thousand by the early 1890s. This growth stemmed from a booming lumber trade, particularly by sea with California, from a favored locale, and from an energetic and entrepreneurial populace. The NP eventually built a stub line up to Seattle, locally known as the "orphan road," but this only whetted the city's appetite for more.

Like town boosters in other frontier cities spurned by major railroads, the Seattle boosters, led by Judge Thomas Burke and his partner Daniel Gilman, formed their own little road, the Seattle, Lake Shore, and Eastern. They raised $1 million and began pushing tracks eastward from Seattle, along Lake Washington and up into the Cascades, and also westward from Spokane. Rumor had it, not surprisingly, that Hill and the Manitoba would buy up the road; but in 1888, the NP made a preemptive strike and secured it instead.

According to his biographer, Thomas Burke "built Seattle." He was, wrote Nard Jones, "a roly-poly little lawyer," a frenetic Irish promoter whose title of judge came from an earlier term on the territorial bench. His appearance, however, belied his true stature. Intelligent, hard-driving, and ambitious, he had years ago demonstrated courage and conviction by defending Chinese victims of local mobs. When Hill's lieutenants Beckler and Clough visited Seattle early in 1890, they sized him up as the best bet to carry the flame for the GN. Hill agreed.

Like Roman imperialists of old, Hill saw in Burke the best representative of the local power structure and thus the best ally to bring his compatriots into the GN fold. Through Clough, he made Burke his man on the coast, with sweeping powers and the charge to bring the city council and other local governance in line and to get Hill the access and sites he needed. The judge proved a good choice and spoke of his new client after their first meeting, "He knows what he wants and isn't afraid to ask for it, and I might add, generally gets it."

Assisted by the Hill minions and their checkbooks, Judge Burke set out on several fronts at once. As unobtrusively as possible, he bought up waterfront and adjacent properties, working carefully to keep prices in line so that one tough precedent would not lead to an escalation in demands. Hill watched him closely; on one occasion, Burke even had to pool money from various secret sources to pay a hard-nosed seller $10,000 for a key acreage without his client's knowledge. Two key strategic locations quickly emerged. At the north end of the Seattle waterfront, the GN purchased sixty acres for its main shops and yards. Well to the south lay an undeveloped area of tidal flats, still submerged, in the seedy area known as Whitechapel. Here, Jim Hill wanted to fill the flats with earth moved from adjacent hills and to locate his terminal and depot facilities.

Burke had earlier succeeded in securing from the Seattle City Council a mile-long, two-block-wide access corridor to the tidelands site from the northern yards along the docks of the "city front," a meandering, yet-to-be-filled route named Railroad Avenue. A 120-foot corridor of the avenue was for rail access, and Burke had gotten 30 feet of this breadth for his Seattle, Lake Shore, and Eastern road, which was now—unfortunately—in the hands of the NP. The GN proceeded to build its waterfront trackage south to a temporary terminal on Columbia Street; but Hill desperately wanted the better site to the south on the tidelands, and for this he needed a sizable share of the remaining corridor on Railroad Avenue.

The Hill forces now found themselves in a hard spot. Even as James himself visited the Puget Sound country, reiterating the possibility of locating his terminal facilities at Everett or Bellingham, the Seattleites knew that he favored their city—that was where the people and the action were. After all, Baring Brothers, the London financial backers of the GN, had already issued a promotional brochure indicating Seattle as the road's western terminus. So they well knew that the GN was not so omnipotent or undecided after all. Thus the city council now became obstreperous, a majority dedicated to ensuring that Burke and Hill would not pry some of their most valuable lands away from them cavalierly or cheaply.

R. H. Thomson, a highly principled city engineer, encouraged them, arguing that the city must have a unified plan of development and not simply cave in to the wishes of a powerful railroad. The NP complicated matters for its rival by hawking its major share of Railroad Avenue access and calling for shared terminal and depot facilities between the two roads. As unpopular as the NP was in Seattle, many local folks agreed that the GN was trying to gouge the city for real estate and prime access. Hill thundered in response: "Sooner than do it, it [the Great Northern] would seek a terminus elsewhere. We want nothing to do with a company so wholly lost to decency and honor."

Tensions mounted, and the game got rough. In the spring of 1890, the Seattle City Council, meeting in secrecy, made a major concession to the GN by granting it 60 of the 120 feet of breadth along Railroad Avenue. There is no question that the Seattle civic leaders made this move out of fear that Hill might yet forsake their town. But critics lashed out both at the secrecy of the process and at the value of the concession. They got even angrier when the acting mayor, who signed the franchise agreement, turned up as editor of the *Seattle Telegraph,* the Democratic newspaper that Burke ran as a spokesman for the Hill interests. Contention over the granting of the concession continued for years, but without success in overturning it. As Seattle historian Roger Sale concluded, the compromise did not turn out to be so bad: the GN had prime Railroad Avenue access, and the NP and other roads could share the remainder of the corridor.

Hill and his cohorts continued to run into a hornet's nest of frustration in their efforts to secure terminal facilities in the southern tidelands. They managed to get the Seattle Chamber of Commerce to kick in $11,650 to assist in purchasing the ground. But the NP, whose right-of-way the GN had to cross to reach the flats, found responsive ears on the city council with its call for shared facilities like the ones the two railroads had, after all, in Saint Paul.

The acrimony dragged on and on, even after Hill returned in 1892, once again extolling the virtues of Everett and the low rates he could charge for hauling Northwest lumber to the Midwest. His foes raised such issues as drainage problems in the area and the loss of access to future industrial sites. As a result, the GN and the NP ended up sharing an inadequate, little waterfront depot throughout the 1890s. Finally, during the years 1902–6, Jim Hill would secure his long-sought, modern terminal-depot facilities by convincing the city fathers of the wisdom of building a north-south tunnel under the Seattle business district to reach the facilities, an idea that engineer Thomson shared.

While things festered in Seattle, the GN group worked more successfully to fashion the "head of the rake" along a north-south axis in western Washington. In 1889 the GN acquired the Fairhaven and Southern line, radiating out of Bellingham Bay. Over the next two years, another Hill line, the Seattle and Montana, laid nearly eighty miles of track along Puget Sound to meet the Fairhaven, so that a "Shore Line" resulted, stretching from Seattle up to the very shadow of the Canadian border. The acquisition of rights to yet another local road, the New Westminster and Southern, gave the GN access to the CP in southern British Columbia and thus to the port of Vancouver. For a decade, these roads operated under separate titles; by 1900, all were melded into the GN. Still missing, for now, was the left end of the head of the rake—from Seattle south to Portland—which would have been built in partnership with the failing UP.

As the head of the rake was pieced together, a final determination had to be made concerning the handle: namely, the location of a workable pass through the Cascade Mountains just east of Puget Sound. The Cascades, unlike the Rockies, are one mighty range, not a cordillera. But this one range is much broader, and steeper in the sense that its base is much lower and closer to sea level. Hill's surveyors had a 125-mile-wide corridor in which to look for their pass: from Stampede Pass, used by the NP on the south, to the CP's route through the steep canyons of the Fraser River, on the north.

Pressed by Hill, John Stevens had his men in the mountains in the spring of 1890. He would always bristle at the suggestion that he accidentally found the pass that his subordinate would name after him. Scouting the Wenatchee River, a westside tributary of the mighty Columbia, Stevens became intrigued by a south fork of the river, the sizable Nason Creek, which he guessed really headed to the west. As he then pondered a low saddle amid towering peaks in this area, he sent a party led by C. F. B. Haskell up to see if this was indeed the head of Nason Creek. The explorers established that it was. Stevens Pass stands at 4,061 feet above sea level, a formidable passage but still less than half the elevation of some of the surrounding peaks.

Snowshoeing the pass during the ensuing winter, Stevens figured that a tunnel at the 3,381-foot level could eliminate the worst of the grades. But until such an expensive tunnel could be bored—and that would be a while—the crossing would be tough, requiring a series of steep switchbacks across the precipitous, avalanche-prone summit from Tumwater Canyon on the east side to the Tye River on the west, which descends into the Skykomish tributary of the Snohomish River, which flows into Puget Sound at Everett.

Now, the pathway westward from Spokane to Seattle became clear. An arc through the productive terrain of southern Washington had never really been an option. This was NP territory, and by agreeing not to parallel its lines into the rich wheat region south of Spokane, Hill gathered valuable bargaining chips with the NP. Similarly, the NP had staked out the lucrative Yakima Valley, spreading just northwest of the twin cities of Pasco-Kennewick, where the Snake joins the Columbia in south-central Washington. Through private and then federal reclamation, this valley was beginning to blossom as one of the chief apple and citrus producers in the country.

And so the GN main line projected due west from Spokane, and tracklaying commenced in midsummer of 1892 across cleft and intermittently forested hills toward Odessa and Ephrata. Here the fragile greenery of the Rocky Mountain rain shadow gave way to the stark and windblown aridity of central Washington, where the towering Cascades to the west allowed precious little moisture to fall. In mid-August, Shepard's crews set the tracklaying record for the Pacific Extension by spiking down 4.3 miles of rail in one day near Harrington. Soon after, they came to the broad south-flowing Columbia River. They crossed it by ferry below the mouth of the Wenatchee River. A huge bridge would have to wait until next year.

Hill and his associates, looking southward at the potential for irrigation in the Yakima Valley, had great plans for the townsite of Wenatchee, on the west bank of the Columbia. Judge Burke formed a syndicate to develop the townsite—with Hill reportedly buying up one-fourth of the lots—and the surrounding irrigable lands. Two canals were dug to deliver water from the Wenatchee River, and Burke donated four lots to the city so that it could compete successfully for the seat of Chelan County.

The GN's Arthur Gunn directed the Wenatchee Development Committee, aimed at duplicating the NP's plans for the Yakima Valley, and Hill loaned him $15,000 in 1896 to form the Wenatchee Power Company. Soon after, when Gunn found himself overextended, the GN moved in to take over the development program directly. But this arid terrain was more marginal farm country than the Minnesota–North Dakota heartland, and progress came slowly. Chelan County boasted only 3,391 inhabitants by 1900.

Now ensued the final, climactic phase of constructing the eight-hundred-mile Pacific Extension, from Havre to the sea. As the crews moved up the challenging Tumwater Canyon through the Cascade foothills from the east, others—under the able Stevens—moved up the westward slope from Everett. For Jim Hill, the pressures became nearly unbearable. Attempting both to manage his regional road in Saint Paul and to oversee construction of a transcontinental, he drove himself to distraction, constantly racing back and forth along the new western tracks in his private car, then succumbing to attacks of rheumatism and cold-flu symptoms that landed him in bed.

When the final realization sank in that he could not complete the road in 1892, he raged at his subordinates and seems even to have come near losing control. He became so exasperated with Beckler that he began bypassing the engineer and issuing orders directly to Shepard and the contractors. Deeply distressed, Beckler confronted Hill, and the old man backed down, but the chief engineer would resign soon after completion of the line.

Now came one, final frustration. Studying the imposing east and west faces of the pass that bore his name, John Stevens saw no alternative—until the summit tunnel could be bored—except to construct what was undeniably every railroad man's nightmare: a horribly costly series of switchbacks over the top. These would total twelve miles of tracks over four and one-half actual miles of terrain, with more than twenty-three hundred feet of curvature, equal to seven full circles! Crossing this obstacle course, twenty-five-unit trains would have to decouple, and engines fore and aft would have to push and pull the trains over in segments of five or six cars per train. In winter, hundreds of men would be required to shovel snow from the tracks. This one terrible bottleneck passage would, in short, drain much of the cost-efficiency from the tightly built GN system.

To everyone's dread, this bit of news pushed James over the edge. Clearing the tracks ahead, he raced full speed westward by special train and rushed up to the summit site. While colleagues stood by quaking, Stevens coolly explained his decision to his highly agitated boss. Then, to the surprise and relief of the group, Hill calmly responded: "That is all right. You could have done nothing else." Without hesitation, Hill raised Stevens's salary by 50 percent!

This marked, as Ralph Hidy and his coauthors noted, "the first time he demanded that speedy construction take precedence over quality of line." In fact, he had no choice. "Death Mountain" would remain highly dangerous, both from avalanches and from runaway trains, and highly expensive until the Cascade Tunnel was completed eight years later, in 1900. Construction of the tunnel would take six to eight hundred men three years to accomplish, but it would replace nine miles of track and seven hundred feet of rise.

Step by weary step, the graders and tracklayers from east and west slowly converged on the summit amid rain, snow, and melts as the year 1892 ground to an end. When the final spike was driven home on January 6, 1893, high on the west slope at a siding now called Scenic, only cold and lethargic work crews were on hand; and even they showed little enthusiasm for the event. Hill was laid up at home with rheumatism; and in any case, this was far from the first transcontinental to be completed and thus was not the superclimax that previous "last spike" ceremonies had been. The first scheduled train crossed the route only one month later.

Saint Paul delayed the celebration of its first true transcontinental railroad until June 9, 1893, with a grand parade and a gala event at the Aberdeen Hotel. The parade passed by for two hours, featuring just about every northwestern theme, from Indians to Red River carts to steamboats and engines, and floats celebrating regional industries. Typically, Jim Hill worked right up until the start of festivities; but he gloried in the kind of tributes that only few people ever know. The *Saint Paul Pioneer Press* featured a large sketch of his face on the front page. Tributes poured in from hundreds of well-wishers, including President Cleveland, and out-of-town dignitaries numbered such prominent men as George Pullman and Marshall Field from Chicago.

Nine days later, the first GN passenger train left Saint Paul and, chugging along behind a Brooks Mogul engine at speeds of up to sixty miles per hour, arrived at Seattle in four days. That city staged its own special celebration on the Fourth of July. Once again, Hill became the hero of the masses, cutting first-class fares below prevailing NP rates, from sixty dollars to thirty-five dollars, and second-class rates from thirty-five dollars to twenty-five dollars, all of which endeared him to westerners eager to travel to the big Chicago World's Fair of 1893.

Jim Hill amply deserved the praise he received that day. Few industrial organizations in America so closely reflected the personality of one, dominant man as did the new GN. Conceding the major contributions of Stephen and Kennedy, it is still right to conclude that Hill had by now come to predominate the financing as well as the management and construction of the road. And its financial strength, quite simply, lay at the heart of the competitiveness of the newly completed transcontinental: it was tightly capitalized at low rates of interest. Although its land grant did not, generally speaking, extend beyond the western border of Minnesota, the GN also possessed other, more subtle advantages.

The GN's major American transcontinental rivals, the NP and the UP, had both been speedily and poorly built and now needed major reconstruction; and both carried heavy burdens of debt, due in no small part to their Pacific Northwest rivalries. In contrast, the newly completed GN had been methodically and well constructed, over comparatively level and unfettered terrain; although it would need improvements, these could be more easily and more substantially made than those of competing roads. With their large and compelling transcontinental land grants, the NP and the UP represented long and heavy trunks, which were only thinly rooted in the rich, agrarian heartlands of the Midwest. The GN's main line, on the other hand, was a strong westward trunk, with a healthy and densely intertwined system of taproots in one of the richest cereal crop regions of the world.

Part of the notable accomplishment of Hill and his associates lay in simple luck, in being forced by the nature of their enterprise to focus their energies for so long on building infrastructure in their Minnesota-Dakota heartland before undertaking the long, costly thrust west. But more important were Hill's talents: his remarkable mastery over every detail of what was now a far-flung operation, his vision of the inevitable triumph of transcontinental through-carriers, his insufferable iron will and work ethic, and his recruitment of an able coterie of men like John Stevens and D. C. Shepard. At the peak of his powers, James J. Hill stood, in the turbulent 1890s, on the national stage.

CHAPTER 5

The "Hill Lines"

JIM Hill was truly fortunate in capitalizing his westward extension during a time of easy credit, but his luck—and the fortunes of other railroaders as well—seemed to run out soon after the completion of the Great Northern in early 1893. With the onset of the Panic of 1893, the nation slid into the worst depression it had yet experienced. Hard times gripped all American regions, but the West in particular, since President Grover Cleveland's decision to take the United States off the silver monetary standard wrought havoc on the mining industry of the region. Profits dried up, industries failed, and unemployment mushroomed. Compounding the problem, a combination of droughts and falling commodity prices struck the agricultural economy. But as in all depressions, for shrewd businessmen like Hill, hard times also brought some wondrous opportunities.

American railroads, heavily indebted and overextended after the big building boom of the 1880s, took the full brunt of the depression. The newly created Interstate Commerce Commission, America's first federal regulatory agency, reported in June 1894 that a remarkable 192 U.S. railroads, owning fully one-fourth of the rail mileage in the country, had fallen into receivership. Among these were the wobbly NP, which went down in August 1893, the equally shaky UP, and the Atchison, Topeka, and Santa Fe, now under the tutelage of Hill protégé Alan Manvel.

It would always be a point of special pride to James J. Hill, and deservedly so, that the well-built and tightly capitalized GN, unlike its federally subsidized competitors, did not fail during the 1893 Panic. As he expressed it to Lord Mount Stephen, "Our company is the only Pacific line paying a dividend on its shares, while three out of the five lines other than our own are in process of reorganization, which must wipe out a great many millions of the capital invested in those enterprises."

The GN did stagger initially under the weight of hard times. Even before 1893, as drought and low wheat prices devastated the railroad's heartland, Hill joined other railroad executives in purchasing seed grain and hauling it free to producers, whom he also pressured to curtail their acreages and to maximize efficiency. He raised loans on Wall Street to assist elevator operators in storing grain for farmers until prices could rise. But prices failed to rise accordingly, and popular anger mounted against railroads and elevator firms, which farmers felt were gouging them. Profits dried up apace.

Yet, the salient fact is that the GN weathered the crisis far better than did its competitors, and soon it was prospering once more. The main reason why lay, as always, in Hill's legendary close management of the organization, as is seen in the following directive, which he issued in the summer of 1893: "Take whatever steps are necessary to reduce track, machinery, stations, and other service to lowest point possible. Take off all extra gangs everywhere, except those relaying steel. Reduce wages section foremen to forty dollars [a month] east and forty-five west, and of section men to one dollar [a day] east and one dollar and quarter west. . . . [T]here will be plenty of men to work at those rates."

The cuts in employment bore out these instructions: GN's work force fell 19 percent between fiscal years 1893 and 1894, from 7,802 to 6,295. Indeed, even as he arrived at the top levels of corporate management in America, Jim Hill kept such a close and overbearing hand on the rudder that a steady procession of his assistants, general managers, and first vice-presidents—including W. A. Stephens and Charles Warren—burned out and moved on. He simply could not delegate authority and live with the outcome.

Yet another factor in the GN's success in weathering the financial storm was Hill's ability to open new markets and add new tonnages to his trains. He now faced a challenging situation: trains heading west naturally carried heaving ladings of manufactured products to newly settled areas, but on the return east, they were underloaded, particularly since they were traveling from one agrarian region to another.

To Hill, who often described an empty railroad car as a "thief," the obvious solution seemed to lie in the magnificent stands of old-growth spruce, cedar, white pine, and other valuable timber in the Cascade Mountains of western Washington and Oregon and, to a lesser extent, in northern Idaho and western Montana. Because of their distance from eastern markets and the dominance of the lumber industry in the Great Lakes region, these superb stands of timber had so far attracted only West Coast developers. Now, as the forests of the Upper Midwest and South were rapidly disappearing, the hour of the Pacific Northwest seemed at hand.

As early as February 1892, Jim Hill lectured an appreciative banquet gathering of Everett civic leaders: "Lumber, gentlemen, is your greatest resource today. . . . What you want, gentlemen, is a cheap railroad connection. . . . You will find that we will treat you well." Soon after completion of the GN to Puget Sound, Hill called together a group of leading Washington lumber operators. Since the prevailing rate for eastbound lumber from the Pacific Northwest stood at a prohibitive ninety cents per hundred pounds, he asked them what rate they would need to tap eastern markets. When they responded that it must be no higher than sixty-five cents, he startled them by responding that—with the efficiency of his new road—he could offer them fifty cents per hundred-weight on cedar and forty cents on fir.

These rates opened a booming market for Northwest lumber all the way to the eastern seaboard and the South, but most particularly in the Upper Midwest, and the shipments increased yearly throughout the decade. Eastbound tonnages soon matched, and even exceeded, those bound west, further bolstering the profitability of the railroad. The future, as we shall see, would hold even greater developments in this key growth industry.

So rich was the GN's midwestern heartland, so solid its management, and so tight its financing that the railroad actually stacked up tidy profits during the depressed mid-1890s. As railroad historian Albro Martin notes, declining costs and increasing efficiency had GN freight trains hauling an average load of three hundred tons by 1894–95. In that one year, this efficiency, abated by depression-induced deflation, allowed the railroad to reduce costs by 13 percent.

Hill actually fretted about excessive profits, which would whet the appetites of a public demanding state and federal regulation, and therefore he plowed even more back into infrastructure and squirreled away over $1.3 million in inconspicuous accounts. He wrote the New York financier Jacob Schiff, "The Great Northern is certainly a most remarkable property to earn money." A few years later, in the prosperous year of 1900, he spoke frankly to Wall Street banker Daniel Lamont: "The Great Northern has about reached a point where its net income is growing faster than its capital can absorb it. Notwithstanding the large increases we have made in capital stock, it looks as if our surplus above dividends this year would be fully five millions of dollars. Of course we cannot afford to make such a showing as this in our reports and will have to cover all we can in such a way as to reduce the amount, but there must come a time when these temporary expedients will end, and the increased earnings will have to be shown."

He further opened his mind to his English friend and investment partner Gaspard Farrer, of the recently failed banking firm of Baring Brothers, which had promoted the recent Pacific Extension bonding: "Our shareholders want to know how well we have done, while the State wants to limit our earnings to a reasonable return on our capital without any guarantee that we will have the traffic to make such return." A new era was aborning, in which businesses, facing government regulation, would keep one set of books for stockholders and another for government perusal.

Meanwhile, in this remarkable era of deflation and of ever more valuable dollars, Jim Hill's personal wealth also defied the national trend and continued to burgeon. His fortune, which had stood at $9.6 million in 1890, rose to $12 million in 1895 and was approaching $20 million in the restored prosperity of the turn of the century. Thus, in an age when a millionaire was truly wealthy, Jim Hill became a true *multi*millionaire, in fact one of America's most wealthy and powerful men.

Of course, the armies of laborers who worked for the GN saw

their earnings headed in the opposite direction; and as their hardships increased, tensions mounted. With the dawn of the critical year 1894, the railroad unions of the Northwest galvanized into activity. The older Knights of Labor, who had earlier boasted over two hundred locals in the four Pacific Northwest states, were sagging after defeats in a wave of strikes several years earlier. Gradually the Knights gave way to a new industrial organization, the American Railway Union, led by the dynamic and articulate socialist Eugene V. Debs.

In the spring of 1894, union rebels, affiliated with "Colonel" Jacob Coxey's vaunted protest march on the national capital, headed eastward, shouting their protests against Cleveland's depression and the abusive powers of the railroads. In Montana, a Coxeyite "army" led by "General" William Hogan actually hijacked an NP train at Butte, fended off federal marshals at Billings with the help of local workers, and got all the way to Forsyth before being stopped by U.S. troops dispatched by the president.

Out on the Montana Central, resentment boiled over when workers got hold of a coded GN directive to fire members of the budding American Railway Union locals at Great Falls, Helena, and Butte. Ignoring the worried counsels of Debs, Hogan ordered a wildcat strike, which quickly spread westward into Washington and eastward into North Dakota and finally all the way to the Twin Cities. Jim Hill never had any use for unions, or for anyone else who defied him, for that matter, but he now faced a situation well beyond his control. Fearful of mobs that threatened to close down the Saint Paul yards and facilities, he implored President Cleveland to intervene once again with the army, something the president, confronted this time by a truly dangerous set of circumstances, hesitated to do.

Fortunately, however, the specter of armed confrontation across more than one thousand miles of railroad frightened everyone involved. So when a group of Twin Cities business leaders led by Minneapolis milling magnate Charles Pillsbury offered to arbitrate the strike, both sides agreed. The group's finding, which both parties promptly accepted, represented a union victory and a comeuppance for Jim Hill, who, to his credit, gamely swallowed it. The American Railway Union won wage parity with the NP for GN workers and, more important, recognition of the union.

For Debs and the American Railway Union, though, this proved to be a pyrrhic victory. Bolstered by a new self-confidence, the union defiantly launched a boycott of the mighty, Chicago-based Pullman Palace Car Company, a boycott that paralyzed rail traffic west of Chicago later in 1894—except for traffic of the recently settled GN. In the end, Cleveland this time intervened with federal troops, breaking the strike and the union as well.

The railroad strikes of 1894 alarmed Hill and other executives, especially since rail-town residents generally sympathized with their neighbors who labored in this dangerous profession rather than with distant management. This was a problem that would not go away. As historian W. Thomas White reveals, the Northwest railroads now sought to undercut union solidarity with a strategy that was gaining favor nationally: mixing various antagonistic ethnic groups together in work parties so that they could not effectively unite. The GN and the NP turned first to Japanese and then more to Slavic and Italian immigrants to achieve this result; by 1912, fully 75 percent of summer construction crews on the GN were Slavs and Italians. The angry response of traditional "white" workers showed the effect. The *Seattle Union Record* commented in 1900, "Jim Hill will have Japs as yardmen, engineers and conductors if a check is not put upon his career of greed."

As the rail brotherhoods enhanced their power in the years after 1894, they became an ever greater worry for James J. Hill, and he continued to face off with them. In 1898, for instance, his General Superintendent Frank Ward bluntly turned down the bid of the GN trainmen and enginemen to secure union recognition and raises to accompany the new prosperity. The GN did prove generous in providing some benefits, such as free travel passes to employees; but it was tardy with others, such as pensions, which it gave only to selected classes of employees until James Hill had passed from the scene. Jim Hill held a very old-fashioned view of laboring; he believed that employees' primary loyalty should be to their employer, and he modified his opinions only slowly. During his final two decades of control, GN salaries slowly crept up to midscale among American railroads, and benefits progressed even more gradually.

The Panic of 1893 had yet another impact on Hill's career in that it prompted a shift in his political loyalties. Unlike most businessmen of his generation, he was not a Republican. Rather, due in large part to his Canadian origins and to the international nature of his business, he believed strongly in free trade, and this orientation drew him to the Democratic Party and its low-tariff policy, as articulated by Grover Cleveland during the 1880s.

Jim Hill loved politics, both the bare-knuckled manipulation of favors and patronage and the philosophical discussion of the issues. He took it as a fact of life that his sweeping economic power—especially political in nature, since it entailed monopolies and near-monopolies over transportation—naturally brought with it political interests and sway. Ever since the frenetic days of 1878–79, Twin Cities rumor mills had claimed that he played rough and mean, bribing or otherwise "influencing" politicians when need be. No one ever proved that Hill gave a bribe, and when a radical "Grit" politician from Manitoba made such an accusation, Jim forced him to retract it. However, Hill never hesitated to give politicians favored deals for stocks and properties. Quite naturally, he quickly became a key Democratic power in Minnesota, and that power soon transcended his home state.

By the time of the 1884 presidential campaign, Hill had come to wield impressive regional and even national political clout. After receiving the assurance of a powerful New York Democratic friend, former presidential candidate Samuel Tilden, that Cleveland was "all right," he contributed $10,000 to Cleveland's war chest and instructed his minions to join the cause. He thereafter struck up a friendship with this first Democratic president since the Civil War, a friendship that would be bruised but not broken by the reservation access controversy that soon ensued. Naturally enough, in this age of spoilsmen at the helm, he expected considerations in return.

And he got them. Minnesota was, by tradition, a Republican state, but it had been seething with agrarian unrest for more than a decade, unrest spearheaded especially by the Grangers and aimed particularly at the railroads. Party lines were, as a result, tenuous at best. Jim Hill got along well with the Irish Democrats of Saint Paul, who dominated their minority party statewide, and he helped them financially. Two of his cohorts, Michael Doran and Patrick Kelly—whom the *Minneapolis Tribune* called "proconsuls for the province of Minnesota"—publicly called the shots. As Doran blithely stated, "Mr. Hill isn't in politics!" Events quickly demonstrated, however, that indeed he was, when the sudden and unexpected accession of the Cleveland Democrats to power brought the blessings of federal patronage to Minnesota politicos not used to having it. Suddenly, as historian Horace Merrill has shown, a nasty chasm opened among the Minnesota Democrats.

Ignatius Donnelly was a chubby, gregarious, and highly articulate agrarian rebel, a consummate crowd rouser and an unabashed romantic who had written a popular book on Atlantis. He had been a leading Granger, and in the decade ahead, he would become a leading Populist. Having served in Congress as a Republican from Minnesota, he shifted parties and in 1884 narrowly lost a bid to return to the House of Representatives as a Democrat. Donnelly figured, reasonably enough, that his prominence now entitled him not only to a voice in slicing the patronage pie but also to a nice federal appointment as surveyor general for his state. He got a rude surprise, though, when the Hill-Doran-Kelly triumvirate stopped him cold. When Donnelly took his case directly to Washington, his foes turned to Hill's friends in Cleveland's home state of New York and to Postmaster General William Vilas from neighboring Wisconsin to keep the reformist pest corralled.

Enraged, Donnelly turned the full and considerable force of his invective against his adversary: "Jim Hill is the *deus ex machina,* the colored gentleman under the woodpile; the new leader of the reformed Democracy of Minnesota. Jim don't approve of my granger legislation in the past, or my granger proclivities in the present, or my granger possibilities in the future." In July 1886, he again excoriated Hill before a large throng of angry reform Democrats in Saint Paul: "Shall the Democratic party of Minnesota be run in the interest of Jim Hill or in the interest of the people?"

Jim Hill had long since learned to ignore such slings and arrows, and in fact, they usually did him no particular harm. For example, Hill's old congressional ally Knute Nelson, now governor, bristled at press criticism that he had been seen lunching with Hill. When Nelson proceeded to rail at the GN as a predator on his state, Hill proved to be remarkably calm, even forgiving. Hill continued, unabashed, in the ensuing years to build a regional base of political power, always concerned to befriend and financially back the allies of his growing transportation empire and to beat back agrarian and labor radicals, like members of the emerging Populist Party, who advocated rail rate controls, soft money, and other heresies.

Like other financial barons of the age, he bought into newspapers to advance his views and interests. He purchased outright the *Saint Paul Daily Globe,* which Norman Kittson had earlier owned, and also bought a substantial interest in the *Fargo Argus* of North Dakota. In Washington, as earlier noted, he had the *Seattle Telegraph,* under Judge Thomas Burke's control; but in Montana, he did not need to worry, since his ally Marcus Daly had a prevalent and powerful mouthpiece with the *Anaconda Standard* and, eventually, other papers as well. Hill even plowed $25,000 into the faltering *New York Times.* All across the GN empire, Jim Hill's private car became a landmark, frequently only a mythical landmark, pulled up on sidings from Fargo to Olympia, Washington—there to dictate policy regarding rail regulation and other pressing issues. He was becoming a legend in his own time, an ogre to many, a force larger than life to nearly all.

In national politics, Jim Hill maintained his support of the Cleveland administration in 1888, despite the recent problems of reservation access. He had little use for the Republican who defeated Cleveland that year, Benjamin Harrison. Once again, however, he demonstrated his hard-nosed pragmatism by calmly paying Harrison's son Russell, a Montana rancher who helped him on the reservation issue, more for some livestock than they were worth. He was pleased to see Cleveland return to the White House in 1892 and was then deeply disturbed as the Panic of 1893 eroded Cleveland's public support. Even when the president refused to send in the army during the 1894 strike, Hill stuck with him, mainly because Hill continued to believe in Cleveland's views on free trade and hard money. With the approach of the 1896 election campaign, he still considered Cleveland "the only safe man for president."

Predictably, to a man of James J. Hill's natural conservatism, the radicalism spawned by the 1893 Panic seemed heretical and highly threatening. He watched in dismay as a new wave of agrarian radicalism, in the form of the Populist Party, swept the nation and particularly his region. Almost everything the farm radicals espoused, particularly their calls for the free coinage of silver dollars to achieve inflation and for a government takeover of railroads, filled him with loathing. When the Democratic Party, at its 1896 convention, dumped Cleveland and nominated a Populist-style orator, William Jennings Bryan, for president, Hill joined other conservative Democrats in looking toward the Republicans, who had nominated a safe, gold standpatter, William McKinley. The tariff issue counted for far less than whether or not the federal government would remain friendly to business!

For Jim Hill, the flight from a Democratic Party that had merged with the Populists proved easier than for some other business leaders of that party. His longtime friend and shipbuilding associate, Senator Mark Hanna of Ohio, commanded the McKinley campaign and was in the process of assembling the largest financial war chest ever attempted in a political campaign. Hill enthusiastically joined him in this enterprise. In mid-August 1896, as Matthew Josephson recounts, the midwestern industrial barons journeyed together to New York City. They traveled by carriage, as the press watched agog, from one industrial headquarters to another—including the Pennsylvania and New York Central railroads and the banking houses of J. P. Morgan and Kuhn, Loeb—arguing their cause for huge donations to fend off

Bryan and his "Popo-crats," albeit to donors who generally needed little convincing.

More to the point, Hill threw the full support of his own personal network and of the GN organization all across the Northwest behind the McKinley campaign. He wrote Hanna in late September, estimating that he and his allies would pour $105,000 into the campaign in Minnesota and the Dakotas alone, $15,000 of it from his personal coffers. The Hill forces focused their attention on like-minded gold Democrats, but they faced some severe problems that their eastern counterparts had trouble comprehending.

In the midwestern heartland, angry farmers could not be weaned away from Bryan and the Populists. Judge Burke faced the same problem in eastern Washington. And in the silver state of Montana, Hill's ally Marcus Daly not only refused to join him on this issue but contributed well over $100,000 to the Bryan cause, making Daly in all probability its largest supporter. In the landslide election that elevated McKinley and swamped Bryan, the three states of Washington, Montana, and South Dakota went Democratic. Under the adverse circumstances, Jim Hill could, nevertheless, take considerable credit for holding Minnesota and North Dakota for the Republicans.

During the ensuing four years, as W. Thomas White points out in his study of Hill's relationships with presidents, the Minnesota magnate enjoyed his most satisfying relationships ever with the federal government. He still did not like the high-tariff proclivities of McKinley and the GOP, and he did not agree with the president's drift toward imperialism and war with Spain. But he very much approved of the administration's hard-money policies and the prosperity that seemed to accompany them; and his friendships with Hanna, especially, and with the president gave him the best access he would ever have to the White House and to the distribution of regional patronage.

In sharp contrast, Hill found his new role of Republican regional power broker to be one of frustration and torment. At the time of McKinley's inauguration, in March 1897, he wrote Hanna, "I have practically had to carry the Republican Party through on my own shoulders, and it has about arrived at a point where the only way to make the party successful will be to have it thoroughly well beaten." Within a week, he wrote Senator Cushman Davis: "The Republican Party in Minnesota today is, if anything, worse than the Populist. A majority of those representing it at the State Capitol are either cowards, afraid to tell the truth, or thieves, desiring to conceal the truth for the money they can make out of it."

In each of the new states served by the GN, Hill faced both the angry specter of Populism and the problem of his own political persona. He seemed to present a Janus-faced image to these watchful frontier people: on the one hand, a larger-than-life captain of industry, and on the other, a manipulative rate gouger and political boss intent on despoiling them.

Washington, for example, now had a Populist governor, John Rogers, whose panoply of reform programs included a railroad commission capable of setting maximum rates and realistic valuations of property. Rogers, however, ran into trouble when the 1897 session of the legislature devolved into a chaos of factional warfare, much of it fomented by a railroad lobby that Lieutenant Governor Henry McBride characterized as "so powerful that measures had to be approved by it before they could be brought to the legislature." An effective rate commission did not come until 1905. As always, Hill relied on his old friend Burke to oversee his political concerns, a practice that did not necessarily help him in eastern Washington, which so resented the dominance of the more populous West.

Unlike Washington, Montana had not yet attracted many farmers to its semiarid plains expanses, and thus Populists here tended to be silver mine owners and workers. Throughout the 1890s, the cadence here was set by the notorious feud between mining barons Marcus Daly, of the Anaconda Copper Mining Company, and his archfoe, the independent operator William Andrews Clark. For the most part, Hill simply supported his friend Daly and his giant customer Anaconda. In the 1894 "capital fight," he unflinchingly threw his resources behind Daly's ill-fated bid to make the company town Anaconda the state capital,

even though the city lay far from his tracks. Clark and the NP
successfully backed the incumbent, Helena. When another good
customer, Leonard Lewisohn, of the Great Falls–based Boston
and Montana Company, also backed Helena—for good, self-in-
terested reasons—Hill berated him for his actions. Hill had,
quite simply, come not only to like and admire Daly but also to
dislike Clark personally.

Of all the GN states, North Dakota, so agriculturally dependent and so near the Twin Cities, was most arguably the bailiwick
of railroads. Alexander "Big Alex" McKenzie had come there
back in frontier days as an army scout and had gone on to become first a land agent and then chief area political broker for the
NP. He kept a suite of rooms at the Merchants' Hotel in Saint
Paul, from which he both received and gave orders; and his "Old
Gang" waxed strongly enough that it could claim credit for the
maintenance of both of the state's U.S. senators, Henry Hansbrough and Porter McCumber. Even here, though, the machine
was far from omnipotent. Farm insurgents managed in 1897 to
legislate a railroad commission, which soon mandated 50 percent
increases in rail property valuations and frightened the carriers
into granting 10–20 percent reductions in eastbound freight.

As his system spread across North Dakota, Jim Hill simply
moved aboard the NP–Old Gang political ship. The two railroads had few differences, by now, in such matters and shared
most of the same concerns. He did not flinch at McKenzie's
methods, and in fact by 1896, the boss had become one of his
main lieutenants. But McKenzie's methods eventually landed
"Big Alex" in trouble. Following federal charges of fraudulent
acquisition of Alaska mining claims, he was imprisoned in 1900.
Hill stood by him, however. Pleading that McKenzie's failing
health would make the sentence a warrant of death, Hill and
Hanna interceded directly with President McKinley; the president, noting that Hill had "presented the case better than any
lawyer" could have, responded with a full pardon the following
year. The precarious state of McKenzie's health was underscored
by the fact that he went on to live for two more decades! The case
demonstrated to all who paid attention that Jim Hill did not

hesitate to work the system, even if this meant consorting with highly unsavory characters.

Despite his increasing involvement in politics, Jim Hill did not follow Hanna's example. Politics never became his primary focus, which remained what it had always been: his businesses. During the mid- and later 1890s, these became far more complex and far-flung than they had ever been before. Most notably, on each end of the new GN, he entered into wholly new endeavors: maritime commerce on the Pacific, and the mining of iron ore in Minnesota.

Since early childhood, Jim Hill had fantasized about the Orient, dreaming even into young manhood of making a career there as an explorer and steamship entrepreneur. Like many other Americans of the nineteenth century, he saw America's destiny as the torchbearer of a civilization—nurtured in the Middle East and Europe, brought westward to fulfillment on the North American continent, and carried full circle to the teeming multitudes of the Far East. This was the proverbial "Passage to India," as articulated earlier by Senator Thomas Hart Benton of Missouri. Only now, in the minds of businessmen like Hill, the civilization they would bring across the broad Pacific would be not only Christian and individualistic but also commercial and based on the cornucopia of American agricultural munificence.

Businessmen-visionaries like James J. Hill became even more enraptured when they considered how the teeming masses of Asia could become good consumers of surplus crops and manufactures that a newly industrialized America had to export if, in their opinion, it was to prosper. This was the vision of the "China Market," millions of potential customers who needed only proper government and education to bring them income and make them good consumers. Hill put it well in a letter to Hanna in mid-1898:

> I believe there will be a commercial development on the Pacific Ocean in the next twenty years which will surpass any commercial growth the world has seen in the last thousand years. China and Japan alone contain nearly one-third of the population of the globe; and the Chinaman, while his education and civilization is [sic] differ-

ent from ours, is commercially speaking capable of the greatest development. When they have a good government, which will not systematically rob them, they will develop very rapidly. . . . Our commercial relations with China can be easily developed to an extent that would take one-third of our agricultural product, including cotton, and a very large amount of iron and steel.

In his conceptualization of the Asian market, Jim Hill was both a prophet and a dreamer. He did foresee the remarkable evolution of the Pacific Rim–Southeast Asian economies that would come to fruition more than a half-century after his demise. And, with his penchant for geopolitical analysis, he commented again and again that America's newest seaport, Seattle, lay less than half as far from East Asia as did its European counterparts via the Suez Canal. What the United States needed was what Europe provided to its producers: a government-supported merchant fleet and marketing subsidies. In contrast, though, the sharp-eyed realist, in this case, ignored some very hard facts. A massive gulf of cultural and economic inertia prevented the impoverished masses of China from becoming Western-style consumers. Any such development would take decades, not years; thus, "potential" had more than one context. The weaning of the Orient from rice to wheat was more an ideal and much less a practical goal.

Before the great surge in transcontinental building during the mid- and late 1880s, San Francisco Bay, controlled by Collis Huntington and his associates and their Central and Southern Pacific railroads, held an unvexed sway over American commerce on the Pacific. Six transpacific steamship lines based their operations on the broad and beautiful shores of the bay by the time of the 1893 Panic. Suddenly, however, new competitors cropped up to the north. The connection to Portland shared by the OR&N, the NP, and the UP was not especially troubling, due to the limitations of that city as a harbor. But the NP's direct passage over the Cascades to Tacoma was, particularly when, in 1892, the NP formed its Northern Pacific Steamship Company. Puget Sound, with its array of good deep-water dockages on a more northern and direct latitude to Japan, competed very well with San Francisco Bay.

Even more dangerous from the perspective of San Francisco, and for that matter of America, was the CP development of the port of Vancouver, British Columbia, by 1888. From the beginning, Hill and George Stephen, and later William Cornelius Van Horne, had planned a Pacific steamship extension to the CP. And in line with British imperial policy, they could count on government subsidies to make these ships globally competitive. This incessantly galled the Canadian-turned-American Jim Hill, since by long tradition, the United States had refused to subsidize a merchant fleet of its own.

As early as 1889, he had belabored a Wisconsin audience about the inanity of seventy carloads of New England cotton products headed for China via the CP. He warned a Senate committee that the British were subsidizing the CP to guarantee themselves an alternate Asian route, in addition to that via the Suez Canal. Now, in 1893, Hill watched the CP's "Empress Line" ships leaving Vancouver; he viewed this with even greater alarm, knowing that such subsidies would continue to allow his Canadian rival to pirate cargoes from American soil and deprive him of the business.

In 1892, even as his entire organization bent every effort toward forging the GN transcontinental, Hill sent one of his most trusted men, Herman Rosenthal, to survey prospects in East Asia. Hill the dreamer was still effectively restrained by Hill the realist. After visiting Japan, Korea, and China, Rosenthal returned with some sobering advice. China, he reported, did not afford much trade opportunity, but rapidly modernizing and industrializing Japan did. Rosenthal recommended the initiation of traffic to both Nagasaki and Yokohama and also an extension on to the international entrepôt of Hong Kong.

The deadening impact of the depression then halted activities for a while, but soon the GN had further incentive to develop ladings for the distant Pacific markets. Burgeoning eastbound cargoes of Pacific Northwest lumber were now, incredibly, creating surplus car capacities on westbound trains. So, early in 1896, Hill dispatched to Asia yet another agent, Captain James Griffiths, to look closer, this time at the actual manifests of ships unloading their cargoes at East Asian ports—no easy task, since shippers guarded such information jealously. He was now ready to move and longed to commission a fleet of large ships, even larger than those the GN ran on the Great Lakes. He aimed to apply the same principles of massive tonnages and low through-rates that he was making work so successfully on his railroads to connecting ocean liners.

The building of a large Pacific fleet, however, represented too formidable a challenge for the moment. It would take time to muster the investment capital and designs and to guarantee the traffic and markets. For now, therefore, Hill turned to the expedient of having Griffiths prepare a contract with Japan's largest steamship line, Nippon Yusen Kaisha, to provide monthly service between Hong Kong, Japanese ports, and Seattle. This represented Japan's first formal maritime link to the United States, and it caused considerable comment in both countries. When the little steamship *Miike Maru* churned into Elliott Bay, Seattle welcomed it with cheers and high hopes.

Jim Hill then set about doing what he did better than anyone else: the construction of through-rates, on basic commodities, that could beat the competition. Once again, he drew on a lifetime of know-how that dated back to his warehousing days on the Saint Paul levee. Soon, he had a stunning three-dollar-per-ton rate on U.S. flour delivered to Japan, less than half the current price from San Francisco, an achievement his direct-line route from the Upper Midwest granaries and mills and his easy grades across the Rockies made possible. He exulted in 1897, "I will make wheat flour as cheap as rice for the millions of the Orient, and our farmers will profit by a new demand." This was a flight of fancy, but Hill had a point in his belief that, by diverting Western grain surpluses to Asian exports, the national price could be bolstered.

Only the future would tell whether such a breathtaking invasion of Asian markets could approach reality. A major determinant would be whether or not the new and still unpredictable Interstate Commerce Commission would permit such special through-rates for international competition and whether it would force these rates to be made public and thus observable by foreign competitors. But even these first stirrings of Pacific commerce from the Northwest had an immediate impact on the entire coast. San Francisco's total maritime tonnage slipped from eighty-six million in 1890 to seventy million in 1904. Between 1898 and 1904, its percentage of America's Pacific exports dropped from 70 to 56, a loss of $14 million, which was matched by an increase of $12 million on Puget Sound alone. The powerful new transcontinental had cast a long and foreboding shadow indeed.

Meanwhile, events at the other end of the GN would prove to be less romantic and visionary but far more profitable. In fact, the fateful movement of the Hill family and the GN into iron ore investments would underscore a seldom stated truth about American business history. The rich often got rich, or richer, by simply walking into unanticipated opportunities that had little to do with either foresight or acumen.

Before the 1890s, the GN had had little interest in the cold, remote, and heavily forested quadrant of northeastern Minnesota. Its Eastern Railway of Minnesota ran north from the Twin Cities to Duluth, which it continued to develop, along with Duluth's sister city of Superior, Wisconsin, as a Great Lakes wheat and coal port; but the entire northern half of this large state gravitated naturally more to the NP, which spanned it due west from Duluth. A booming steel industry would now abruptly change all of this.

The so-called Lake Superior Iron Ore Region constituted one of the greatest cornucopias of natural wealth that the United States ever counted among its many blessings. These deposits of easily extracted, granular ferric oxides lay in a series of "iron ranges" stretching from Michigan eastward across Wisconsin and into Minnesota along the forestlands of the Great Lakes plain. Although the eastern ranges were the first to be developed, the richest by far were in Minnesota to the west. They were so fantastically rich, in fact, that by 1910 the three Minnesota ranges—the Vermillion, the Mesabi, and the Cuyuna—would be yielding two-thirds of all the iron ore mined in the United States. The Mesabi Range, lying seventy miles northwest of Lake Superior, would in turn prove to be the largest and richest of the three.

Hill first came on this northern Minnesota prospect as a result of his traditional interests in rails and wheat, not iron. His Eastern Railway line north to Duluth, the giant grain elevators constructed there, and the Buffalo-bound ships that gave the GN its own route to East Coast markets, an alternate route from that through Chicago—all these had a natural corollary. It now made sense to forge a new line directly eastward from the Red River valley granary to this new GN hub at the ports of Duluth-Superior, thus avoiding the long bow to the south along the GN main line. By 1888, the year the Eastern Railway of Minnesota was completed and all other work was set aside to complete the transcontinental, forty-six miles of this new line had been constructed—from Crookston, which lay just east of Grand Forks on the Red, eastward to Fosston.

Complications, however, soon intruded on the other end of the projected line. An inconspicuous little road with typically grandiose ambitions, the Duluth and Winnipeg, had begun building out of Duluth-Superior, aiming along the same route that Hill had in mind. The Duluth and Winnipeg suddenly took on a new potential and importance when the Merritt brothers brought in their pathbreaking Mountain Iron Mine on the Mesabi Range and built a rickety little railroad connecting to it. The Duluth and Winnipeg soon ran into trouble as other lines joined the Mesabi to Duluth-Superior; but for now, as the Duluth and Winnipeg solidified its lines and developed major ore docks at Allouez Bay on Lake Superior, it posed a major threat to the GN. The little road seemed able to build a shorter and better line westward than Hill could build eastward in competition.

Hill immediately moved, naturally, to acquire the Duluth and Winnipeg, but he received a severe jolt when he learned that his old foe, William Cornelius Van Horne, had slipped in and acquired it for the CP. Van Horne rubbed salt in the wound by gloating over "Mr. Hill's defeat," and in truth, the defeat was twofold. James Hill not only lost the competitive road he direly needed but lost it to his chief adversary, the foreign carrier that he was determined to keep off American soil. Once again, however, he got lucky. The Panic of 1893 intervened, staggering both the little railroad and its new parent. And once again, his friends Sir George Stephen and Sir Donald Smith, anxious to keep some measure of peace between the two railroads in which they were each interested, pressured Van Horne to back off.

So, in mid-1897, facing the fact that he could not afford to make the road competitive, Van Horne agreed to sell the Duluth and Winnipeg, now renamed the Duluth, Superior, and Western, a road that in fact promised him little, to Hill and the GN. The fortunate recipient then speedily welded it into the GN's shortened line from Crookston to Fosston, through the maze of lakes and woodlands north of the Mississippi headwaters at Leech Lake, and on to Superior. On the completion of this heavy-tonnage line, in September 1898, the latter city staged a mighty celebration; by then, as one thousand cars per day were dumping wheat on its docks, the Duluth, Superior, and Western had become a main arm of the GN for transporting grain eastward from the Minnesota-Dakota heartland.

In buying a wheat carrier, Jim Hill quickly found that he had acquired an iron ore carrier as well. Although the Duluth, Superior, and Western had plenty of competition in bidding for the traffic of iron ore flowing from the Mesabi to Duluth-Superior, he readily saw that this flank of his new road could be made into his kind of railroad: a hauler of heavy tonnages over efficient tracks. Interestingly, however, he did not immediately jump to the next obvious opportunity—buying up Mesabi mines.

He had become quite cautious over the years about buying into ancillary industries along his lines; and he remained so, even though he had acquired some mine properties with the railroad purchase and even though the arrival of the Carnegie and Rockefeller interests on the scene clearly indicated that good buys were beckoning. Instead, his sons, Louis and James, who knew the area well due to their work on the Eastern Railway, pressured him to invest. Eventually, he came to agree and thus moved, crablike, into one of the best investments he, or anyone else, ever made.

In addition to the sizable properties they bought with the Duluth, Superior, and Western, the Hills focused their interest on the holdings of A. W. Wright and Charles Davis. Wright and Davis had built the Duluth, Mississippi River, and Northern Railroad into the heart of the Mesabi district and, more important, had accumulated impressive acreages of both iron-rich lands and timberlands, the crown jewel of which was the Mahoning Mine near Hibbing.

After a prolonged negotiating session with old Wright and his partner in Chicago late in 1898, Jim Hill worked out a purchase price of $4,050,000 for the combined properties, completing the transaction in January 1899. He wrote the check personally, aligning his newly purchased iron roads with the Eastern Railway of Minnesota, whose CEO was his son James, and holding the acreages for speculation. Meanwhile, Louis took to the field, buying up seventeen thousand more acres to enhance the package; and the Eastern Railway, more than tripling its stock to $16 million, built a high-quality system of lines north to the Mesabi.

Hill and the GN got a nice welcome from Duluth-Superior and the "Iron Range" country. The predatory and dreaded Rockefeller interests had, after all, been rumored to be after the Wright and Davis properties. Earlier, the *Duluth New Tribune* had feted Hill: "Duluth is fortunate in many respects but in none more so than in being the main lake port of such a line of road as the Great Northern, headed by such a man as James J. Hill."

The Eastern Railway hauled its first ores to Duluth-Superior in 1898. Soon afterward, Hill began transferring both this highly valuable railroad and the terminal facilities of the Allouez Bay Dock Company at cost to the GN. Then, in a remarkable and farsighted move in October 1900, he transferred over the iron ore properties themselves—now including not only the Mahoning but also the Bennett and Longyear mines—to the Lake Superior Company, Limited, a technically separate entity from the GN but in fact a limited partnership of its directors.

By the terms of the Manitoba-GN charter, the railroad could not legally own or operate metal mines. And, in addition to these legal problems, the direct acquisition of these increasingly valuable mining properties would have added to the valuation of the GN and thus have immensely complicated the issue of rate equity and regulation. So, in a true sense, placing the iron properties into an ostensibly independent but actually a GN-controlled corporation represented a subterfuge. The GN stockholders would own them and profit from them, but the railroad could argue at the same time that they were not taxable railroad properties. This would lead to legislative problems later.

In another sense, however, Hill's transfer of the iron properties from his personal portfolio to the Lake Superior Company, and thus to the GN stockholders, represented a truly magnanimous and intelligent decision. As he put it, "I always had a rule that if I could make money for myself in a transaction connected with the company I could make it for the shareholders." He well understood that he and his family would profit considerably from a pro-rata distribution of ownership in the iron ore investments to the GN shareholders in any case and that he did not really need yet another bonanza to add to his own fast-growing fortune. And he well knew that the trust of those shareholders, which he already enjoyed, would be bolstered anew, as indeed it was. He would later describe this as the most satisfying move he ever made.

Thus, instead of the full value of the Mesabi–Lake Superior Company package, the Hills got only their proportionate share as GN stockholders: one hundred thousand of the 1.5 million shares issued. How vastly profitable these iron lands might be would not become clear until the new century, when the Minnesota Iron Range became the largest supplier for a world-leading American steel industry. The Hills, and the other GN investors, were about to reap a dual harvest: from the rich mines themselves, and from freight rates levied on the massive tonnages of ore hauled from the Mesabi to Lake Superior.

Thus, throughout the hectic decade of the 1890s, the scope of Jim Hill's interests and activities steadily broadened—into whole new fields of endeavor such as Pacific commerce and iron ore, into regional and national politics, and into philanthropy. Yet, as always, what he cared about most was his railroad, and what he loved most was making and executing grand transportation strategy. And again as always, the forging of strategy for his railroad involved him inevitably and intimately with his two major competitors to the north and to the south: the CP and the NP.

From its inception in the late 1870s until the end of his life, the CP posed threats and frustrations to James J. Hill; and his raging preoccupation with it sometimes caused him to act in ways that defied his true self-interests. As Ralph Hidy and his coauthors demonstrate in their history of the GN, the struggle between the two roads, and between the Canadian-turned-American Hill and the American-turned-Canadian Van Horne, stretched across the continent from Lake Superior to the Pacific.

Hill simply could not live with the facts that the CP, with its government subsidies and protection, could rob traffic from American soil via its Minneapolis, Saint Paul, and Sault Sainte Marie Line, or Soo Line, and that the GN did not have extensive competing lines into Canada. He seldom paused to ponder the fact that Van Horne had problems of his own. For example, the CP had a longer, bending route westward, through truly tortuous western mountains; and it faced the political wrath of the "grits," prairie radicals who demanded a socialized road that would bring them lower rates. Neither side cared a whit about cooperation. Although the two lines linked on both the east and the west, they refused even to cooperate by prorating rates and exchanging cargoes.

Generally speaking, the CP held the upper hand in its competition with the GN in the eastern—or midwestern—theater. Hill could access Winnipeg, Brandon, and other Manitoba traffic points via the feeble lines that the NP had secured there earlier, lines that, as we shall see momentarily, now served him as well. But, even after the CP gave up the Duluth and Winnipeg, the CP's Soo Line hounded the GN mercilessly. This situation would motivate Hill to turn to the west to harass the CP in British Columbia, more in the spirit of mischief, and in the hope of forcing an overall compromise, than of constructive competition.

The Soo Line complicated matters both in the Minnesota–

Great Lakes sphere and well on to the west. Hill parried the Soo intruder with his Crookston-Duluth route and maneuvered it away from the treasure of the Mesabi. But the Soo now had a long extension, completed back in 1893, that crossed North Dakota on a northwestern tangent and stretched 320 miles to Regina, on the CP main line in south-central Saskatchewan. It advertised this long incursion through the GN heartland as "the shortest line from Minneapolis and St. Paul to the Pacific Coast." In 1897, Hill begrudgingly formed a traffic-sharing understanding with the Soo Line, but almost immediately Van Horne was complaining that Hill broke the agreement, specifically in denying Van Horne his fair share of Montana wool ladings.

Farther west, however, the advantages and vulnerabilities were reversed. In the remote mountain fastnesses of the interior, southern reaches of British Columbia, a scattering of bustling little mining cities had arisen, far below the tracks of the CP to the north. Like their plains brethren to the east, these Canadian frontier folk felt slighted by their "monopoly" railroad and resented it. Jim Hill knew these emotions from long experience and knew how to play on them. Even though the markets in question were small, difficult to reach, and of dubious worth, he could scarcely resist the nice strategic ploy they offered him. He figured, wrongly as it would turn out, that if he could build up to and capture them, he could use them as a prize of war to force the CP, by trading hostages, from the American soil occupied by the Soo Line.

By the turn of the century, Jim Hill had forged several routes into British Columbia. In 1898, he merged the Seattle and Montana Railway, the Fairhaven and Southern Railway, the Seattle and Northern Railway, and the capital stock of the Westminster Southern Railway into the Seattle and Montana Railroad Company. This offered a unified system reaching from Seattle north to Vancouver, albeit by a clumsy ferry crossing of the large Fraser River and entrance to Vancouver via an interurban line.

That same year, he acquired the 217 miles and four lines of D. C. Corbin's old Spokane Falls and Northern system from the NP. This system, quaint as it was, offered direct access due north from strategically located Spokane to the mining towns of Nelson and Rossland, British Columbia. Yet two more, even less promising lines projected north: from Bonners Ferry, Idaho, to Kuskonook on Kootenay Lake, and from Jennings, near Kalispell, Montana, toward the lesser Canadian mining centers of Fernie, Swinton, and Michel.

The point of all this became clear when, to the cheers of the British Columbia antimonopolists, Hill secured the charter of the Vancouver, Victoria, and Eastern Railway and Navigation Company in 1900 and began building it eastward out of Vancouver, up the Fraser River canyons through the southern reaches of the province and toward a connecting loop with his lines running north from Spokane. The CP had at first responded lethargically to Hill's moves, evidently reasoning that the prizes were not worth the candle, but then it finally came to life—aiming two countervailing roads, the Crow's Nest Railway and the Kettle Valley Railway, to block the intruder and forming the Crow's Nest Pass Coal Company to mine the ores. Before long, though, Hill and his associates countered by securing a 30 percent share of the Crow's Nest firm and soon had majority control, forming the Crow's Nest Southern line to haul its output into the United States.

As the old century ended, one fact about this situation was clear enough to any neutral observer. The only circumstance in which either contestant in this struggle for such a far-off and underpopulated hinterland might make money would be if this frontier entered a greater era of prosperity than any that seemed to beckon. For now, all that appeared certain was that both parties seemed committed to a wasteful competition, almost military in intensity, which neither party was able or willing to end. In the midst of this, during the centenary year of 1900, Hill's old adversary Van Horne quit the CP to build railroads in the Caribbean. His successor, Thomas Shaughnessy, would prove to be an equally stubborn and formidable challenger.

The NP had, of course, been as much a scourge to Jim Hill as had the CP; but now, in contrast, it suddenly offered a priceless opportunity. When the rickety NP skidded into bankruptcy and receivership in August 1893, it was not because the GN had set out to destroy the railroad, although many people thought so. Rather, it simply cost the NP 50 percent more per ton-mile to haul freight than it cost the NP's well-constructed competitor. In addition to Jim Hill's age-old worries about the NP—that it fostered reckless competition by building spurs that could never make money and that it started rate wars in an equally reckless manner—there suddenly emerged an even greater concern. In receivership, the NP found itself freed both from interest payments and from profit expectations. It could now, ironically, cause more trouble in receivership than it had before.

Not surprisingly, therefore, Hill and Lord Mount Stephen returned to their previous ideas, which they had considered before building the GN westward, about acquiring control of the NP. Luckily for them, other powerful people now agreed with them about the NP's misdirection, its conferring of unearned dividends, and its wasteful spur construction. These people included the influential Jacob Schiff of the Wall Street firm of Kuhn, Loeb. Schiff, a stately and dignified Jewish banker and a national leader in rail finance, commanded enormous respect on "the Street." He had assisted Hill in financing the GN expansion and had become a corporate director in 1892. Also concurring were the directors of the Berlin-based Deutsche Bank, which held a large block of NP stock. They believed, as did Hill and Stephen, that the NP could be salvaged only by consolidating it with the GN, thus bringing it under Hill's expert guidance and also eliminating wasteful competition between the two roads.

Hill stood nearly alone, however, in believing that the NP held a vast, if hidden, potential for profit. Confiding his thoughts, for now, only to such close associates as Stephen and Farrer, he maintained that, with sizable up-front investments in grading, bridges, and heavier rails, the NP could turn a profit within two to three years. He wrote Stephen in October 1894: "If the Nor. Pac could be handled as we handle our property and all the wild and uncalled for rate cutting stopped it could be made great property. Its capacity to earn money is good, and with all unnecessary expenses, commissions, and train service abolished it would I think astonish even its friends, but the main trouble has been that it has not been run as a railway for years, but as a device for creating bonds to be sold, and part at least of the proceeds to be divided on the inside." Soon after, he continued: "The Nor. Pac. has never in my opinion known what economy means. The main line is largely laid with 56-lb. steel which is too light for modern engines or cars and their equipment is generally too light and out of date."

Hill and Stephen were very much in the vanguard of forward-looking rail executives of their generation. They wanted a quick end to wasteful competition, which they viewed as contrary to the interests of investors and consumers alike, since it resulted only in overconstruction, rate instability, low returns, and poor service. They believed that these two transcontinental giants could be and should be joined in a "community of interest." True enough, such a strategy seemed to run directly afoul of newly passed federal regulatory laws—the Interstate Commerce Act of 1887 and the Sherman Antitrust Act of 1890, both of which seemed clearly to disallow any such moves toward constraining competition and toward structuring monopolies. But, the two men reasoned, the courts did not seem inclined to literal interpretation of these laws and in fact seemed inclined toward emasculating them.

Jim Hill's mounting interest in the NP, one of America's largest and best-established corporations, truly brought him into the halls of Wall Street finance for the first time. Hitherto, he had relied on Stephen and J. S. Kennedy, and on other banking agents like Schiff, for such service and expertise. But now, firmly in command of one of America's biggest corporations and eyeing another, he strode confidently onto the center stage of American commerce, a man who by now understood the complex world of finance very well, through years of experience.

Indeed, he soon came into contact with America's premier capitalist and leading proponent of rail consolidation and "community of interest," J. Pierpont Morgan, who had had the NP as a client for fifteen years. Morgan, with whom Hill would be closely identified until the former's death in 1913, was presently coming into his prime as the key leader of American finance. The son of a prominent Anglo-American banker, Pierpont Morgan presided over the firm of Drexel, Morgan, and Company, which was about to become J. P. Morgan and Company. During the years since the fall of Jay Cooke, he had climbed steadily to the forefront of American finance; and in the panic year of 1893, he demonstrated his hegemony by coming dramatically to the rescue of President Cleveland and the administration's failed treasury policy.

Morgan was brilliant, irascible, and domineering; often scowling in demeanor, he was famed for his bulbous nose and, as the author John Dos Passos unforgettably put it, his "small black magpie's eyes." With his famous yachts and art collections culled from across Europe, his mansions and bequests, even his barely disguised adulteries, he epitomized the waxing might of Wall Street and investment banking. His legendary stature arose from the fact that his firm, now becoming known, ominously, as the "House of Morgan," dominated the fin de siècle era in which Wall Street investment bankers ruled the American economy.

By presiding over the "rationalizing" of wastefully competing businesses, and by providing the necessary capital, these men rose inexorably to rule the corporate boards of the companies they reorganized and amalgamated. This heyday of the investment bankers would endure well into the twentieth century, until new industrial and commercial corporations grew to such dimensions that they could break the dominance of the financiers; but the image of the age of Morgan lives on in the American mind as the stereotypical halcyon time of unfettered capitalism. The Morgans, as Ron Chernow pointed out in his recent study, stood at the apex of the Anglo-Saxon elite while Jacob Schiff and Kuhn, Loeb led the important Jewish contingent.

Morgan made his specialty the refinancing, reorganization, and rationalization of America's badly overextended and overcapitalized railroads; his "clients" included some of the largest, such as the Erie, the New York Central, and the Pennsylvania. None figured larger than the NP, to which he devoted much of his attention during 1893–95. He had known and liked old John

Kennedy for years, admiring his traditional, gentlemanly style of business. And when he first met James Hill, at an Episcopal Church conference in 1895, he was immediately impressed by Hill's self-assurance and amazingly detailed knowledge of railroads, particularly of this railroad, whose inner workings James had pondered for years, sometimes with the help of spies.

Morgan rapidly came to see an obvious point. The large groups of NP investors—his own firm, the Germans, the Hill-Stephen contingent, which had been buying heavily into the depreciated NP both to speculate and to gain a voice in its management, and reportedly even the old NP faction led by Frederick Billings—all agreed that the NP should be merged with the GN, under the managerial genius of James J. Hill. In this manner, wasteful competition could be abated, markets could be shared and divided, and Hill's techniques could remake this hurriedly and shoddily constructed road, just as E. H. Harriman was making over the similarly misconstructed UP.

With remarkable speed and ease, the factions came together behind a plan to reorganize the NP in linkage with the GN. J. P. Morgan and Company, represented by senior partner Charles Coster, one of a number of Morgan associates who would work themselves to death for the cause, led the consortium that would underwrite the financing of the reorganized company. The Hill-Stephen associates, including Farrer, Edward Tuck, and other loyalists, agreed to head the effort by guaranteeing a $175 million bond issue of the reorganized NP and in turn were guaranteed a majority of one on the reorganized board of directors of the railroad. For the domineering Morgan, this represented a stunning vote of confidence in Hill. In May 1895, James Hill secretly sailed for England, where he and an enthusiastic Lord Mount Stephen met with Thomas Skinner, representing the Deutsche Bank, and penned the "London Agreement," cementing their strategy to revamp the NP.

Hill returned home elated at the prospect of merger, but he should have known better; matters of such large import seldom go down that easily. Predictably, in fact, Henry Villard and the current management personnel of the NP came out in strong opposition to submerging their identity into that of the GN. Then there was the problem of the court-appointed reorganization committee that was currently managing the NP. Its egotistical chairman, E. D. Adams, a scion of the legendary presidential family, led a group that harbored grave doubts about giving up its lucrative sway over the giant railroad. And the notorious New York attorney William Nelson Cromwell, who was counsel to the committee (and who would later prove his cunning in prying Panama away from Columbia so that the United States could build a canal there), worked feverishly against the merger in order to protect his handsome annual retainer.

Political and legal threats proved even more imposing. Antimonopoly and antirailroad sentiment ran strong all along the routes of the two roads, and Hill's fulminations against Chicago imperialism over the Northwest did little to counter it. Minnesota had an antimonopoly statute that seemed likely to disallow the GN guarantees of the NP as provided in the London Agreement; but the organizers' high-priced counsel advised, inadvisably, that the law would not apply, since the charters for the roads predated it.

Eager to secure an answer, Hill encouraged an old associate and GN stockholder, Thomas Pearsall, to file a test case arguing against the legality of the merger. After a circuit court judge ruled against Pearsall, the Minnesota Supreme Court found in his favor. Thus, the high hopes of 1895 that a friendly merger might be easily attained proved illusory; and even before the supreme court decision, both Hill and Morgan had come to accept the fact and to act accordingly.

Clearly, at least for the near term, the GN and the NP must, therefore, remain independent. And the main NP ownership groups—the Hill-Stephen bloc, the old NP crowd, the House of Morgan, and the Germans—must reconfigure accordingly. They generally agreed, though, that the old, wasteful competition had to be ended, and this meant that a new accord would have to replace the shattered London Agreement. Morgan now stepped forward to play the dominant hand that everyone knew had been his all along.

Working with Deutsche Bank representatives, the House of Morgan formed a reorganized firm called the Northern Pacific Railway Company, controlled by a five-year voting trust dominated by Morgan partners. Then, in early April 1896, a most formidable group of men—Morgan, Hill, Stephen, and Arthur Gwinner of Deutsche Bank—gathered at Stephen's English estate to hammer out the strategic terms that would govern the relations of the two railroads, which would be legally independent but would be harnessed in a community of interest. The "London Memorandum" that they structured spoke directly to the point, in terms that must shock those who still believe the folklore that nineteenth-century capitalists manfully sought out a robust competition. According to the memo, the two railroads would form a true alliance: "The Great Northern Railway Company and the re-organized Northern Pacific Railroad Company shall form a permanent alliance, defensive, and in case of need offensive, with a view of avoiding competition and aggressive policy and of generally protecting the common interests of both Companies. . . . Neither party shall in future ingress into the other's territory by new construction or purchase or acquiring control of existing lines."

For Hill and Stephen, this new agreement represented a mixed blessing. On the positive side, the NP would now end the worst competitive abuses of the past, and they could and did continue to buy into it. They agreed, speaking for their group, to invest at least $3 million more into the reorganized NP; by early 1897, after pouring in over $4 million more, they held nearly $8 million in NP stocks and bonds. But to the impatient Hill, the negatives still outweighed the positives. The House of Morgan and Deutsche Bank controlled the board; indeed, the GN faction had, for now, not one member on the board of directors. And when Morgan unilaterally chose first Edwin Winter and then Charles Mellen, two men whom Hill considered overrated underachievers, to be president of the NP, he boiled with indignation.

As the last years of the century unfolded, the capable but terribly overworked Coster tried hard to keep peace between the Morgan and the Hill factions. Jim Hill took some solace from the fact that, as a major owner, he could wield some influence over the NP—for instance, he could pry the Spokane and Northern away from it. In addition, the NP finally began turning a profit. But, with a characteristic lack of tact, he railed against the unfairness of the voting trust, complained about stolid and unrealistic management, and viewed the road as still harboring silly plans for undercutting the GN.

Mellen, he wrote Morgan partner Daniel Lamont in 1898, had "no sound level headed judgement." To Coster he complained, "The Northern Pacific was wrecked by the acquisition of a lot of worthless branches, and it is apparently making efforts to repeat its former experience." As a major owner, he complained that the NP was severely overcapitalized—by at least $50 million, in his estimation—causing a drag on the organization he referred to as a "bag of wind."

A true measure of Jim Hill's mettle was the simple fact that he could and did face off with the great "Jupiter" Morgan. Demanding concessions, particularly an end to the one-sided voting trust, he issued Morgan a letter of ultimatum in the fall of 1898. Either his group received board representation and greater management prerogatives in the NP—especially to modernize its infrastructure and increase its profitability—or members of his group would begin selling their holdings. This presented a realistic threat now that the NP was turning a profit. Finally, after wearily countering Hill's complaints with counterarguments pointing out GN aggressions against the NP, a realistic Morgan began to see the light, realizing that Hill really had the answers and the ability to make his will felt. Changes in NP management began to occur, and in mid-1899, Hill's friend J. S. Kennedy was elevated to the NP board of directors.

The first year of the new century brought to Jim Hill the prize he had so long sought, the helm of the NP. Worn out by the struggle, Coster died in March; and his able successor, Morgan partner Robert Bacon, worked willingly and ably with the Hill group, not wanting to follow Coster to the grave by shouldering so much of the burden by himself. Morgan himself came, with each passing month, to respect Hill more and more. He increasingly sought Hill's advice about the affairs of other client roads, such as the Erie; and as he watched the rising star of Edward Harriman over the UP and the Southern Pacific roads, allied with his enemies the Rockefellers, he saw Hill ever more as an invaluable, even indispensable ally.

The two men met once again in England in May, agreeing on their joint strategy. At a subsequent conference on the banker's prized yacht, the *Corsair*, Morgan told an elated Hill that he would give up his solitary control and even agreed to purchase ten thousand shares of the GN. Finally, in November, came the long-awaited message: the voting trust would end with the first of the year. With the Morgan and Deutsche Bank investors firmly behind his leadership, Jim Hill could now fulfill his dream of operating the two great transcontinentals in tandem.

He immediately set about doing so. Although the law clearly precluded an outright merger, Hill seemed to have all the latitude he needed to bring the GN and the NP into a practical and fruitful cooperation. Thus, whereas he immediately stopped the objectionable NP practice of building and maintaining wasteful spur lines, he also gave to the old road much in return. The remarkable management system that he had developed for the GN, which had been generating such ample profits that they could become embarrassing when disclosed, could now be used to improve the infrastructure of the NP.

And Hill did not hesitate to share the GN's most prized and dearly won traffic, notably eastbound blister copper from Montana and lumber from the Cascades, with its sister road. Meanwhile, he set about isolating Mellen from any effective role in the NP and brought over capable Darius Miller from the "Katy" (Missouri, Kansas, and Texas Railroad) to work with his son James Norman as second vice-president of the GN, thus freeing Hill for work on the NP. And he continued to plow more of his own money into the NP. The $1.5 million he had invested in it by early 1901 would increase sixfold in the next five years.

His rise to the corporate leadership of the NP represented a dizzying triumph for the one-time impoverished Canadian lad, a leap nearly as great as the forging of the GN into a transcontinental ten years before. He now consorted on the national and international levels with the world's leading capitalists, men like Morgan and Schiff, who were genuinely astonished by his managerial abilities, his mastery of railroading details, his knowledge of finance, and his willfulness. Still, his greatest challenges and most heralded venture onto the national stage lay directly before him.

CHAPTER 6

Northern Securities

THE remarkable career of James Jerome Hill owed much not only to his remarkable abilities and perseverance but also to chance, luck, and timing. He was fortunate, for example, to have been born in that remarkable generation that, coming to maturity during the Civil War, moved forward to lead in the industrializing of America during the late nineteenth century. And it would prove highly significant, as well as symbolic, that he would die in 1916, at the very peak of the mileage and influence of American railroads—before the automobile and federal regulation would cause the decline of the railroads, a decline that Hill foresaw. It is also interesting that he reached the peak of his fame and influence with the dawn of the new century. As a "captain of industry"—or a monopolist, depending on one's point of view—he moved to the center stage of national attention amid the wave of new industrial consolidations that now crested, changing America forever. This would be the James Hill that readers of American history know and best remember.

With the epochal dawn of the new century, James J. Hill had much indeed to look back on and much yet to anticipate. Now in his early sixties, he still enjoyed quite good health, especially so considering the terrible work regimen that he still followed, although he was beginning to let up a little. The symptoms of colds and congestion still hit him in rhythmic fashion, as they had for years. But these had clearly become a part of his method for coping with stress: by periodically forcing him to bed for days on end, they afforded him badly needed rest. Also, as he entered what in those days was truly old age, he increasingly suffered from several afflictions that inevitably come with advancing years, particularly hemorrhoids, the result in part of his long hours at the desk and aboard trains. He dreaded and avoided surgery for the problem. Overall, though, he remained remarkably robust and energetic, savoring life in all its aspects.

If anything, the trademark Hill persona of aggressive, self-confident assertiveness became more, rather than less, pronounced with the accumulating years. Whatever he lost in energy seemed more than compensated for by the aura of a reputation that by now had become truly legendary. Few doubted, and seemingly no one questioned, the great Hill. In countless invited addresses, he set forth his views to obsequious audiences, driving home his fervent assertions with stabbing and chopping gestures. His gray beard and fringe of unruly gray hair surrounding his bald pate gave him an even more unkempt appearance than before. And his growing portliness, the result of a sumptuous lifestyle, took nothing away from his visage of strength and authority. He looked and acted like a Scottish chief of clan, which in a true sense was exactly what he was.

Continuity and good fortune also characterized his domestic life, which truly did mean more to him than even his business. Mary stoically tolerated, as she always had, his waspish disposition and his preoccupation with business affairs; she remained, without exaggeration, totally devoted to him, as he was to her. Although she was eight years younger than her husband, her health seemed more precarious than his. She suffered both from a heart condition and from what was now clearly diagnosed as tuberculosis. While resting at their Jekyll Island, Georgia, retreat in the spring of 1905, she collapsed and very nearly died. For the next year, she had to follow a cautious regimen of recuperation, in the New York Adirondack Mountains during the warm season and in the South during the winter, before returning to Minnesota.

By now, of course, the brood of children had passed almost entirely into maturity. Jim and Mary continued to dote on them, just as always, along with the ten grandchildren that had arrived by 1910. As they took measure of their nine children, however, they encountered a range of experiences—from elation to disappointment—that seem to resemble modern times more than the stereotypes of regimented and blissful family life during the Victorian era.

Both of the two oldest children, Mary and James Norman, concerned their parents with the passing years. "Mamie," the oldest, grew up to be a dark-complected, slender, and attractive woman of moody disposition. Her heralded marriage to Sam Hill led year by year to estrangement. Sam was a true bon vivant, who loved world travel and focused his energies particularly on the far Northwest and the "Good Roads" movement. Like many another railroad man, including his father-in-law, he did not yet see the threat that the car posed to the train. Mamie, in contrast, favored the East Coast and spent most of her time there. Their detachment never led to the ultimate Victorian stigma of divorce, but it severely distressed both their children and Mamie's parents.

After starting out on the Eastern Railway of Minnesota, James N.—one of the brightest of the Hills—had risen to a Great Northern vice-presidency by 1899. But it soon became clear that the demanding life of management did not suit him, part of the reason being his long bouts with rheumatism. By 1905 he had settled in his favorite spot, New York City, with nominal responsibilities. His timely investments in what was becoming the petroleum giant Texaco made him very wealthy, but his insouciant and independent status caused his father considerable frustration. When James N., a longtime bachelor, married a divorced woman, his mother drew the Roman Catholic line at accepting her into the family circle. Indeed, Mary would not even allow her daughter-in-law into her drawing room.

Their second son, Louis, in contrast, became the apple of his father's eye. Jim loved to remark that if he could make Lou over, he would change nothing. Mary had to live with the fact that Louis's attractive wife, Maude, required that their children be raised Episcopalian, but both grandparents doted on the three grandsons that moved with their parents into the home next door on Summit Avenue. Courtly in bearing, trim and upright, with a meticulously trimmed beard and wire-framed glasses, Louis Hill was much more gentlemanly in appearance and much more reserved than his father, and he readily submitted to the directions that the old man never hesitated to give. But he was also capable and much more attuned to the public and its whims than his father. James moved Louis steadily closer to him in managing the GN. In 1907, the senior Hill gave up the GN presidency to Louis and took the still-active title of chairman of the board.

The younger Hill girls soon began to leave the nest. In 1901, the same year that Louis was wed, Charlotte became the bride of yet another railroad man to join the Hill ranks, George Slade; and in 1902, Ruth married attorney Anson Beard. Gertrude became the wife of banker Michael Gavin in 1906. Clara and Rachel remained at home for several more years, the former devoting her energies especially to charity work and to traveling with her father as a substitute for Mary, who chose more and more often to remain in Saint Paul. But they too eventually became wed, not long before the death of their father: Rachel to Egil Boeckmann and Clara to Erasmus Lindley. The youngest child, Walter, meanwhile, got away with far more than did his older brothers. He was a carefree chap, who loved to shower money on his friends and to have a gay time and who showed little predilection for business. After he married Dorothy Barrows in 1908, his father accepted the situation and abided his wishes, setting Walter up with the princely Northcote Farm in the Red River valley.

Jim Hill drew a sharp line, as he had ever since those long-ago days in the warehouse on the levee, between his business life and his family life. On the former, he lavished little; on the latter, he lavished everything. All of his three business offices—the one on Nassau Street in New York and the two in Saint Paul—were stark and foreboding in appearance. In the Saint Paul Great Northern Building at Rosabel and Third, he kept not only his own GN head office but also another staffed by seven employees under John Toomey, who also looked after Hill's personal, now far-flung investments.

Even his own private business car was anything but luxurious. Whereas other executives named their cars after wives or daughters and outfitted them with luxurious appointments, Hill unceremoniously called his the "A-1!"—a rather clear statement that outward sentimentality did not rank highly among his concerns—and furnished it rather plainly. East of Chicago, he

The Hill family at wedding of daughter Ruth, 1902. Courtesy of James J. Hill Papers, James Jerome Hill Reference Library, Saint Paul, Minnesota.

normally traveled by drawing-room bookings rather than by routing his car on other roads.

At home, however, he proved to be anything but a "thrifty Scot." Twin Cities people loved to follow the comings and goings of the Hill clan, and rumors recurred that they would leave the old hometown for New York, where Jim Hill spent more and more of his time. In 1906 he abandoned the apartment he had kept there for years and bought an expensive and elaborate townhouse just off Fifth Avenue on East 65th Street. This proved to be both a good investment and a fine abode, and he kept it fully staffed at all times. He also maintained his apartment at Jekyll Island, Georgia, where his wealthy neighbors included J. P. Morgan, but he finally gave up the Paris apartment he had kept for several years and seldom used.

Actually, the Hills never really considered giving up their superb home at Summit Avenue in Saint Paul, where they loved being surrounded by family and friends and where Jim gloried in entertaining and in exhibiting his art. Mary oversaw a large troupe of servants at the mansion, and Jim kept another contingent at the North Oaks farm, where the family still relished weekend escapes. Eventually, they would build a mansion here too, and Hill continued to add more land until the farm totaled five thousand acres, with ample expanses of woods and a nice lake. It seems likely that the attractions of weekend and summer stays at North Oaks offered one more reason for remaining in Saint Paul. This was the only hometown the children had ever known, and it seemed certain to remain the permanent center of the Hill enterprises.

North Oaks, which took two hours to reach by carriage, soon became much more accessible, thanks to the automobile. Sons Louis and Walter and son-in-law Sam quickly became motoring enthusiasts, and the old man followed their example with his first purchase in 1906, a Pierce Arrow, soon followed by a Studebaker and a custom-made touring car. Like most Americans, he quickly became not only addicted to but thoroughly dependent on his automobiles.

So averse to vacations, Jim continued to make one major exception: his annual pilgrimage to the Saint John tributary of the Saint Lawrence River in Canada to fish for the sporting Atlantic salmon. By 1901, he had built a substantial log retreat there and had bought up the fishing rights to a long stretch of the stream. He loved to retire there with his business friends and savor the rustic life. He took former President Grover Cleveland in 1901, and to the delight of everyone except Cleveland, the overweight old fellow managed to get stuck in a canoe.

Hill's most extravagant pleasure, considering how little use he made of it, was his yacht, which he seldom used except to cruise up to his Canadian fishing haunt. Perhaps he had Morgan's famous ship the *Corsair* in mind when he purchased the oceangoing steam yacht *Eleanor* in 1900. It was a substantial ship, 243 feet in length, with ten staterooms and a steam laundry, and it required a crew of forty-three. He renamed it the *Wacouta* and planned to use it for transatlantic voyages, which he never quite managed to take. Though he paid out $150,000 for it, and spent $60,000 yearly to maintain it, the *Wacouta* remained almost always docked at New London, Connecticut. The ship represented Hill's closest approximation to what his peer Thorstein Veblen aptly called "conspicuous consumption."

Rather strangely, in light of the philanthropy later bestowed by the Hill Family Foundation and its successor, the Northwest Area Foundation, the founders of the dynasty initially struck a quite conservative posture in giving away part of their fortune. James Hill cast a skeptical eye by now at both the Protestant and the Catholic Churches and at public colleges and universities. Rumors that he had donated up to $1.5 million for the Roman Catholic cathedral that rose up to block his view of downtown Saint Paul were entirely false. In fact, the structure angered him. It was his son Louis, instead, who promoted that project.

Hill felt that state-funded colleges should rely solely on government and tuition support and favored instead the philanthropic promotion of private, denominational colleges, such as Macalester, which he did support. His stance would prove ironic, since the two medium-sized states at each end of his tracks— Minnesota and Washington—would nurture two of America's best public universities, universities that excelled through private as well as public support. Thus, for now, he proved quite parsimonious, but he continued to foster, especially, the Saint Paul Seminary and to contemplate what would, in his last years, become his favorite project: a reference library for the people of Saint Paul and Minnesota, a library that would bear his name.

As much as he loved the leisure and amenities that great wealth brought him, Jim Hill found, as always, true pleasure only in activity. Increasingly, that activity came to include presenting his thoughts to the public, especially in speeches. By the early years of the twentieth century, he had become not only one of America's legendary success stories but also one of its most sought-after public speakers, invited to address countless throngs, from formal banquets to state fairs, in and out of the Northwest. He also set forth his thoughts in essays and in lengthy magazine and newspaper interviews. In short, Jim Hill was becoming a pundit, and he was thoroughly enjoying the role.

Although he had always scoffed at the suggestion of writing his memoirs, Hill needed little persuasion to gather together a collection of his writings on various subjects. Even after his Saint Paul newspaper, the *Globe,* closed its doors, he kept its obsequious editor, Joseph Pyle, around to handle publicity and related matters. Pyle would later write a fawning, two-volume "official" biography, published after his employer's death.

When Walter Hines Page, the prestigious publisher of the *World's Work,* approached Hill about a book of essays to be issued by his firm, Doubleday, Page, and Company, Hill promptly agreed. The book appeared first as a series of published articles, then under the collection title *Highways of Progress,* in 1910. As even a perusal of the book reveals, its author held fervent views on many subjects, views that he had honed for many years, that he advanced with massive informational support, and that he propounded without even a hint of self-doubt.

Jim Hill might appear, to the casual observer, quite conventional in his thinking, an uncritically smug Victorian who believed unflinchingly in the inevitability of materialist progress, of

American world domination, and of business above all other interests. Like many others who hear too much of their own pronouncements, he could ensnare himself in clichés. For instance, he complained frequently of unrealistically misguided "tack-head philosophers and preachers" and noted: "I don't believe in the college education which turns the young man out a full-fledged prig with a disgust for practical business. . . . [I]t has not been proved that the higher education makes the most successful man." Most Americans nodded at the prevailing views in his statements: "It is not so much the high cost of living as the cost of high living that afflicts the country." Or: "Just so the wealth of the country, its capital, its credit, must be saved from the predatory poor as well as the predatory rich, but above all from the predatory politician."

In many respects, he quite accurately reflected the views of his countrymen. He was a true believer in the virtues of unfettered capitalism; he winced at the thought of federal regulation and controls and shuddered at the prospect of socialism or, as he put it, "the menacing figure of public ownership." Like Andrew Carnegie, he believed that individual initiative provided the key to prosperity and that, given the right opportunities, all could prosper.

Like most other nineteenth-century Americans, he saw the expansion of the agrarian frontier as good and wilderness as something to be subjugated to human betterment. "Land without population," he wrote, "is a wilderness, and population without land is a mob." In the same vein, he was also a typically American heir of Thomas Jefferson, despite being a Canadian transplant. Like Jefferson a century earlier, Jim Hill decried the siren song of industrialism and urban life—a rather ironic feat, given the fact that no man ever pressed the machine into the American garden more ardently than did he.

Virtue lay, instead, in the soil and on the farm. "A profitable husbandry is the very fountain from which all other occupations flow and by which they are nourished in strength. . . . The farm is the basis of all industry." In his own life, even as his railroads pressed the march of factory and city westward, his heart pulled him toward the belief that the farmer would be and must always be the true and virtuous American.

A closer assessment of Hill's speeches and writings, however, clearly reveals that he in fact was a serious thinker who pursued issues to a logical conclusion and who defied deft categorization. He could be, on occasion, either optimistic or pessimistic, nationalistic or cosmopolitan, materialistic or idealistic. For instance, he bristled at jingoism and nationalism and fit well the judgment of the school of historians who emphasize the fact that businessmen opposed war with Spain in 1898.

Though he frowned at this brief and popular war, he correctly predicted that it would be short and successful. Hill wrote Minnesota Senator Knute Nelson in April: "The jingo sentiment, which first manifested itself in political platforms, has gotten such momentum that it would be difficult to arrest it at present. . . . With our present navy, a few weeks should settle the whole question." Similarly, when the Philippine Islands fell into America's lap as a prize of war, he approved President William McKinley's agonized decision to annex them.

The Minnesotan seemed even more insightful in his thoughts, four years later, on the question of an isthmian canal. Hill felt the same national pride as did his countrymen in President Theodore Roosevelt's vaunted campaign to dig the Panama Canal, but he also had severe misgivings, for reasons both of self-interest and of strategic insight. Sizing up the narrow system of locks and gates along the canal, Hill saw that they could never handle the "ships of the largest carrying capacity" that could "be operated at a low ton-mile cost"—ships of the type, as we shall see, that he was even then constructing.

The passage of over a half-century and the emergence of supertankers would demonstrate the truth of his foreboding: "Broader and better methods will have to prevail in the future, both on land and water, and it would be very unfortunate if, after the general government had spent the enormous sum proposed for building an Isthmian canal, should it turn out that the growth of the traffic and size of the ships was greater than the capacity of the canal." It is equally true, of course, that in questioning the

canal, he, like other railroad men, simply protected his self-interest. His concept of a "land bridge" of low-cost rails from sea to
sea—in other words, of a globally integrated system of large ships
and large trains—ran directly counter to a government-funded
canal system.

Hill especially loved to hold forth on four subjects near and
dear to his heart: free trade, resource depletion and conservation, agriculture, and of course, railroading. Like his friends John
S. Kennedy, George Stephen, and Donald Smith, he was an An-
glophile who held a nineteenth-century British attachment to
the merits of unfettered commercial intercourse. His Canadian
roots and trade affiliations also fed this proclivity, as did his
desire to avoid paying tariffs of up to 50 percent on high-grade,
imported British and German rails.

Hill took up with special gusto the cause of tariff reciprocity
between the United States and Canada, a cause that did not play
well among northwestern farmers fearful of Canadian agricultural imports. In 1911, he strongly supported President William
Howard Taft's campaign for Canadian reciprocity but saw it fail
when Canadian industrialists and unions, likewise fearful of
American imports, caused it to be defeated.

In a number of cases, Jim Hill was more pessimist than optimist. Like such contemporaries as President Roosevelt and historian Frederick Jackson Turner, he viewed the vanishing frontier
with trepidation. He figured that the nation's supplies of coal
and iron might not last the century, the best soils would last less
than half that time, and the best stands of Cascades timber would
be depleted in less than twenty years. Thus he readily, and quite
early, took up the cause of conservation: "The era of unlimited
expansion on every side, of having but to reach out and seize any
desired good, ready provided for us by the Hand that laid the
foundations of the earth, is drawing to a close. . . . The principle of
the conservation of natural resources as the foremost and controlling policy of the United States henceforth is coming to be seen by
many, and must be heartily accepted by all, as the first condition,
not only of continued material prosperity, but also of the perpetua-
tion of free institutions and a government by the people."

Not surprisingly, though, Hill inclined toward the mainstream idea of "multiple-use" conservation, as put forth by Roosevelt and Gifford Pinchot, rather than toward the pristine preservationism advocated by John Muir and others. Ever the pragmatist and developer, he wanted no more federal forestland withdrawals than were absolutely necessary to protect watersheds and other critical areas and thereby parted company with more advanced progressives like Roosevelt. Indeed, in 1910, he found out just how unpleasant these people could be when the San Francisco reformer Francis Heney, getting the facts badly confused, attacked Hill to his face, in front of a Saint Paul conservation gathering, as a despoiler of giant federal land grants.

More than any other subject, even railroading perhaps, agriculture was Jim Hill's favorite topic of discussion. Fervent and well-informed as he indisputably was on the subject, as Howard Dickman reveals in a discerning study, Hill actually adhered quite closely to the conventional wisdom of the time. Thus, assessing the glutted markets of the 1890s, he preached exports. Then, when a paucity of natural products seemed to pose a threat, he shifted toward an emphasis on reinvigorating a threatened productivity.

The perennial Jeffersonian, he preached the physiocratic axiom that family farms form the backbone of society and that farms must remain small and intensively cultivated. "Every people is thus reduced, in the final appraisal of its estate, to reliance upon the soil." "This is preeminently and primarily an agricultural country." "The farms of the future will be smaller and closer together and social conditions improved, which will be as it should be." "If any considerable part of the United States were farmed as Denmark is, we might feed the world."

He proved a terrible prophet here, both in predicting the viability of small family farms and in failing to foresee the emergence of the great commercial cereal farms and livestock ranches that would reconstitute the agricultural economy of the Northwest in the years ahead. That is understandable, for he could no more anticipate than could others the impetus toward large-scale agriculture that would come with mechanization, hybrid grains and genetically improved animals, synthetic fertilizers, and pesticides and herbicides.

But this misapprehension naturally led him to a second, fundamentally mistaken prophecy. "We are approaching the point," he proclaimed, "where all our wheat product will be needed for our own uses, and we shall cease to be an exporter of grain. . . . Our own people, whose mineral resources will by that time have greatly diminished, must find themselves thrown back upon the soil for a living." The new world of highly capitalized, often corporate-owned, and federally subsidized agriculture lay far beyond his ken, or his generation's, as did the huge commodity surpluses that America would one day export to the rest of the world. Some of Hill's other theories proved wrongheaded as well. He persisted, for example, in advocating the use of manures as the best fertilizer long after agricultural scientists had determined otherwise.

But many of his other points were persuasive and constructive. Alarmed at the depleted soils and unproductive farms along his tracks, he ceaselessly urged the need to rotate plantings, introducing especially hay crops like alfalfa and oats, and to raise livestock that could bring in extra dollars and keep idle hands busily employed during the long winters. The result would be economically balanced and viable family units. "Our agriculture will take a place midway between the miniature garden-farm of Japan and the vast estates of countries like those in eastern Europe that still support a landed gentry."

Hill was most influential as an advocate of model demonstration farms and plots, where working farmers could learn the latest applications of agricultural science. During these years after the 1890 Hatch Act began adding experiment stations to the budding land-grant colleges, he stood as one of the country's main advocates of this new federal role. Playing off the major armaments-race issue of the time, he proclaimed: "If I could have my way, I should build a couple of warships a year less. Perhaps one would do. I would take that $5,000,000 or $6,000,000 a year and start at least one-thousand agricultural schools in the United States at $5,000 a year each, in the shape of model farms." He meant it; for as we shall see, he was busily constructing the world's largest system of private agricultural experimentation and extension farms during these final, climactic years of his life.

With the dawn of the new century, James J. Hill stood alone as the grand old man of American railroading. His views were sought and respected, and he had thought them through very analytically. He did not, naturally enough, as a practical business-man, waste much time pondering first principles. He continued to argue, as he always had, that what was good for the railroad was good for its hinterland and vice versa—in other words, community of interest. "The only community of interests that can exist permanently is the community between the producer of tonnage and the carrier. The railroads depend for their existence upon the products of the land they serve."

He meant this, feeling deep in his soul that no successful road could or would long exploit the producers of its region and continue to profit. To his critics, particularly among distressed farmers, this meant that he turned a blind eye—no pun in-tended—to the issue of excess rates; but to him, the rates were not excessive. Rather, they represented not only the return of an honest profit to shareholders but also vitally necessary reinvest-ments in infrastructure. On the latter point, he made a good case. After all, he did in fact plow earnings heavily back into the business; and after all, rates were yearly declining, even if not so fast as producers felt they could and should, given the new econ-omies of railroading. If the railroads continued to reinvest in modernizing their systems, Hill reasoned, they could keep the rates down and thus blunt criticism.

To Jim Hill, the railroad trunk lines and their spreading branches formed a living, vital organism, which constantly needed to be replenished. His life's passion lay in straightening curves, lowering grades, laying new ballast and high-grade steel rails, re-placing wooden trestles with steel ones and wooden culverts with masonry structures, raising tonnages hauled by ever-larger cars and engines, and lowering rates and extending ladings over ever-longer distances. He cared most about *freight*, never frills; and he apparently never considered that newfangled automobiles, trucks, and hard-surfaced roads could challenge rails as the basic transportation infrastructure of America and of the world.

To those critics who argued that he and his peers should place greater emphasis on the niceties of passenger traffic, he juxtaposed an interesting thought about economic democracy: "The so-called 'travelling public' forms in reality but a small, and the more fortunate class of the community; while the freight payers, direct and indirect, include all. Hence, justice requires that railway systems, like the Manitoba . . . should be cautious not to favor passenger traffic at the necessary expense of freight payers." One of his best-remembered observations was that passenger trains were like the male teat—neither functional nor particularly pretty!

Seldom mouthing the simplistic bromides of laissez-faire, he did like to speak in terms of tooth-and-claw social Darwinism; but the product of such fierce competition among railroads, he thought, would not be a singular monopoly. Rather, the result would be groupings of regional "combinations," each ascendant in its own area—and each integrating with its neighbors. "The fortunes of railroad companies are determined by the law of the survival of the fittest. This has already grouped the railroads of other countries into a few great systems, operated in harmony with one another."

Like any other intelligent businessman, Hill saw cutthroat competition as wasteful and as something to be ended. "Combination," therefore, was natural and necessary—"merely an incident on the road to efficient service." The only losers in the process were middlemen, who made no real contribution anyhow, and inefficient competitors, who were doomed to extinction. The winners consisted of all consumers, who received better service at lower rates. The problem, of course, lay in how to combine effectively without running afoul of the Interstate Commerce Act of 1887 or the Sherman Antitrust Act of 1890, both of which seemed—albeit in vague terms—to disallow "restraint of trade." Hill had never liked the informal and ineffective "pooling" arrangements of earlier days. But now, as an advocate of formal consolidation of regional roads, he faced a far more

serious challenge than mere competitors who cheated on pooling
arrangements—namely, government regulators.

Not surprisingly, Jim Hill resembled his business peers in his
hearty dislike of federal and state regulators, whom he castigated
in 1905 as "a lot of doctrinaires, . . . mainly either politicians
seeking office or college tack-head philosophers and preachers."
But he was far more practical than that and was in fact ready to
accept some measure of federal regulation of railroads, with the
hope that it might curtail such abuses as rail rate rebates demanded by large producers and free passes hustled by politicos.
Thus when the Interstate Commerce Act of 1887 passed, he
wrote: "While the interstate law, if enforced as it is written,
would destroy the producers of the Northwest, I have no fear
that an intelligent commission, having authority to suspend its
effect, will allow the bill to work any material damage to any
interest concerned. If they should, there would be no doubt but
Congress would at the next session repeal the obnoxious clauses
very promptly."

The fact that Hill accepted the inevitability of federal regulation did not mean, however, that he welcomed it or felt that he
really benefited from it. His example fails to uphold historian
Gabriel Kolko's famous assertion that rail executives supported
and then secured federal regulation and that they won from it a
benevolent federal oversight of the industry, oversight running
counter to the public interest. Hill's perspective tends, rather, to
affirm the interpretations of Edward Purcell, Albro Martin, and
others: railroad men divided over the nascent Interstate Commerce Commission (ICC), grudgingly accepting its political necessity but sharing gains and losses with producers and other
interested groups.

Hill and other railroad leaders watched approvingly during the
conservative 1890s as the U.S. Supreme Court ruled that the ICC
lacked the authority to set maximum rates. Similarly, the courts
cut the railroads considerable slack regarding Section Four of the
Interstate Commerce Act, which nebulously outlawed the notorious "long-and-short-haul," whereby railroads charged higher
rates to inland cities than to ports even when the interior city lay

nearer the point of embarkation. The law had muddied the situation initially by defining such rulings to apply only in "substantially similar" situations—whatever that meant. In the Alabama Midlands case of 1897, the Supreme Court ruled that long-and-short-haul discrimination could stand if "alternative" sea routes forced the railroads to reduce their competitive rates to distant ports.

With the dawn of the new century, however, came a wave of "progressive" sentiment that called for a far tougher regulation of railroads, in the public interest. For years, the "Inland Empire" hub city of Spokane had petitioned that it suffered from severe long-and-short-haul discrimination; it now hired the distinguished Brooks Adams to help make its case. The port cities of Seattle, Tacoma, and Portland all enjoyed better rates because of maritime competition; in fact, Spokane's rates were equal to those all the way from the Twin Cities to the Pacific ports and then back to Spokane! As a result, Portland merchants could invade Spokane's hinterland via the Columbia and Snake Rivers and underprice its own merchants.

In 1902, Hill addressed two angry meetings in the eastern Washington towns of Colfax and Davenport. He counseled, "You can legislate until the barn door has fallen off its hinges with rust, and you will not succeed." But even after Charles Mellen, of the NP, dropped grain rates by 10 percent, the Inland Empire seethed with unrest.

Congressional enactment of the sweeping Hepburn Act of 1906 and the Mann-Elkins Act of 1910 tightened the screws on the long-and-short-haul standards, and in 1911 Spokane finally won a sweeping ICC ruling that granted its shippers "terminal rates" equitable to those of its coastal competitors. Even then, the railroads appealed to the Supreme Court, so that it took until 1918 to solidify these hard-won gains. By then, completion of the Panama Canal allowed the coastal cities, ironically, to win back much of the interior trade they would have lost. Nonetheless, federal regulation did allow the capital city of the Inland Empire to become and remain one of America's major rail centers—and Spokane gloried in besting the Hill railroads.

Jim Hill fretted less about this marathon case than he did about other, farther-reaching ICC rulings. The ICC steadfastly refused, for example, to allow lower rates on rail shipments to the Northwest Coast of "through" cargoes bound for the Orient via his big, new ships, described below. Of course, this meant that American rail-ocean commerce with the Orient would likely not prove competitive with European ships using the Suez Canal. By 1910 Hill had lost hope in the idea: "America is not a commercial nation, and until she has to make greater efforts to support her population than has been necessary in the past, I do not see how she will become important among the leading exporting nations of the world."

As he slipped into old age, the grand old man of western rails grew ever more negative as he contemplated the conundrum of the American rail system. Mounting inflation and the pressing need to expand and renovate infrastructure demanded increasing present rates and attracting new investments. But as fate would have it, just at this moment in history, the progressive regulation campaign finally won a series of sweeping enactments that made such increases politically difficult, slow, and exasperating: the Hepburn and the Mann-Elkins Acts, and the Railroad Valuation Act of 1913, gave the ICC the final rate-setting tool of actually setting values on rail properties for that purpose. The railroads thus found themselves unable to respond to market pressures, even as a fledgling but imposing new competitor loomed in the form of cars, trucks, and hard-surfaced roads and highways.

Hill understood the situation pretty well, and he chafed angrily at it. He testified before congressional committees, always stressing the same theme: don't set rates by government fiat, but instead let the rail managers establish rates flexibly, for instance in granting preferential rates to promote Pacific Northwest lumber shipments to eastern markets. If wrongs appeared, they could be corrected either by act of Congress or through the courts. But, aiming a critical eye especially at President Roosevelt, he concluded that politics, not reason, would prevail. He ended up likening governmental regulators to horseflies, who could sting their host into anguish and torpor but could never reanimate or redirect it. The business in which he had triumphed came to seem increasingly confined and unpromising, and he urged Louis to abandon it before his son reached age forty.

The epic battle of American railroad history began in 1901 and centered on control of the strategic Chicago, Burlington, and Quincy Railroad (the "Q"). Once Hill and Morgan had consolidated the NP with the GN under Hill's effective tutelage, it made more sense than ever to forge a connecting link between the Twin Cities–Duluth termini of the two railroads and the great rail hub of Chicago, the "gateway" point for transfers of East Coast traffic with the regions farther west. This would create the sort of regional consolidation that Hill had been envisioning; at Chicago, the "Hill lines" could join to other regional main lines, such as the Atlantic-bound Pennsylvania and New York Central railroads.

Three major roads connected the Twin Cities to Chicago: the Chicago, Burlington, and Quincy, the Chicago and Northwestern, and the Chicago, Milwaukee, and Saint Paul. Whereas Morgan preferred the Milwaukee, Hill had always favored the Burlington, whose Burlington and Northern subsidiary already had a community of interest with the GN and already had Hill dollars invested in it. In this case, the well-informed Hill had the better argument.

The "Q" was truly one of America's best and most-profitable roads. Well capitalized, well constructed, and well managed by two of the giant figures of American railroading, John Murray Forbes and Charles Perkins, along with their New England associates, it served a densely populated and fertile agrarian hinterland stretching across Illinois and Iowa, down into Missouri and out into Nebraska and Minnesota. Beginning in 1889, it had extended westward into South Dakota and Wyoming, and in 1894 it drove this potential transcontinental track up to join the NP main line at the most strategic location on the northwestern Great Plains, the Clark Fork Bottom of the Yellowstone River, where the Montana city of Billings was emerging as a major rail hub.

The "Billings Gateway"—a forced marriage extorted from the NP under threat to build westward toward Butte in direct competition—gave the Burlington transcontinental access and saved the railroad the frightful expense of building on west. It also made the road a natural partner of the emerging Hill lines. And a valuable partner the Burlington would prove to be, for it offered the NP and the GN access not only to Chicago but also, via later extensions, to Denver and eventually southward all the way to the Gulf of Mexico at Galveston. Most significant, it offered the potential of opening the entire vista of midwestern and even southern markets to northwestern natural products and vice versa. The problem with the Chicago, Burlington, and Quincy lay in the fact that it was so alluring that it naturally attracted other well-heeled suitors. Indeed, at this very moment it attracted the man who was about to become Jim Hill's archrival, Edward H. Harriman, of whom it was once said that he feared neither God nor J. P. Morgan.

Harriman was a truly remarkable man, one of the most brilliant railroaders and formidable capitalists in American history, whose genius has been somewhat masked behind a partially deserved reputation for shady dealing. In his early fifties at the dawn of the new century, he resembled a clerk more than a captain of industry—slender, balding, with wire-rimmed glasses and drooping mustache. He came to railroading from the world of finance, having bought a seat on the New York Stock Exchange at the tender age of twenty-two, and learned the trade first as a director and then as a vice-president of the Illinois Central. Already understanding well the intricacies of money and markets, he now learned with remarkable haste the same lesson that Hill had mastered earlier: the need to engineer grades, curves, and roadbeds for maximum, heavy-tonnage efficiency.

Harriman made his great ascent by taking over and rebuilding the rickety, old, bankrupt UP, which had been built hastily by speculators to secure its lucrative federal land grant and had then lapsed into sad disrepair. He became a director of the UP in 1897 and chairman of the board a year later. With the full backing of Hill's friend Jacob Schiff, of Kuhn, Loeb, and then the support of

E. H. Harriman. Courtesy of James J. Hill Papers, James Jerome Hill Reference Library, Saint Paul, Minnesota.

the enormously wealthy and rapacious Standard Oil group led by Henry Rogers, William Rockefeller, and James Stillman of the National City Bank, he raised $75 million to erase the debt and renovate the UP into a highly competitive carrier. As a result, its earnings would soar a remarkable 90 percent during the decade following 1899.

To rationalize and round out his railroad, he reacquired the combined Oregon Short Line and OR&N, the UP's transcontinental line to Portland, Oregon, which had earlier been lost in bankruptcy. And then, after the death of crusty old Collis Huntington, he secured and similarly renovated the Central Pacific, the UP's Siamese twin, which brought his tracks across the Nevada deserts and the towering California Sierras to San Francisco Bay. As one success spectacularly followed another, he and his powerful syndicate of coinvestors soon proceeded to take over the Central Pacific's larger sister line, the Southern Pacific. Blessed with an enormous land grant through California's agricultural heartland, the Southern Pacific stretched from San Francisco Bay across southern California and the arid lands of Arizona, New Mexico, and Texas to the mouth of the Mississippi, as well as northward from San Francisco to Portland. By 1906, the Harriman group controlled roughly 25,000 miles of track—a genuine empire, which rivaled that of Hill and Morgan.

To Harriman, the "Q" offered the same advantage it did to Hill: superb access to Chicago and the Upper Midwest. But to him it also offered the counterincentive of a threat; the Nebraska-Billings Gateway extension of the Burlington, in the hands of Hill and Morgan, would allow the NP-GN lines to invade freely the central midwestern heartland of the UP. Thus, in 1899–1900, Harriman had Schiff begin buying up Burlington stock on the open market.

This ploy held some hope of giving him a voice in management of the road, but it held little possibility of gaining him control of the line itself. Burlington stock was a reliable and sound dividend payer and was thus widely prized and dispersed. The only hope anyone could have in securing majority control would be to have the current management, under Perkins, secure a very high price for it and then advise the trusting stockholders to deliver it for exchange.

An eminently practical man, the courtly Perkins knew well what Hill had earlier ascertained: that even profitable regional roads like the "Q" must either expand to the sea, in order to secure the transcontinental through-rates they needed to compete, or be absorbed by other such systems. He knew that it would be wiser for the Burlington to consolidate than to build on its own westward, through thinly populated country, in such a time of rising costs.

Perkins's first inclination was to go with Hill and Morgan, rather than Harriman, not only because his railroad already had a community of interest with theirs but also because he highly regarded James J. Hill. He articulated this regard more than once, paying Hill truly the ultimate in compliments: "Hill is in many ways a wonderful man, not only a prophet and a dreamer, but he has a very unusual faculty for figures. . . . He is a great man—there is no mistake about it." Perkins added: "Mr. Hill has seen more clearly than any of us that the fittest to survive would be the railroad which could work at the lowest rate per ton mile. That has been his central idea, and he has educated everybody on his road to make everything subordinate to it."

Perkins now found himself in a very strong position, and he naturally took advantage of it. He presented the same tough terms to both Harriman and Hill, namely that he would recommend to his board and to the shareholders that they turn over their stock, but only at the steeply increased purchase price of $200 per share. This was too much for Harriman, who was heavily overextended with his Central Pacific–Southern Pacific acquisitions, and it was nearly too much for Hill and Morgan as well.

But they understood that the hour of decision was at hand, and thus they elected to raise the necessary purchase funding through the issuance of 4 percent bonds jointly by the NP and the GN. So, in a marathon series of negotiations between Hill and Morgan's man George Baker on the one hand and Perkins and his team on the other, the two sides came to terms in April 1901. The Burlington directors easily persuaded their stockholders, who could choose either the princely $200 per share return or the 4 percent bonds, to turn over their shares, and the Hill-Morgan team now had the key railroad they needed to round out their regional railroad empire.

As Richard Overton, the historian of the Chicago, Burlington, and Quincy, has demonstrated, the marriage to the two northern transcontinentals proved to be a good one for the "Q." Perkins felt the same, commenting later in 1901, "Great Northern and Northern Pacific combined with the Burlington is [*sic*] going to make a stronger and better property than the Union and Southern Pacific under Harriman." And a half-century later, in 1957, rail leader Ralph Budd reaffirmed Perkins's judgment: "The Hill Line Association has been good for the Burlington."

Indeed, the merger looks very good when contrasted to the fate of the Burlington's main peers. Following a conservative course of standing pat and unintegrated, the Chicago and Northwestern stagnated. On the other hand, the Chicago, Milwaukee, and Saint Paul soon built on to the Pacific alone, during an era of mounting costs, and ended up in a succession of bankruptcies that would finally prove fatal.

From his perspective, Jim Hill also came to a quick appreciation of the marriage, which turned out to be well worth the high price. He now saw that the profitable Burlington, with its rich agrarian hinterland, was the most valuable of his three lines. He wanted to bring John Stevens in as general manager of the "Q," and when Stevens turned him down, the old man went into one of his notorious rages and ordered his car uncoupled from the train to which it and the younger man's own car had been hitched. Instead, Hill elected to work with George Harris, who had succeeded Perkins, and brought in to assist him two young executives who would both become prominent leaders of the next generation, Daniel Willard and Darius Miller.

During the ensuing years, the Burlington system, which Jim Hill had acquired primarily for its west-east connections, proved to be equally valuable for its north-south extension. The trackage down to southern Illinois, and then on into Kentucky, provided lucrative, high-grade coal, both to market and to consume in his own engines, as well as access to prime farmlands there and in Missouri. In 1908, Hill would direct the purchase of the Colorado and Southern line for the "Q," which gave it access all the way south to Galveston on the Gulf of Mexico, so that the Hill lines now touched the waters of both the Pacific and the Atlantic. Via the Nebraska-Montana linkage to the NP, he could market Northwest lumber and minerals not only to the Midwest but also to the South and could bring cotton and other commodities on return, some of which he hoped to export to Asia.

So momentous was the GN-NP acquisition of the Burlington that it raised concerns across the land that the new leviathan would soon reach eastward beyond Chicago to become a true coast-to-coast transcontinental. Hill's long friendship with the Baltimore and Ohio fueled such speculation; but of course, such a strategy did not fit the Minnesotan's regional philosophy, nor did it fit the schemes of the House of Morgan. Hill thus hastened to reassure nervous rival executives, such as Alexander J. Cassatt, of the Pennsylvania Railroad: "There is no intention, present or remote, to carry this combination further East or South than Chicago or St. Louis. I do not believe it is possible to make a strong combination covering the country between the Atlantic and the Pacific. The ownership on [*sic*] much the largest portion of the traffic from the West breaks at the Great Lakes or Chicago, and I want to give you my personal assurance that the three interests—Great Northern, Northern Pacific, and Burlington— have no desire to be in any manner a disturbing element, either east of Chicago or elsewhere."

Blandishments about disinterest in becoming "a disturbing element" may have mollified detached observers like Cassatt, but they did nothing to pacify Harriman and his friends. Harriman worried, with good reason, that in the dynamic hands of Morgan and Hill, the Burlington now represented a blade poised at the heart of his UP empire. The "Q" represented lost access to Chicago and also the threat of invasion from the north and east. He felt, furthermore, that he had been badly used.

Hill calmly stated that he had actually helped the UP by ensuring that the "Q" would not build a westward line parallel to Harriman's; the explanation fell, naturally enough, on deaf ears. And although Jim Hill always maintained that he had kept the Harriman group informed of what he was doing, Schiff stoutly argued that Hill had misled them. Harriman and Schiff pressed for the allowance of a one-third interest in the Burlington for the

UP, to achieve a soothing community of interest. The Morgan-Hill forces turned them down flat. Such an accommodation, they purred, might represent an illegal "restraint of trade" under federal statute.

To understand the fierce struggle that now erupted, one must first realize that it involved not just a railroad, or even a group of railroads, but also a contest for supremacy on Wall Street itself. The Rockefeller–Standard Oil–National City Bank interests, fortified by the massive earnings they had taken from their Standard Oil monopoly, stuck with Harriman out of loyalty and also because they had invested not only in the UP but also in another Burlington rival, the Milwaukee Road.

More than that, however, they hated and resented the House of Morgan and were determined to show the world that they too held a place in the sun—as indeed they did. This was less true of Schiff and Kuhn, Loeb, who were pulled from their earlier ties with the GN by their much closer ones to the UP, than it was of Stillman, Rockefeller, Rogers, and George Gould, son of rail tycoon Jay Gould, who had now joined the alliance as well. As Hill explained to Kennedy after the battle had ended, "I am sure the main motive was truly expressed by Stillman and others who said they would show the world that Morgan was not the only banker in America, &c, that all other banking houses were nothing more than his clerks, and talked of cutting his wings, &c."

For sheer grit and audacity, Harriman had few rivals, and he now proceeded on a daring, even reckless corporate raid that would shake Wall Street to its very foundations. Since Morgan and Hill had stonewalled his request for a one-third holding in the Burlington, he would proceed to attack them from the rear. He would, instead, stealthily buy control of one of the two parents of the "Q"—the NP! This not only would give him, thereby, 50 percent control of the "Q" but also would rend apart the northwestern rail empire that his enemies had so painstakingly created and would leave the mighty GN itself isolated, weakened, and endangered.

Even for such a prosperous group as the Harriman-Schiff-Rogers combination, however, surreptitious purchase of the mighty NP would pose a daunting challenge; and the burden it placed on the overextended UP–Southern Pacific systems amounted to irresponsibility. Morgan and Hill, along with their allies, held roughly $35 million of the total $155 million in NP stock, as Harriman accurately figured, and Harriman hoped to make sizable purchases while Morgan was absent on one of his widely heralded sorties to Europe in pursuit of its artistic treasures. Harriman succeeded. As Kuhn, Loeb quietly made its purchases, unnoticed, from a variety of different brokerages, the price of NP common stock slowly rose from 101 to past 117. Unsuspecting, the NP directors and the House of Morgan even sold blocs of their own shares to take a profit.

Interestingly, it was not the Morgan partners, temporarily led by the debonair Robert Bacon, who noticed that something was wrong. It was Jim Hill, out in Seattle, who first smelled a rat. Increasingly suspicious of the steadily climbing stock price, Hill boarded a special train late in April and sped eastward. The media presented this journey as an epic, roaring train ride over cleared tracks, with the furious captain of industry flying against his foes, and this incident then took its place in the hagiography of Hill legend. But in fact, Jim was more controlled than that, and he strode gentlemanly into the Kuhn, Loeb offices on May 3, 1901, to confront his old friend and new foe, Jacob Schiff. What the calm and dignified Schiff told him, however, brought his Scottish blood to a fast boil. The massive purchasing campaign, Schiff said, had landed the Harriman forces a majority of the NP stock: $42 million of the $75 million worth of preferred shares and $37 million of the $80 million in shares of common stock!

Exactly what happened at this meeting, and at another one later that night, is unclear. Schiff later maintained that he informed Hill that Harriman did not plan to displace James from management of the NP but wanted only to gain a voice in the road and to assure more reasonableness than he had been accorded regarding the Burlington. Hill, to the contrary, said that Schiff and Harriman tried to "bribe" him with offers to stay on in charge of the NP, offers that he indignantly declined. The Minnesotan was highly agitated. He told his wife, no doubt with considerable exaggeration, that if Harriman succeeded, he would divest the GN, since his enemies would have him cornered by controlling the UP, the NP, and half of the Burlington. He now found himself, in fact, embroiled in the most climactic struggle of his life.

From the Kuhn, Loeb offices, Hill proceeded to the House of Morgan. When he learned that Morgan Bank and the NP had actually sold stock, so that the Morgan-Hill forces now held less than $25 million of NP common stock, he loosed the fury of his wrath upon them, one of the few recorded instances of anyone ever chewing out a group of Morgan partners! A wire immediately went off to an equally enraged Morgan, who was at the Alpine retreat of Aix-les-Bains, seeking authorization to purchase $15 million of NP common on the open market in a desperate bid to regain control. Morgan's approval promptly followed.

To their great relief, the group soon realized that the opposition had, meanwhile, erred seriously. Although Harriman and his group now held a majority of common and preferred stock combined, they did not hold a majority of the common alone. This could be used to defeat them: according to the corporate charter of the NP, a majority of common stockholders had the legal right to vote to retire the preferred shares on the first day of 1902, which of course would make the preferred shares irrelevant in directing the corporation. Thus, since a total of $80 million in NP common stock had been issued, the Hill-Morgan minions set out to buy up enough of the outstanding stock "on the street" to boost their total past $40 million.

The Harriman group, incredibly, found itself holding only $37 million—just short of a majority—because Harriman, sick in bed, had ordered Kuhn, Loeb to buy $4 million more, but Schiff had been worshiping at the synagogue at that moment, and the order had not been executed in time! The frenzied search for the scarce remaining shares needed to make a majority for either the Morgan-Hill allies or the Harriman group now set off one of the wildest episodes the stock market has ever witnessed.

When the market opened on Monday, May 6, 1901, the price of NP common stock stood at a robust 114. The Morgan purchases sent it soaring, dramatically, during the day to 133. As market watchers began to scent what was going on, word spread that Hill and Morgan had lost control of the NP. Instinctively, brokers and speculators moved to sell NP stock "short"—that is, to sell off more shares than they actually had at the artificially high price, figuring they could buy the shares in good time at a lower price for actual delivery and never guessing that the shares would not be there when needed, since by then the shares would be locked safely away in Morgan vaults. Once this happened, NP stock would be "cornered," with more shares obligated than could be delivered—the sort of crisis that would drive prices to astronomical heights, sucking investments from other stocks, and that could blow the whole market.

The pace of buying quickened on Tuesday, as the Morgan men continued their quest and as short-sellers began grasping about madly for shares to cover their sales and their behinds. By the end of the day, the Morgan allies had spent their money and, breathing easier, had the shares they needed—420,000, of which the Hill group held 223,800. However, it was now becoming apparent that their campaign had resulted in a cornering of NP common, with the price approaching 150 at the end of trading. On Wednesday, tension mounted steadily as the "shorts" desperately sought the shares they needed, almost regardless of the price, driving it to 180. Neither the Morgan nor the Harriman forces, together holding almost all the stock, could or would show them mercy. As speculators sold off other stocks to rush toward the NP stock, its meteoric rise began to disrupt the stability of the entire market.

Genuine panic and bedlam occurred on Thursday as the cornered "shorts" bid up the vanishing stock in a final effort to save themselves. In a spectacular surge, the few shares of remaining NP common passed 300, 700, and even touched 1,000! This led, of course, to some choice Wall Street stories, like that of the New Englander who had just earlier bought NP for 84 and now sold it for 700, netting $60,000, which was enough to retire on in those days.

But the real results were extremely dangerous. As other stocks plummeted, in the heaviest single volume of trading the market had ever seen, and as money dried up, the interest rate in the call-loan market shot up to a devastating 75 percent. A true and pro-longed panic threatened. A typical headline proclaimed, "Money Kings in Death Struggle." Even the sedate *New York Times* lectured the protagonists for acting "like cowboys on a spree . . . shooting wildly at each other in entire disregard of the safety of the bystanders."

Even as the foundations of Wall Street seemed to tremble, however, the establishment worked to quell the storm. Throughout the long hours of May 9, the leading figures at Morgan Bank and at Kuhn, Loeb hammered out the terms of a truce; and late that afternoon, Hill joined them to hear what a beleaguered Schiff proposed, on behalf of Harriman, who was still laid up with appendicitis. If the Morgan group would offer up enough shares of NP to bail out the shorts, and thus restore the stability of the exchange, Schiff would pledge his best efforts to bring Harriman into a compromise regarding both the NP and the Burlington. The Hill-Morgan team could afford to accept, since they now held an ample majority of the shares, and they agreed.

As for Hill, he seemed calm in victory, asking one of Schiff's associates, Felix Warburg, how the old man was standing up. When Warburg responded "not very happy," Hill said, "He takes these things too seriously." Publicly, Hill shrugged the whole thing off: "The truth is, that I have been engaged in no fight—although there are some people who have been throwing stones into my yard." Asked at another moment for a comment on the whole affair, he quipped: "I have no statement to make. I have been too busy today buying locomotives."

In one sense, he could well afford to be flippant, for he and Morgan had beaten back the attack and now held firm control of both the NP and the Burlington. The "Northern Pacific Panic," furthermore, quickly flared out. NP stock immediately fell back, well below 200, and the panic did not lead to depression but instead was rapidly eclipsed by a mounting prosperity. Yet the victorious allies had, in fact, paid a heavy price. The public, particularly the investing elite, looked askance at these behe-

moths, especially Morgan and Harriman, who had nearly en-
gulfed them in chaos while battling one another. And a rising
group of reformers, calling themselves "progressives," counted
this as another glaring illustration of the need to regulate an
unrestrained capitalism.

Savoring their triumph, Morgan and Hill then proceeded to
have their way with both the NP and the Chicago, Burlington,
and Quincy. The NP preferred stock was slated for retirement,
and Morgan fashioned a board of directors that clearly reflected
his and Hill's control. Harriman received a directorship on both
boards, and his ally Rockefeller also sat on the NP board. But this
gave the defeated speculators only a minority voice and nothing
more, aside from saving face. They still held a huge bloc of NP
stock, though: $37 million worth, compared with the $42 million
held by the Morgan-Hill forces.

In reality, the victors were quite chastened themselves, as well
they should have been. Hill henceforth had little good to say
about Harriman. In 1904 he wrote Stephen, "All they [Harriman
and Stillman] want to make them crooked is an opportunity to
cheat someone." And a year later, he confided even to Schiff: "I
do not agree with you that the fight has been a fair one. I think it
was the foulest and most unnecessary fight that I have ever
known." Having very nearly lost control of the NP, he became
obsessed with protecting his properties from further piratical
raids. He had his staff purchase for him personally all the NP
stock they could find at reasonable price; he soon had a large
portion of his wealth, $13 million, invested in the NP.

He wanted and needed more security than that, however. For
some years, Hill had thought about the creation of a "holding
company," which could secure the majority shares of both the
GN and the NP and thus would house the Burlington as well.
Such an arrangement would unify the management of the three
roads, and more important, it would combine their capitalization—which would be raised so high as to make it nearly impossible for raiders like Harriman to sneak in. Such holding companies were becoming ever more popular at the time, in part as
a strategy to gain monopoly control over operating companies

Cartoonist "Ding" Darling on the Northern Pacific stock frenzy, 1900. Courtesy of James J. Hill Papers, James Jerome Hill Reference Library, Saint Paul, Minnesota.

while arguing to sympathetic courts that the Sherman Antitrust restrictions on "restraints of trade" were not being violated.

All of this was a part of what Robert Reich has called "America's first great merger boom," which crested during the years 1898–1902. In that brief, four-year interval, over twenty-six hundred business mergers took place in the United States, involving assets worth more than $6.3 billion. This sharp trend toward monopoly, or at least oligopoly, produced new supercorporations, or "trusts," as they were popularly known. Patterned after John D. Rockefeller's behemoth and dreaded Standard Oil Company, they came to number such familiar names as American Tobacco, American Telephone and Telegraph, and two of J. P. Morgan's prime creations: International Harvester and the $1.4 billion U.S. Steel Corporation. The public watched these dizzying events with mounting anxiety, fearing especially monopolistic price gouging and a loss of their political power to the new corporate order. Politicians, of course, sensed and shared this concern and proceeded to act on it.

Jim Hill had little difficulty convincing Morgan of the need for such an incursion-proof, "super" holding company, since "Jupiter" was already at work designing others like it. Harriman proved a harder sell because he and his friends had no hope of controlling it, although they would benefit from stabilizing the situation. Furthermore, some of Hill's key coinvestors, such as Gaspard Farrer in England, balked at the idea of converting their GN and NP stock for less-certain issues of the new holding company—whose shares, if typical of the coming trend, might well be watered.

Hill had to convince them, however, since shouldering the NP load without them was straining his and even Morgan's finances. By late summer of 1901, such were the powers of his persuasiveness and of their confidence in him that his key, major coholders of GN-NP stock agreed to exchange it for stock in the new holding company: Lords Mount Stephen and Strathcona and Mount Royal, Kennedy, and finally Farrer. Surely, their decision would tend to bring smaller holders in with them.

The Northern Securities Company was chartered on November 12, 1901, in New Jersey, the state so permissive and friendly to the new corporate order that it had become known as the "Mother of Trusts." Capitalized at $400 million, it ranked from the outset as one of the country's financial giants. Controversy surrounded it from the beginning, with critics maintaining that fully $122 million represented pure "water"—bloated valuation that could pour unwarranted profits into the pockets of those on the inside. No less a personage than U.S. Attorney General Philander Knox not only soon criticized this stock watering but also ominously speculated that such behavior might well augur the holding company's inclination to rate-gouge the public.

Northern Securities held near-complete control of the NP, with 96 percent of its shares, and firm control of the other two roads as well, with 76 percent of the GN. Harriman, Schiff, and Stillman sat on its board; but obvious board control lay firmly in the hands of Hill and his associates, including Kennedy, Samuel Thorne, William Clough, Nicholas Terhune, Edward Nichols, and D. Willis James, as well as their Morgan allies, who numbered among others Bacon, Perkins, and Daniel Lamont. The board promptly elected James J. Hill to be its president.

Clearly, both sides in the recent dispute now felt they had gained security in Northern Securities. For the Hill-Morgan faction, any party that pondered raiding either the NP or the GN would have to raise over $200 million to do so, a practically impossible task. As for Harriman, together with his allies, as one observer has commented, their three votes would allow him to forestall "the nightmare of a Hill-controlled Burlington creeping into his territory."

Given the obvious, fast-mounting public concern over the trust issue, the Wall Street barons who created Northern Securities entered into this project with remarkably little concern about the likely public, political, and legal fallout. Even as late as February 1902, Hill was reassuring Farrer that public opinion in the Northwest generally favored the merger. They should have known better; Northern Securities came near being a monopoly of railroad traffic in the region between Minnesota and Washington—even nearer when one considered that although the UP was not in the holding company, it was under the control of participant Harriman.

The CP's Soo Line offered only limited competition, and the Milwaukee Road had not yet built on to the Pacific Coast. Northern Securities looked, indeed, to be an effective monopoly. However, corporate lawyers steadily advised the lords of Northern Securities, not irresponsibly, that the courts would probably not interfere. So far, earlier mergers had withstood the test of the Sherman Antitrust Act, and the Supreme Court had balked only at outright rate-setting agreements.

Hill, the only one of the major architects of Northern Securities who actually inhabited the affected region, stumped hard in favor of the trust and its benefits. Once again he preached, at countless fairs and banquets, about the community of interest between the railroads and the producers; and he pointedly reminded his listeners that his recent foes were, after all, advocates of other regions who had tried to take over the railroads of this region. This approach won him some favor. Although almost everyone disliked the idea of monopoly, some regional spokesmen phrased their concern carefully, stating it as relating only to what might happen when the benevolent hand of J. J. Hill was gone. Others leveled their aim at both Hill and his creation. The *Rock County Herald* of Minnesota stated, "The laws of this state will be upheld and enforced, and for once and at last James J. Hill will bow to the will of the people he has so contemptuously and haughtily defied."

Of course, this antitrust sentiment found quick reflection in regional politics. Governor Samuel Van Sant of Minnesota, for instance, who had earlier attempted to block the GN takeover of the NP, orchestrated a suit in state court to void the Northern Securities merger on the grounds that it violated a Minnesota statute disallowing the joining of competing, parallel rail lines. He also organized a meeting of northwestern governors at Helena, Montana, a meeting that resulted in a predictable denunciation of the trust. Clearly, Van Sant was plumbing a deep current of anti–Wall Street feeling. In 1901, facing a hard prospect for reelection, he vigorously pursued an antitrust and generally progressive campaign and claimed a comfortable reelection victory in 1902.

Antitrust suspicion of the new Northern Securities behemoth also surfaced at the national level, although with a lesser sense of urgency. Some even worried that the regional monopoly might presage a giant, nationwide rail consolidation. The popular magazine *World's Work* speculated: "If a securities company can lawfully get control of two roads why not of ten? and if of ten why not, conceivably of all? The courts have seldom if ever had a case before them which involved such enormous commercial interests." More than that, though, the public simply stood in awe of the new moguls of industry. An imaginary dialogue between teacher and student put it this way, as rendered by *Life Magazine,* a precursor of the later picture weekly:

> Question: Who made the world, Charles?
> Answer: God made the world in 4,004, B.C., but it was reorganized in 1901 by James J. Hill, J. Pierpont Morgan, and John D. Rockefeller.

Things suddenly turned drastically worse for the creators of Northern Securities on February 12, 1902, when Attorney General Knox formally announced the imminence of a federal suit to break up the holding company as a violation of the Sherman Antitrust Act. Knox obviously acted at the direction of the young, new president, Theodore Roosevelt, who had just come to office months earlier on the assassination of President McKinley. The announcement of this epochal suit stunned McKinley's mentor and Republican Party leader Senator Mark Hanna of Ohio, Hill's old friend, and it stunned the nation at large.

Hanna commented: "I warned Hill that McKinley might have to act against his company. Mr. Roosevelt's done it." But Hanna could offer his old friend no help, for the president was adamant, considering Northern Securities not only an especially ugly example of the new plutocracy but also an especially vulnerable one, in that it involved transportation and thus interstate commerce, which the constitution clearly made liable to federal regulation. The *New York Tribune* termed the announcement "a sudden and severe shock." This was true enough, for all at once the probusiness Republicanism of McKinley seemed disrupted by a move toward trust-busting by his young and unpredictable successor. Jim Hill's new company suddenly seemed likely to become the first casualty of a new and anticorporate direction in federal trust policy.

No one was more shocked by the news than Morgan. Entertaining dinner guests when he heard it, Morgan blurted out that it had caught him flat-footed. He then hurried down to Washington, closeted himself with the president, and angered him with the imperious statement, "If we have done anything wrong, send your man to my man and they can fix it up." His declaration not only failed to move Roosevelt but also won him a citation in many American histories for a special rendering of corporate arrogance. When Morgan went on to query the president about whether this suit signaled an all-out offensive against his phalanx of new supercorporations, "TR" replied no, unless they had "done something" that Roosevelt regarded as "wrong." Clearly, a new day seemed at hand in the ever more tangled relationships between Wall Street and Washington.

Jim Hill did not yet know the president and had no immediate access to him, but he poured out his anger and resentment in a letter to D. Willis James:

> What you say of President Roosevelt is very true. He is undoubtedly honest and desires to serve his country, but he is so vain and self-willed that he has no judgement. The only motive he has in bringing suit against the Securities company, is to aid his chance of renomination in the middle west, where he thinks it will help him. . . . It really seems hard when we look back at what we have done and how we have led all western companies in opening the country and carrying at the lowest rates, that we should be compelled to fight for our lives against the political adventurers who have never done anything but pose and draw a salary.

According to George Mowry, a close student of Roosevelt, Hill was largely correct in his assessment. As the *New York World* commented, TR would be loved "for the enemies he . . . made," although he would admittedly have to revisit some of these "enemies" when it came time to finance his 1904 election campaign.

The president's dramatic prosecution of Northern Securities immediately won him popular acclaim as a virile "trustbuster"; and, true enough, over the following seven years, his administration would launch forty-four more antitrust suits against other large corporate combinations, among them such giants as Standard Oil and American Tobacco. But TR was more a politician than a progressive. In fact, he never really believed in breaking up the new supercorporations as a matter of policy.

He believed, instead, that they represented the efficient way of the future and that they simply needed to be regulated by federal authority in the public interest. Only those that did wrong, or seemed likely to do wrong, would actually be prosecuted. Thus, he would follow a "rule of reason," selectively prosecuting only those that seemed to need it. But no one knew this at the time; and the precedent of Northern Securities seemed to signal that the president meant to break up the hated trusts across the board. The youthful president's popularity waxed accordingly.

The years 1902–4 proved as hard as any Jim Hill had ever endured. In addition to overseeing the affairs of three major railroads, he insisted also on exercising a hands-on management of the mounting litigation involving the Northern Securities prosecution. The case meant far more to him personally than it did to Morgan, who had many other corporate irons in the fire; for Hill, the merger truly represented the capstone of his life's work. His own railroad attorneys played a major role in the preparation of the case, and his family and associates worried at his feverish preoccupation with it.

In April 1903, the defendants received a rude jolt when the U.S. Circuit Court of Appeals in Saint Paul ruled against them. The court pursued a very narrow line of thought: instead of following any flexible rule-of-reason approach, it literally argued that the mere ability or potential to restrain trade constituted a violation of the Sherman Antitrust Act. Now, the case headed on appeal toward the U.S. Supreme Court itself, where Hill remained optimistic that his point of view would yet prevail.

The U.S. Supreme Court made its long-awaited ruling in the case of *Northern Securities Company* v. *U.S.* in March 1904, and for Hill and Morgan, the news once again was very bad. Speaking for a narrow five-to-four majority, Chief Justice John Marshall Harlan found that the holding company stood in violation of the Sherman Act. Harlan stated, "The act is not limited to restraints of interstate and international trade or commerce that are unreasonable in their nature, but embraces *all* direct *restraints"* (Harlan's emphases).

The majority argued that, as Martin Sklar has paraphrased it, "any direct and substantial restraint constituted a prima facie violation of the law." There was no room for compromise here. This proved especially galling in light of the brilliant dissent filed by Roosevelt's new appointee to the court, Oliver Wendell Holmes, Jr., who reasoned, "Great cases like hard cases make bad law." Holmes pressed the common-law proposition that no restraint of trade occurred until or unless the guilty party actually did something demonstrably to curtail competition. In fact, Holmes argued mischievously, since the Sherman Act was a criminal statute, if the law had indeed been violated, then the men who created Northern Securities should be prosecuted personally—something no one in government envisioned.

Heralding, as it did, the Supreme Court's seeming acceptance of Rooseveltian trust-busting, the *Northern Securities* case was highly popular with the public. So was the president who launched it; newspaper cartoons featured Roosevelt, flashing his teeth and, wielding a large stick, clubbing corporate monsters to the ground. Ironically, however, behind the hoopla and the flurry of antitrust prosecutions that followed the case, Holmes's dissent—which so angered the president, who had just appointed him—proved to be prophetic.

Buttressed by the Hepburn and the Mann-Elkins Acts, the ICC would soon burgeon to regulate the trusts; and this trend, rather than court-enforced "trust-busting," would become the true way of the future. By the time of the "Rule of Reason" cases of 1911—in which the Supreme Court found both the Standard Oil and the American Tobacco companies guilty of restraining trade but allowed them to be reorganized rather than forcing their elimination—the court itself would come to accept the reasoning of Holmes rather than that of Harlan. Thus, the bally-hooed case of Northern Securities would eventually prove to be an anomaly rather than a true augury of the future.

Railroad executives could not know this, of course, in the immediate wake of the 1904 decision; as an immediate result, a pall descended over the consolidation movement. They could continue to operate commonly controlled railroads, like these three, informally and outside the law, in a general community of interest. But they could not merge the roads under a unified and cost-efficient management. They would have to watch the rising ICC carefully, and they would have to be able to demonstrate in court that they were not stifling competition.

Thus, only after several frustrated tries and the passage of sixty-six years would the GN, the NP, and the Chicago, Burlington, and Quincy be formally merged—this time not into the Northern Securities Company but into the Burlington Northern. As the friendly and respected railroad authority Balthaser Meyer of Wisconsin stated at the time, the court had mandated the "impossible doctrine of protection of the public by railway competition," a doctrine that should have been "cast away more than fifty years ago."

Outwardly, Jim Hill seemed to take the court's decision casually, commenting: "Two certificates of stock are now issued instead of one. They are printed in different colors. That is the main difference." That was not the main difference. In fact, the demise of Northern Securities meant a severe backpedaling in the extent to which Hill's three lines could now be managed in a shared community of interest—they could not be truly or meaningfully unified at all. He well knew this and vented his real feelings in a public reaffirmation of social Darwinism several months later: "Competition is the test which proves the survival of the fittest. The laws of trade are as certain as the laws of gravity." In fact, he bitterly resented Roosevelt's prosecution of his holding company, and he never really got over it.

The deconstruction of Northern Securities began. Afterward, members of the Harriman group began selling off their holdings in the three Hill railroads, since they now needed all the resources they could muster in order to secure control of the great Southern Pacific system and weld it into their UP empire. Meanwhile, the dissolution of the holding company led to yet another Hill-Harriman imbroglio.

Harriman wanted the shares of Northern Securities to be returned to investors on the basis of how many shares each investor had initially held either in GN or NP stock; this would restore to him his nearly one-half control of the NP. Hill argued that shares in the trust should simply be redistributed according to the proportion of shares in each of the two railroads held by Northern Securities, without regard to any investor's initial holding in either line.

Once again, the Supreme Court had to adjudicate the case, and once again, Hill's position prevailed. Ironically, however, Harriman actually benefited from the ruling. Although he argued that he was being disadvantaged by a gain in NP relative to GN stock, this trend reversed during the big rise in railroad stocks during 1905–6; ironically, millions of dollars in GN profits were put into the pockets of the man who had tried so hard to undermine that very road.

Thus, Jim Hill's attempt to merge and monopolize the three premier railroads of the Northwest crashed in failure. Perhaps, though, it is more accurate, considering his entire strategy— dating back to securing control of the NP and the Burlington in 1901—to term the attempt instead as a long-term success blunted by a final setback. For Hill was quite correct in noting that the same group of investors still held firm control of all three roads. Their only frustration, admittedly a major one, was their inability to consolidate the roads. This marked a highly significant defeat, but it did not negate the tremendous aggregation of power and profitability that Hill and his partners had achieved during the first four years of the new century—as the coming decade would amply demonstrate.

CHAPTER 7

The Baron of the Northwest

ENTERING the final, busy decade of his life after the Northern Securities affair, James J. Hill, now in his mid-sixties, seemed more than ever larger than life, a flesh-and blood monument to unrestrained, nineteenth-century capitalism. Some viewed his awesome might negatively; according to Brooks Adams, Hill commandeered the Northwest region "precisely as a Roman proconsul might have plundered a conquered province." Others were kinder; John Kimberly Mumford wrote about Hill, the "Old Man of the North," in *Harper's Weekly* in 1908: "The manner in which the Great Northern Railway reflects his personality, with all its diversifications, is one of the most interesting things to be encountered in the study of American institutions and conditions. Save in a purely statistical way it is impossible to dissociate the man from his creation . . . a virile anachronism—a one-man railroad, and the only one remaining since Sam Sloan and Collis P. Huntington passed away from the field of their great accomplishment."

The accuracy of Mumford's depiction was all the more striking in that it coincided with Hill's formal departure from the positions of leadership he had held for so long. In 1907, the same year that the various Great Northern subsidiaries were reorganized into "one homogenous system," James J. Hill resigned its presidency, a position he had held continuously since 1882. The old man had the double satisfaction of seeing his son Louis succeed him in the position and of being able to note that, in all those twenty-five years, even during the 1893 Panic, GN stockholders had never once failed to receive a dividend on their investment.

He stayed on as chairman of the board for five more years, resigning from this position in 1912, at which time he could remind the loyal shareholders of yet another impressive fact: "At no

Jim Hill and son Louis. Courtesy of James J. Hill Papers, James Jerome Hill Reference Library, Saint Paul, Minnesota.

time have I accepted any salary for my services as President or Chairman of the Board of Directors, since I have felt that I was sufficiently compensated by the increase in the value of the property in which my interest has always been large." To Jim Hill, the remarkably high salaries of corporate executives in modern America, and the "golden parachutes" that sometimes cap them off, would have seemed unthinkable.

The fact was, of course, that Hill actually relinquished only some of the strategic and detailed control of the road that he had held so tightfistedly over the years—a fact that stoic son Louis accepted with little apparent discomfort. True enough,

James Hill did now have a broadly based administrative support system that liberated more of his time. But, given the sweeping vistas that opened before him, his unabated understanding of the industry, his status, and his love of immersing himself in the details of railroading, it was simply inevitable that he would continue to hover over his giant creation, even after the 1912 "retirement."

One reason the grizzled railroader could not retire was simply that the new opportunities to amalgamate, assimilate, and expand his new empire were too inviting. For instance, for more than a decade preceding 1907, the year in which Louis replaced him, Hill and his associates had been steadily gathering all their railroads and other assets under the broad umbrella of the GN. Now, in July of that year, they completed the formal GN purchase of all assets of fourteen separate corporate affiliates; and in November they added the old Manitoba itself, which had been leased. During the ten years preceding 1907, the GN had issued $125 million in new shares. Its capitalization per mile of track was very low, compared with that of other railroads, and its annual net income averaged about $17 million. The cadre of GN stockholders was rapidly increasing, and they loved the old man for the 7 percent dividend that he perennially secured for them.

Like all other "robber barons" of the time, Jim Hill had his critics. In 1907, a popular muckraking magazine, the *Outlook*, carried a piece entitled "The Case against the Great Northern," by William L. Snyder. Snyder accused the GN of overcapitalizing, of rate-gouging, and most pointedly, of using its "excessive" earnings to buy up monopolistic control of competing roads instead of improving the line itself, yearly called on to carry more traffic. The GN, said Snyder, had been increasing its mileage less than 1.5 percent annually, whereas business activity along its lines was burgeoning at an annual rate of 10 percent. Rather easily deflecting Snyder's roundhouse charges, Hill's fellow railroad man and Summit Avenue neighbor A. B. Stickney pointed out in a companion article that, in truth, the GN's valuation had indeed more than doubled since 1890 but so too had its trackage— from 3,000 miles to over 6,100. As for Snyder's argument that

Hill should have built a first-class paralleling line to handle the increasing GN traffic, the obvious point was that he had accomplished much the same end by acquiring the NP.

Snyder's attack on Hill and the GN reflected the continuing progressive indictment, especially within Minnesota, of the monopolistic implications of the attempted Northern Securities merger. One court action, pressed by the state attorney general, attempted to forestall the issuance of a new $60 million stock issue until the Minnesota Railroad and Warehouse Commission approved it; another sought to cancel the original Manitoba charter on the grounds that it had been completely subsumed by the GN. In 1905, when the Minnesota legislature enacted a law raising taxes imposed on railroads in the state from 3 to 4 percent, the GN countered by arguing that the Manitoba still legally existed—along with its charter guarantee that it would never be taxed by the state at a rate higher than 3 percent. Well fortified with expensive legal expertise, the GN, like most of its sister roads, managed in this and other cases rather easily to protect itself from regulatory attacks by the states it traversed.

These concerns represented, in Hill's homely analogy, the stings of flies that distracted the old workhorse, but they did not divert him from what had always been and still was his main concern: making and remaking his railroad. One reason he could not bear to leave his position was because so many lifelong efforts now seemed ready to come to fruition. In addition, new technologies were proving exciting and productive.

An example was the powerful new 2-6-6-2 compound Mallet steam locomotives that the GN began mass purchasing in 1906–7, first for mountain crossings and then also for the heavy iron ore tonnages on the Mesabi run. By the time of Hill's death in 1916, these were, in turn, rapidly giving way to the new Baldwin "Mikado" engines, which commanded nearly 61,000 pounds of tractive power. Also by that time, as Ralph Hidy and his coauthors reveal, the GN had increased its fleet of freight cars from 35,000 in 1906 to 56,000 ten years later. The average carrying capacity of these cars had more than doubled, to an average of nearly 38 tons. To the very end, Jim Hill unfailingly applied his lifelong philosophy, by these and many other such applications, of plowing earnings back into improved infrastructure.

Even in old age, Jim Hill loved the laborious, detailed work of increasing efficiency, tasks that most men his age would have gladly passed to others. GN engineers led the field in continuing to press forward the work of moving earth and blasting rock to reduce grades and curves and in installing more durable and reliable trestles and culverts. By 1911, the cumulative grade from Saint Paul all the way to Minot was 0.3 percent, from Whitefish to Havre 0.8 percent, from Havre to Williston 0.4 percent, and from Spokane to Wenatchee 1 percent.

Atop towering Stevens Pass, the GN made its largest investment in cost-per-ton-mile reduction when it built, between 1897 and the close of 1900, the Cascade Tunnel. This 2.6-mile bore, built by up to eight hundred workers at a time, eliminated the terrible sprawl of switchbacks over the summit known as "Death Mountain," taking out nine miles of track, 700 feet of rise, and 2,332 feet of curvature and bringing the approaching grades on each side to maximums of 2.2 percent.

All of this guaranteed that the GN, which already bested its competitors in line efficiency, would continue to do so. Increased efficiency did not, however, end all of the troubles associated with challenging mountain crossings. In March 1910, a terrible avalanche descended on the west side of Stevens Pass at Wellington and killed 101 people in the worst such incident yet seen in the history of the West. This and other accidents would prompt the building of an even longer tunnel in 1929; at eight miles, it was the longest in the Western Hemisphere.

Simple statistics graphically demonstrate the wide margin of the GN's competitive superiority. Whereas back in the early days, in 1881, the Manitoba had charged an average rate of 2.88 cents per ton-mile, by the inflationary year of 1907, the rate stood at .77 cents. These rates derived, of course, mainly from the heavy tonnages that GN trains could carry over excellent and easy roadbeds. During the twelve years following 1893, Jim Hill nearly doubled the tonnages carried on his GN trains, whereas those carried by his competitors increased by only one-half. And by then, the average tonnages of his trains amounted to 447, compared with 339 on the NP—already being reconfigured to resemble its sister road—325 on the Southern Pacific, 378 on Edward H. Harriman's improving UP, 279 on the CP, and 269 on the Santa Fe. As always, attention to and investment in infrastructure formed one of the two core elements in mapping strategy for the GN.

The other core element lay, as always, in meeting and besting the regional competition. Now that the NP was under Hill's influence, although not under his outright control, that long-term competitor presented few problems; but two others, the UP and the CP, continued to bother Hill, as did yet another westward-building transcontinental, the Milwaukee Road.

Unlike its main rival, the Burlington, which chose the merger route, the Chicago, Milwaukee, and Saint Paul took the risky gambit of building its own tracks to the Pacific. President Albert Earling and the Milwaukee directors, who included Harriman's ally William Rockefeller, of Standard Oil, figured that, with a modest indebtedness of $116 million and annual earnings over three times the amount required to service interest on the estimated construction cost of $60 million, they could pull it off.

Thus, beginning work in the fall of 1906, construction gangs pressed rapidly westward from Mobridge, on the Missouri River in northern South Dakota, across central Montana between the NP and the GN lines, and then paralleled the NP route via Butte and Spokane to Seattle. The line to Seattle, nearly fourteen hundred miles long, was completed by the spring of 1909, and its midportion across the Rockies soon became the longest electrified expanse of railroad in the world.

Jim Hill seemed to be unruffled by the intrusion of yet another transcontinental rival through the heartland of his realm; he repeatedly commented that the fast-growing region could easily support another road. Speaking in Seattle in 1908, he publicly advised the Milwaukee: "By all means build to the Coast; extend your road—if you do not, somebody who has more enterprise than you will take the business and will keep it on their rails and you will have to fight to get a share of it."

And he seemed actually to mean what he said, since he was positioned to block or at least hinder the Milwaukee's progress and failed to do so. For example, lying astride the railroad's projected route through central Montana was the Jawbone Railroad—so named because its builder, Richard Harlow, frequently relied more on promises than on hard cash in dealing with his workers. The Jawbone presented the Milwaukee either with a vital part of its main line or, conversely, with the necessity of a costly detour. Hill held a mortgage on the heavily indebted Jawbone and thus could keep it away from his rival; but strangely, whether from neglect or indifference, he did not do so. In 1909, while Hill was in England, the Milwaukee simply funded the Jawbone to pay off the mortgage and then took it over. The Minnesotan was angry at being outflanked, but in any event, he did not seem to be terribly threatened by the invading road.

One reason for his lack of concern may have been that, from the date of its completion, the Milwaukee, now rechristened the Chicago, Milwaukee, Saint Paul, and Pacific, had faced greater challenges than it could handle. It was built late, during a time of rising costs, and its construction bills ballooned to an astronomical $257 million; and like the other western roads, it now faced a new competitor in the ships that were crossing the Panama Canal. It also faced the enmity of the combined "Hill lines," which railroad historian John Stover aptly described as a "very vicious competition." Thus the Milwaukee would prove a weak competitor to the Hill lines, and once hard times set in, it would falter and then buckle under a series of bankruptcies.

Hill's larger competitive worries came from two longtime adversaries, the CP and the UP. Now that his old allies Donald Smith and George Stephen had long since departed the CP, Jim Hill's relationship with the Canadian road was purely adversarial, with no one to mediate differences; and William Van Horne's successor, Thomas Shaughnessy, proved equally as uncompromising as his predecessor. These final international struggles took place on both sides of the boundary, and even more than the

earlier ones, they proved to be unproductive and even embarrassing to both parties—the final, futile spasms of a blood feud in
which the real stakes had given way to sheer emotional enmity.

Jim Hill's attempts to confront the CP on its own territory
sputtered out during these closing years of the rivalry. He now
had lines, both of the GN and of the NP, probing into Manitoba,
all the way to Winnipeg; but although these tracks forced the CP
to keep its rates down, they yielded Hill's roads little profit. And
his blustering about building a rival line from Vancouver to Winnipeg frightened no one in particular, since such a move was
clearly beyond even his ken or self-interest. CP officials dismissed
this threat as "pure wind"; observing the rivalry from retirement, Hill's old foe Van Horne cagily commented: "I don't
know what Mr. Hill's plans are. I know that he is a very able man,
and when he talks about doing what is clearly a foolish thing, it is
safe to assume that it is a cover to something which is not foolish." In this case, Hill was simply trying to get the CP off his
back.

Similarly, his incursion into the remote mining region of the
lonely forests out west in British Columbia, an incursion under-
taken to look for hostages in his war with the CP, now sputtered
out in indebtedness. He continued pressing his Vancouver, Victoria, and Eastern Railway eastward into the remote West Kootenay mining district; and when the line reached the town of
Princeton in 1909, he enjoyed a good laugh as the local folks
renamed the Similkameen River the "Jimhillameen." But as anyone could see, there was little here for him. Despite the attacks of
the regional population, who resented the CP's economic colonialism and its neglect of them, the CP simply drove its Kettle
Valley Railway into the area to checkmate Hill. And by linking to
the north-building Spokane International Railway, the CP constructed an allied connection that could match Hill's own connection between the Vancouver, Victoria, and Eastern and the
Spokane and Northern.

Thus, although the Americans could tap the interior of British
Columbia from Spokane, they could not truly pry economic control of it away from Vancouver, the CP, and Canada. In 1916, the

year of Hill's death, the GN had over $36 million tied up in its Canadian capers, and hardly any of these pursuits were paying a dividend. Within three years of his death, the GN would sell the Vancouver, Victoria, and Eastern and begin phasing down its investments in British Columbia. As Ralph Hidy and his coauthors conclude, "Clearly when the Empire Builder made an unsound investment decision, he made a big one."

The CP, with its government support, proved able once again to cause Jim Hill much more trouble on his turf than he could render them on theirs. In 1905, the CP's Soo Line drove a westward extension, its "Wheat Line," directly into the heartland of the GN, from Thief River Falls, Minnesota, to Kenmare, North Dakota, invading the strategic area lying between the GN and the Canadian border. In so doing, the Soo was touching Hill where he was tender.

Ever cost-conscious, Hill had built few spur lines north into these remote reaches, leaving farmers the choice of either continuing to haul their grain to the nearest elevator by wagon or trying—usually futilely—to build their own branch lines. Indeed, Hill had left himself doubly vulnerable to such inroads through his political alienation from North Dakota, whose liberal regulatory and taxation policy and prairie radicalism he had long denounced. Back in 1898, he had announced that he would henceforth curtail investments in a state "where the disposition of its officers" was "to confiscate the investment already made."

In directing this momentous thrust into GN territory, Shaughnessy and Soo president Edmund Pennington pursued a real opportunity for new business, not just an attempt to twist the tail of James J. Hill. But they failed to anticipate the toughness of his response, as well as that of son Louis, who was moving into his presidential position and was eager to prove his own mettle. When Pennington refused to back off, Louis first threatened full-scale war on all fronts and then began the more sensible strategy of simply forging spur lines northward from the main GN line into the disputed territory.

Clearly, though, these spurs would not suffice to hold the North Dakota northern tier within the GN realm in the face of a direct Soo invasion; and so, finally, in 1910 the Hills announced a grander strategy that would kill two birds with one stone. They would construct a new and better line westward to Minot, north of the current main line. This new road, the "Surrey Cutoff," would both improve and shorten the main line and, lying for the most part within twenty miles of the Soo's Wheat Line, would take it on head to head. With the veteran firm of A. Guthrie doing the construction for the GN's subsidiary Dakota and Great Northern Railway, the Surrey Cutoff took shape during 1911–12 at a cost of $9 million. But the Soo Line struck back with another line of its own, the Fordville-Drake extension, which wormed its way into the territory between the old and the new GN lines. New prairie towns, with their cathedral-like grain elevators and their webs of farm-to-market roads radiating outward, sprouted like mushrooms along the new stretches of track.

This corporate jousting, so military in style, seemed likely to go on indefinitely. In 1912, the Soo grandiosely projected an extension far to the west, either a road through Lewistown, in central Montana, and possibly on to a linkage with a southward extension of the CP somewhere in the Rockies, or even a crossing of the Rockies via the tortuous Clearwater drainage and Lewiston, Idaho, and a road all the way to the Pacific Coast via the Snake and Columbia river systems. Facing this threat to add yet another line to the terrain between the NP and the GN, the Hills countered with a plan of their own: the "New Rockford West Extension," reaching from New Rockford, North Dakota, also to Lewistown, which already lay at the end of a GN spur line that would soon reach all the way from Great Falls to Billings.

In this orgy of overbuilding, however, reality had to intervene sometime, and it did in 1913, as both railroads called off their building plans for western North Dakota and east-central Montana. "North Dakota's railway war of 1905," as historian John C. Hudson aptly called it, ground to a halt. Viewed in context, it was not unique but was rather an illuminating chapter in the final proliferation of lines and spurs that built—and overbuilt—the American rail system to its peak mileage in 1916. As Hudson notes in his studies of the period, most of the mileage constructed along the Wheat Line and the Surrey Cutoff and most of the more than fifty towns and hamlets that arose along them are still there today. But the economic lethargy that has fallen on them, and on the entire northern plains region, presents a sad and ironic counterpoint to the boom atmosphere of eighty years ago.

Meanwhile, a far greater conflict arose to the west with another established rival of both the NP and the GN, Harriman's burgeoning Union Pacific. The question here involved a classic turf issue. The UP's primary dockage lay at Portland, Oregon, accessed by the old Oregon Railway and Navigation Company's tracks along the south bank of the Columbia River. Since the NP and the GN both had lines running to Puget Sound in Washington to the north, and since the UP and the NP both had a north-south line running between Portland and Puget Sound, two sets of issues naturally arose.

On the one hand, the UP eyed the traffic lying north of the Columbia in Washington, whereas the NP and the GN looked longingly southward into Oregon. On the other hand, the really meaningful issue lay in the trade triangle formed by Spokane on the east, Seattle-Tacoma on the north, and Portland on the south. Could, and would, the adversaries—even now, fighting over the Burlington and the NP—establish a community of interest here, or would they once again go to war?

In several face-to-face meetings with Harriman, even before 1900, Jim Hill had argued for an apportionment of traffic within the triangle; but neither side really tried very hard to accomplish such a prickly task. In the meantime, the aggressive Hill pined for lines southward into Oregon—both into the wet, fertile and densely settled Willamette Valley to the west, served by Harriman's Southern Pacific extension northward from California to Portland, and into the arid lands of east-central Oregon, which were less agriculturally productive than the rich farmlands of eastern Washington.

Speaking expansively at the Lewis and Clark Centennial Exposition at Portland in 1905, Hill received a "mighty ovation" and pointedly commented that he wanted to "help with the development of this great state." He told the Portlanders that, if they could deepen the channel of the Columbia to more than thirty-two feet, he would bring them ocean steamships, and he promised them "a road of such character" as had not "been built west of the Rocky Mountains, of low gradients and slight curvature." He added, "It will be completed ready for trains to enter Portland by a year from Christmas." The *Oregonian* reflected local feelings of neglect by responding, "Oregon is at last free from the Harriman thraldom."

In fact, over the preceding five years, Jim Hill had been surreptitiously buying up access routes, facilities, and properties within the "City of Roses." The key to the situation lay along both banks of the mighty Columbia, the access from the interior, through its breathtakingly beautiful gorge, to Portland and the sea. Even though the UP-controlled OR&N claimed the more strategic and more open south bank, Hill continually pointed out to Harriman and to others the feasibility of building a better line along the rocky north bank, on the Washington side, for as little as $5 million. This promised to be a better and cheaper access, he argued, than could be had by coming to terms with the OR&N.

Hill's instrument to build along the "north bank" route would be the newly chartered Portland and Seattle Railway, soon rechartered as the Spokane, Portland, and Seattle (SP&S). Jointly owned by the NP and the GN, and christened "The Northwest's Own Railway," the SP&S would build a new line eastward from Portland along the north bank of the Columbia and then would depart the north-bending Columbia at Pasco-Kennewick in southern Washington via a new line northeast to Spokane. With both the NP and the GN main lines connecting the latter city to Puget Sound, and with the NP's already existing line joining Portland to the Sound, the SP&S would thus join the three sides of the trade triangle.

Anticipating the threat, Harriman had already begun an attempt to block his adversary on the north bank, surveying a line there for two companies he called the Columbia Valley and the Cascade railroads and buying up strategic properties. His crews even began tunnel work at strategic Cape Horn. Harriman succeeded in forcing Hill into extensive litigation, but his ploy was so transparently one of obstruction that it could not succeed.

In the meantime, Jim Hill managed to obtain from Congress eminent-domain land certificates for right-of-way; in Congress, his ally North Dakota Senator Henry Hansbrough provided valuable assistance as chairman of the Senate Public Lands Committee. By the spring of 1906, armies of grading crews spread out along the north bank, building a high-quality line in an expensive hurry. UP crews still harassed them, for instance by attempting to occupy strategic Cascade Locks, and there were even some scuffles; but clearly the SP&S was now destined to succeed.

The Spokane, Portland, and Seattle was speedily and well constructed. In March 1908, the golden spike was hammered into the ground at Cascade Locks on the main portion of the line, from Kennewick westward to Vancouver, Portland's sister city on the north bank of the river. Vancouver would serve as the primary freight depot, but the line also spanned the Columbia by bridge, connecting to Portland's North Bank Station; further trackage ran downstream to the deep-water port of Astoria, which could handle the new super ships that, as we shall soon see, Hill was developing. In 1909, the eastward extension of the SP&S was completed northeastward to Spokane.

As for the Portland-Seattle span, Hill never intended to build it; rather, he would simply double-track the existing NP line. The SP&S proved to be the superb line that Jim Hill had promised; in fact, it was the best road he had ever built. It had gentle curvature and very good gradation, with maximum lifts of 3 percent. But it also proved to be frightfully expensive, with the most costly mileage, through the Columbia Gorge, exceeding $100,000 per mile, in addition to the cost of tunneling. To the consternation of such key financial partners as Gaspard Farrer, the final price tag exceeded $40 million.

Jim Hill faced further frustration with his costly new railroad. To his disappointment, he found that his managers on both the NP and the GN continued to route their westbound freight via the straightaway main lines over the high Cascades rather than down the dearly constructed water-level route to Vancouver,

Portland, and points north and south. He also found that the hardheaded new managers he had moved into the NP, men like Howard Elliott, did not hesitate to stand up to him in defending their railroad against shouldering an unfair proportion in the joint ownership arrangement of the SP&S. Finally, to get things in order, he persuaded his brilliant stalwart employee John F. Stevens—who had left the GN to take over for a time the direction of the slowly building Panama Canal—to come back and put the new railroad in order.

In one sense, however, the great old war-horse had once again succeeded with the SP&S: he now stood poised to move four-square into Harriman's central Oregon domain and perhaps beyond that, farther south even into the promised land of California. Since Harriman's Southern Pacific held a firm lock on the Willamette Valley to the west, Jim Hill seized on the Deschutes River, flowing northward into the Columbia along the eastern drainage of the Cascades through central Oregon, as his best avenue of invasion. High upstream, in the shadows of the Cascade summits, lay the small city of Bend, and this became his primary strategic destination.

From there he could, if events should seem fortuitous, project his line on a long grade downhill to the south, on to Klamath Falls and perhaps even to a linkup with George Gould's new Western Pacific line through northern California. Interestingly, the aridity of the hills along the Deschutes did not seem to dampen his enthusiasm for the agricultural potential of the area or to deter his irrepressible ambition—a harbinger of troubles to come. He seemed to look past such pragmatic concerns, driven by the ambition to extend his empire and probably to repay Harriman for past wrongs, and assumed that he could make even this apparent desert "blossom as the rose."

A derelict, projected line, called the Oregon Trunk Line, lay along the Deschutes route, and Hill's man Stevens quietly secured its charter. Stealthily, using assumed names and staying in fleabag hotels and inns, Stevens then journeyed through the area, buying up key parcels of land for the road. Harriman, whose minions had made some effort to secure this corridor, quickly caught on and fought back, contesting the validity of the Trunk Line charter and forming his own line, the Deschutes Railroad, to compete with it.

Construction gangs of both sides—each numbering over twenty-five hundred workers, those of Hill commanded by the Porter Brothers firm and those of Harriman by the Tuohy Brothers—fanned out facing each other across the river. The crunch came in the narrow defile of the Deschutes Canyon, which afforded access for only one road. Imaginative "Wild West" historians have dubbed the ensuing contest the "Deschutes Canyon War," but in fact this "war," like most others on the frontier, was really no war at all. Construction crews did scuffle with one another on occasion, aiming curses, stones, and even dynamite at each other and rendering some casualties. But clearly, the stakes here did not warrant a war.

And then suddenly, in September 1909, Edward Harriman fell ill and died of stomach cancer at age sixty-two, removing Hill's most dangerous adversary and depersonalizing the issue. Jim Hill sent no condolences to the Harriman family, commenting mercilessly that the fallen adversary had been "trying to carry a load bigger than he could bear" with his far-flung empire.

Before his demise, though, this fierce competitor left Jim Hill other worries for the future. In 1908 Harriman had directed the building of a UP spur north from Saint Anthony, in southeastern Idaho, up to West Yellowstone, Montana, there to siphon off some of the growing tourist trade that the NP was garnering from Yellowstone National Park. This western portal to Yellowstone would eventually grow to become the main entrance to the park.

Much more menacingly, Harriman also backed the veteran plunger and UP man Robert Strahorn, whose North Coast Railroad sought to weave a web of rails across the state of Washington with Yakima at its center, thus siphoning off trade from the NP and the GN into UP hands. Years later in 1914, this line, now gathered into the UP's Oregon-Washington Railroad and Navigation Company, finally overcame the opposition of the Hills and built into Spokane, where a grand new Union Station was erected and shared with another Hill adversary, the Milwaukee Road.

Under the leadership of "Judge" Robert Lovett, Harriman's smooth confidant and protégé, the UP quickly came to terms with the Hill lines in joint usage of the line through the Deschutes Canyon. In fact, although the NP-GN forces seemed to have the upper hand, the UP-Deschutes Railroad actually had them checkmated by holding control of a key homestead at "Mile 75," where the Oregon Trunk Line had to cross the river. Thus, the two sides agreed the following spring to build the final fifty-three miles jointly into Bend. Incongruously symbolizing this forced marriage was a little town along the track improbably named "Hillman" after the two remorseless competitors who could never suffer one another. Its name was later changed, appropriately, to a less contrived and more cheerful "Terrebonne."

Functioning as a property of the Spokane, Portland, and Seattle, the Oregon Trunk Line was completed in 1911, bridging the Columbia from the SP&S at Wishram, Washington, on the north bank and extending south to The Dalles on the Oregon side and then on to Bend. Speaking to an enthusiastic crowd in October at Bend while driving home the golden spike, Jim waxed warmly about the virtues of bringing population and prosperity to this remote locale. He did not seem to mind when someone in the crowd exuberantly shouted out, "I have known you since 1858 and you are the best man that ever lived, Mr. Hill."

For the time being, the forlorn spur road, which the NP and the GN interestingly advertised as the "Inside Gateway"—seemingly to California as well as south-central Oregon—did not probe on toward California. But Jim Hill simultaneously made yet another move in that direction in 1910 by acquiring the Oregon Electric Railway. This little road, which the Southern Pacific had not dared to acquire for fear of antitrust prosecution, headed southward up the populous Willamette Valley from Portland to Albany; and Hill soon built it farther south to Eugene.

Although Hill's railroads stood poised to strike on southward into southern Oregon and California, they failed to do so during the few remaining years of his life. For one thing, the Southern

Pacific, divorced from Harriman's UP by court action in 1913, defensively beefed up its system there; and for another, an NP-GN extension to a San Francisco connection would have probed well beyond the boundaries of what Hill normally liked to define as his regional domain.

Eventually, during the 1920s, as Don Hofsommer has shown, the ICC would permit the Oregon Trunk Line to use a combination of its own new lines and those of the Southern Pacific to access Klamath Falls, Oregon, and ultimately, in 1931, Bieber, California, on the Western Pacific line. Thus Hill's dream of an "Inside Gateway" from the Pacific Northwest to San Francisco would materialize long after his death. But, like the foray into British Columbia, this thrust far beyond the Columbia would prove extraneous and unprofitable, a prime example of overconstruction during the heady and competitive days that characterized the apex of railroad construction in America.

The efforts to strengthen and expand the contours of the Hill railroad domain actually counted for less, in the long run, than did those to build up the economy within it. As always, Jim Hill focused his attention on enhancing the output of natural products, knowing that such growth would directly enhance the profits of his railroads. During these halcyon years, he paid special heed to his favorite nonrailroad enterprise, agriculture, and also to two industries that had attracted him back in the 1890s, lumbering and iron ore, all with considerable reward. However, his other new enterprise of the 1890s, maritime transportation, ended in failure. Interestingly, the relatively new thrust of his railroads during these years—into tourism—owed less to his efforts than to those of his son Louis.

Of all the growth industries in the Northwest during these prosperous years of the early twentieth century, lumbering was the most spectacular, and James J. Hill's role in fostering its rise was considerable. As noted earlier, he had already begun its promotion a decade earlier, motivated especially to fill the ladings of eastbound boxcars that would otherwise return home mostly empty. Succeeding in that, he now turned to truly big-time promotion, encouraging his prosperous lumbermen friends from the Great Lakes region to begin transferring their bases of operations from the cutover woodlands of the Upper Midwest to the wondrous and barely tapped old-growth forests of the Pacific Northwest.

The foremost of these was his close friend and Summit Avenue neighbor Frederick Weyerhaeuser, one of America's premier lumbermen. A reclusive German immigrant, Weyerhaeuser had made a fortune in his well-managed logging businesses in Wisconsin and Minnesota and had thoroughly directed his brood of offspring into the system. For years, he had listened to and absorbed Hill's speeches about the virtues of the bountiful old-growth forests of the Pacific Northwest. Now, he finally succumbed to the compelling bargain his friend offered him, after Hill had triumphed in securing a dominant voice in the affairs of the NP and its still sizable land grant.

After organizing his Sound Lumber Company in 1899, Weyerhaeuser inked his name the following year to one of the largest and most advantageous land transactions in American history. For a purchase price of six dollars per acre—roughly a dime per thousand board feet of wood—he received, through Hill's auspices, title to nine hundred thousand acres of prime woodlands from the NP land grant in Washington. Soon his acreage had ballooned to two million acres. By 1913, incredibly enough, his Weyerhaeuser Timber Company owned over 26 percent of the privately held timber stands in Washington. Together with the NP, Weyerhaeuser came to own nearly 46 percent of the nongovernment-held woodlands of Washington and, together with the Southern Pacific, over 22 percent of those in neighboring Oregon.

Weyerhaeuser's acquisitions marked a highly significant movement of the center of gravity in American lumbering from the Great Lakes to the Pacific Northwest. Some observers considered his move a gamble, since huge distances from eastern markets threatened to eat up the profits to be made in virgin timber stands; but Hill's preferential rates offset much of that risk. Soon, lumber camps and mills dotted the slopes of the Cascades, and the world's largest lumber mill took shape at Everett, Washington, where the GN met the sea. From an initial capacity of twenty-eight million board feet per year in 1902, the mill expanded to a capacity of seventy million by 1912.

Hill also enticed other Minnesota notables to the forests of western Washington, men such as former Minnesota Governor David Clough, whom he escorted out in his private car in 1902. Clough, assisted by his son-in-law, future Washington Governor Roland Hartley, also established a cluster of profitable lumber companies around Puget Sound: the Clark-Nickerson Lumber, Clough-Hartley, and Clough-Whitney companies. The huge mills of these and other concerns made Everett a hub of the American lumber business.

The Northwest lumber boom soon moved also into the interior of the region. Weyerhaeuser had a hand in nine companies working the lush white pine forests of the Idaho panhandle, among them Boise Payette, the forerunner of today's Boise Cascade. Here too, hundreds of camps and small mills dotted the landscape, and Potlatch became the familiar, dreary company town. The impact of all this was truly enormous. Even by 1905, Washington had shot upward to become the nation's leading lumber state. Oregon, whose beautiful stands of old-growth timber in its southwestern quadrant attracted development more slowly, ranked second, eventually replacing Washington as first.

The Pacific Northwest reached a peak of production before the World War I boom in 1913, with a harvest of 7.46 billion board feet; by then, over 90 percent of the producers had joined together in the West Coast Lumbermen's Association. Jim Hill could, and did, take much satisfaction in these developments. Although the pendulum swing of lumber supremacy from the Great Lakes plain to the far Northwest was, in hindsight, inevitable, he made it happen, both by the risky granting of preferential rates and by his inimitable personal persuasion.

At the other end of the line, another natural product, iron, developed less spectacularly than did lumber; but it meant even more to the Hills and their railroads, since they profited not only by carrying but also by owning and mining it. After personally acquiring a sizable acreage of Mesabi Range properties, Jim Hill had proceeded, astutely, to share them with the GN stockholders at cost by gathering them into a legally separate but actually GN-controlled firm called Lake Superior Company, Limited, in 1900. This arrangement was necessitated by the GN charter provision that prohibited it from acquiring mining properties. Now, he proceeded rapidly to develop the properties and the rail facilities to serve them.

Hauling such massive iron ore tonnage southeast from the Mesabi area 107 miles to Duluth-Superior on Lake Superior perfectly fit the Hill system of efficient mass transportation over well-engineered roadbeds. His only regret here lay in the unavoidable necessity of carrying back empty cars to the point of origin. GN engineers soon had multiple-track lines along the route reduced to maximum grades of 0.2 percent.

Larger and larger locomotives were adapted to the route until, in 1912, the 2-6-6-2 engines, first used in the western mountain crossings, were fitted with 22,000-gallon tenders and sent down the tracks to Allouez Bay, where new concrete-steel dock-storage facilities were added to the old facilities, building to a massive, 378,000-ton capacity. To the boss's enormous satisfaction, these steam-powered giants were soon pulling average columns of 175 cars and nearly 15,000 tons apiece in round-trips barely exceeding ten hours. Rail observer Duncan Kerr marveled, "The movement of iron ore from the Mesabi Range to Allouez is probably the greatest mass transportation job in the country."

Meanwhile, the Hills continued acquiring ore-bearing lands in the Mesabi until, by 1906, their holdings totaled more than sixty-five thousand acres. In that year, Jim Hill terminated the Lake Superior Company, Limited, and replaced it with a new firm, Great Northern Ore Properties, which, like its predecessor, stood apart from the GN but was controlled by its corporate family and paid dividends exclusively to its shareholders. These dividends now swelled to awesome proportions when Great Northern Ore Properties promptly signed an agreement with J. P. Morgan's new supertrust, U.S. Steel, whereby the steel giant would pay a hefty lease to extract ores from its lands.

U.S. Steel maintained its lease arrangement with Great Northern Ore Properties for eight years, from 1907 until 1915, when it canceled the lease by prearrangement out of fear of federal antitrust prosecution. As Hill commented, U.S. Steel had ample reason to fear such prosecution—"buck fever," as he put it—since the supertrust now controlled three-fourths of the Mesabi at a time when that region produced two-thirds of the iron used in the United States. During the eight-year lifetime of the lease, Great Northern Ore Properties distributed $9.75 million to stockholders of the railroad.

Although Hill received much acclaim, which he deserved, for turning these properties over to the GN stockholders, this arrangement aroused considerable and predictable controversy. The railroad was legally barred from owning mineral lands; but its profits had purchased these properties, its officers controlled them, and its shareholders banked the profits. This arrangement, furthermore, secluded the large revenue stream of iron ore earnings from the valuation of the GN and thus from the calculations of state regulators and tax authorities. Minnesota politicians, particularly a select committee of the legislature, bemoaned this situation but could do little about it.

On top of all that, the GN made enormous profits on carrying the huge ladings of iron ore to Allouez Bay. As historian Joseph Wilmer Thompson astutely described the situation: "By 1911 iron ore was furnishing over 50 percent of the Great Northern's total traffic, whereas grain contributed approximately ten per cent. . . . [I]n 1911 the Great Northern Railway Company, with over 7,000 miles of railroad, was receiving about 50 per cent of its traffic tonnage from the approximately five per cent of its lines devoted to ore traffic."

With the best-graded and most efficient system, the GN supplanted all rivals to become the main Mesabi carrier by 1911, and the profits mushroomed accordingly. If critics at the time were correct—that the GN rate of eighty cents per ton was at least twenty cents too high—then they were also correct that the railroad made $7 million in "excess" profits between 1907 and 1911. In any case, this most intensively capitalized and utilized segment of Jim Hill's rail empire proved to be an enormous cash cow, and it would remain so for many years into the future.

Not everything, however, that this remarkable man initiated led to success. A number of his lesser investments ended in failures, and so did at least one of his major undertakings. When Jim Hill first ventured into maritime commerce between Puget Sound and the Orient, he fully planned soon to increase his commitment, applying the same philosophy of heavy tonnages moved at low cost that had served him so well in rails. Thus, while he continued his carrying agreement with the Japanese line Nippon Yusen Kaisha, he now set about the high-risk task of constructing his own line of steamships to enter the business directly. The ships would haul his region's basic commodities, along with some manufactures, across the sea to the beckoning markets of Asia, bringing back silk and other imports to the United States. He did so confidently, since he had been running big steamships on the Great Lakes for years.

Jim Hill at first planned four giant ships for his Great Northern Steamship Company, but he backed off to two at the time of commissioning early in 1900. The first to be constructed was the *Minnesota,* which his daughter Clara christened with the customary champagne bottle while forty thousand people looked on in April 1903; the second was the *Dakota.* Built to carry well over twenty thousand tons of freight, with five acres of tonnage space, as well as two hundred first-class passengers, these were for a time the largest ships of their day.

When the *Minnesota* made its maiden voyage in 1905, it laded twenty-six thousand tons of Hill's favorite export commodities: lumber from the Northwest, copper from the Rockies, and cotton from the South via the Burlington connection. Return ladings were less reassuring, although imports of silk did prove remunerative as special, high-speed trains rushed them eastward from Seattle. Unfortunately, though, the size of the ships meant that they traveled slowly and were capable of only four round-trips per year.

Almost from the outset, Hill found his maritime venture, which proved so dissimilar from his railroad experience, a source of unending frustration. Wealthy travelers proved reluctant to book passage on such slow vessels, and Japanese and other competitors could outbid even him with their government subsidies. The Minnesotan pleaded for similar export subsidies from his own government, to no avail; but in truth, he faced a far greater governmental frustration than this one. Once again, the culprit was the ICC, which ruled in February 1904 that railroads must publish both their domestic and their export rates, a requirement that left them totally vulnerable to fully informed foreign competitors. Hill blamed this edict for the collapse of his flour exports to Asia and plaintively commented, "I would rather undertake to build a thousand miles of railway than to build two ships."

Even by the time the *Minnesota* was launched, Jim Hill was already contemplating a retreat from his shipping enterprise, clearly seeing the handwriting on the wall in the form of subsidized foreign competition and impossible federal regulations. Disaster then hastened his decision when, due to captain's error, the *Dakota* struck a reef off the coast of Japan, broke up, and sank, the largest vessel ever lost at sea. Hill proceeded to sell off the smaller NP liners *Trenton* and *Shawmut,* for the same competitive and regulatory reasons, finally leaving only the *Minnesota* at work. This old ship, badly needing repair, worked on until World War I, when the U.S. War Shipping Board took possession of it as part of the government's effort to create an instant maritime fleet in 1917–18, and the ship did yeoman work in transporting troops and materiel across the Atlantic while avoiding German submarines.

Two years after Hill's death, in 1918, the company sold the *Minnesota,* thus symbolically ending its involvement in ocean transportation, even though the Great Northern Steamship Company lived on as a legal entity until 1927. Also sold were two other ships—the *Great Northern* and the *Northern Pacific*—which had been brought on in 1915 for service in the coast trade from Astoria to San Francisco. These had also failed to make a profit. Like his great adversary Harriman, who had even envisioned joining a Pacific fleet to railroads in Manchuria, Hill the dreamer had been unable to fulfill his lifelong vision of intercontinental transport and global economic development into reality.

This is not to say that his vision was faulty, only that political and economic realities forced him out of that realm and back within the land-bound confines he knew so well.

The promotion of tourism never figured largely in the mind of James J. Hill; he had grown and prospered in the domain of basics—ledgers, bottom lines, ladings, and infrastructure. As he bluntly stated to E. H. Beckler back in 1890, amid the fevered transcontinental construction campaign: "We do not care enough for Rocky Mountain scenery to spend a large sum of money in developing it, either on the Spokane or elsewhere. What we want is the best possible line, shortest distance, lowest grades and least curvature that we can build between the points to be covered."

Yet, in these last years, he followed the lead of his son in this direction. Just as, for obvious reasons, the NP had played a key role in making Yellowstone America's first national park back in the early 1870s, so the GN now played the key role in developing the enchanting mountains astride its northern Montana crossing of the Continental Divide, a process that resulted in the creation of Glacier National Park in 1910.

As early as 1902, Hill put up some funds to build trails from beautiful Lake McDonald to Sperry Glacier and to Gunsight Pass; but much larger investments came from Louis, who clearly saw the potential for rail- and car-bound tourists among the millions of newly affluent Americans. One park historian figured that Louis and the GN "spent almost $10 there for every one spent by the government" in these early days and concluded that Louis Hill "did more than any other to put Glacier National Park on the map." Louis loved the area and took his family there for extended summer outings.

He directed the building of hundreds of miles of roads and trails and many lodges and chalets, including the soaring, fir-logged Glacier Park Lodge in 1913 and the giant Many Glacier Hotel in 1915. Actually, Louis proved to be a more adept promoter than his father. He came up with the mountain goat "Rocky," perched high atop a crag, as the logo of the railroad; he adopted the slogan "See America First," hired artists such as Winold Reiss to paint the local Blackfeet, issued playing cards and me-

mentos with Indian graphics, and even took Indians to Chicago and New York to appeal to impressionable audiences. These promotions soon began to bear demonstrable results. In 1912, the very first year that true hotel-class rooms became available in Glacier, the park drew eleven thousand recorded visitors.

In 1913, Louis Hill came up with yet another promotional idea: an automobile tour from Minneapolis to Glacier Park. That same year, he staged a gala train tour for all twenty-five-year employees of the GN to honor his father on Hill's seventy-fifth birthday. A year later, he incorporated the Glacier Park Hotel Company to manage all the firm's park investments, which now totaled over $2 million annually and included everything from a fleet of White passenger busses and touring boats to hotels and chalets.

By this time, the GN was spending roughly $300,000 annually on tourist promotion, placing Glacier Park promotional materials in the hands of over one hundred thousand people. The railroad also promoted other choice locales along what its bound timetable called the "National Park Route." These included lovely Lake Minnetonka and the Lake Park region in Minnesota, Hayden Lake near Spokane in northern Idaho, which had its own first-class, chalet-style lodge, and Soap and Chelan Lakes in central Washington. Jim Hill's prosaic wheat, ore, and lumber road was entering a new era.

In each of these instances, the Hill railroads acted as basic promoters of economic development, both in their own self-interest and in the interest of the region they served. Agriculture, the pursuit that Jim Hill loved more than all others, except for railroading itself, remained, during the early years of the new century, overwhelmingly the basic industry of the Northwest. Hill, it will be recalled, had long devoted much time and money to its promotion. Now, he mustered the last great thrust of his still formidable energies to an imperial promotion of modern agriculture all across the breadth of his domain, particularly across the semiarid expanse of barely occupied lands in its central portion. For good and bad, this campaign would leave behind one of his most enduring legacies.

A robust, well-established agricultural economy anchored each end of the GN-NP systems. In southern and western Minnesota and the Red River valley, of course, vast fields of corn and wheat provided the bounty that had long fed the coffers of both roads and provided their basic stability. And in the rolling hills of southeastern Washington and north-central Idaho, opened to wheat production in the 1880s, harvests proved so abundant, in parched but remarkably rich volcanic soil, that by 1910 Washington's agricultural economy was based fully 45 percent on wheat, and only North Dakota ranked as a more wheat-reliant state.

The problem with most of the Northwest, as regional boosters like Hill saw it, was that huge swaths of its real estate were arid or semiarid and thus remained devoid of settlement. Across the hundreds of miles of western North Dakota and eastern Montana prairie, only marginal grazing prevailed; and in the true desert of central Washington, even that was impossible. Inveterate frontier promoter-optimists like Jim Hill, however, could not and would not accept the notion that these arid lands lay beyond the reach of agrarian productivity: new technologies could make these lands yield crops. As the new century dawned, two approaches to developing these areas seemed to promise the answer: reclamation and dry farming.

Jim Hill's most direct promotion of irrigated agriculture centered on the town of Wenatchee, which his railroad had spawned along the dry Columbia River foothills in central Washington. Along with Judge Thomas Burke and other lieutenants, he made one effort after another to prime the pump of local development here, for example by arranging the immigration of German Dunkers, who numbered among his favorite farmers, from North Dakota.

More important, the Hill group purchased the bonds of the Wenatchee Water Power Company, the East Wenatchee Land Company, the Washington Canal Company, the Washington Bridge Company, and other budding local enterprises and thereby nurtured their growth. By 1905, thirty thousand acres of apple and other fruit orchards had resulted, and the Wenatchee area showed every promise of reflecting the performance of the NP's citrus domain in the Yakima Valley to the south. To the north, the GN similarly nurtured the West Okanogon Irrigation district, mainly also by buying up its bonds; and by 1916, seven thousand acres were under irrigation there too.

So intensive was the railroad's promotion of Wenatchee and surrounding locales that the prominent publisher and promoter Rufus Woods felt compelled to warn his compatriots, "Fruit men are not always going to get through by leaving it all to God and the Great Northern." The GN brought its first refrigerator cars on line in 1902, and by World War I its famed "Red Ball Express" trains were pounding eastward at record paces and in record numbers. By that time, both Wenatchee and its sister apple capital of Yakima had full-fledged marketing associations; modern packing and storage plants had evolved; and the best citrus lands in the Wenatchee, Yakima, and Okanogan Valleys were yielding $1,000 to $2,000 per acre in annual returns. Washington, by 1917, produced fully 20 percent of the nation's apple production, and wondrous to tell, one of its choicest varieties was the "Jim Hill."

Hill's other favorite irrigation project lay along the Milk River. The valley of this large, east-flowing, northern tributary of the Missouri afforded the GN passage through northern Montana. Like many other regional promoters of the time, he at first believed that federally sponsored reclamation held the only real key to the limited agricultural possibilities of the dry northwestern Great Plains—that broad swaths of the plains might be made to "blossom as the rose" by diverting the few and fragile rivers. Always the pragmatist, he did not oppose but rather favored federal initiative in this sphere, since large-scale reclamation quite clearly lay beyond either state or private capabilities.

Thus, he enthusiastically supported the Newlands Act of 1902, which created what became that mighty engine of federal development, the Bureau of Reclamation. The bureau embraced the Milk River as one of its early projects. To his intense displeasure, the Milk River Project evolved very slowly, however, due both to the laborious workings of the bureaucracy and to the wet cycle of 1909–18, which worked to favor dryland farming and thus to draw away the appeal of reclamation. Hill felt strongly enough about the bureau that he became a tireless critic of its plodding, as well as an advocate of easing the repayment burdens placed on farmers on the irrigated lands. The project eventually watered over ninety thousand acres but did not come to maturity until long after Hill's time.

Hill also favored federal initiative in the form of the Hatch Act of 1889, which provided funding for a network of agricultural experiment stations affiliated with the state land-grant colleges and universities. As these programs slowly gestated within the states of his realm, he quickly adopted policies to collaborate with them, donating 480 acres near Crookston for a branch of the Minnesota Experiment Station, offering farmers free fares for demonstration visitations, and beginning in 1906, providing the experiment stations with supplemental funding directly from the GN and the NP.

The Hill lines now joined the nationwide campaign to create statewide systems of "cooperative extension," which would carry the agricultural know-how thus generated to the dispersed farm population. In 1913, the Burlington Road adopted the novel strategy of offering any of the counties in its service area $150 annually to help support extension agents; and by 1912–14, the GN had established its own private extension network, disseminating publications and information to nearly eight hundred Minnesota and North Dakota farmers. According to Roy V. Scott, "Observers claimed that the Great Northern's effort constituted the largest private system of agricultural extension in the nation." Finally, in 1914, the passage of the federal Smith-Lever Act formed a nationwide system of cooperative extension, in partnership with the states and counties. Here again, the Hill organizations readily embraced the new federal program.

As he always had, Jim Hill contributed to, and networked with, a number of other regional agricultural organizations, drawing Twin Cities business allies along with him. County fairs continued to provide him excellent forums for elaborating his own views. His address to the Minnesota State Fair in 1906, entitled "What We Must Do to Be Fed," was carried in *World's Work* and won considerable acclaim. He loved mixing with people at the fairs, extolling farm life and discussing agriculture as a science; and he especially enjoyed showing his prized Shorthorn-Angus crossbred cattle, which he heralded as a combined dairy and beef breed, even though many professional and other critics panned this idea.

Typical of the state and regional organizations promoted by the Hill lines were the National Soil Fertility League, the West Central Development Association in Minnesota, the Better Farming Association in South Dakota, and the powerful Better Farming Association of North Dakota. The GN pumped $15,000 into the last organization, created in 1911, and the NP and the Soo Line also made major contributions. The Better Farming Association of North Dakota claimed to have direct contact with over 40 percent of all the people in the state.

Year by year, Hill and his railroad organizations assembled an elaborate system of agricultural research and promotion. To the greenhouses erected behind his Summit Avenue mansion, he now added laboratories for soil and plant analysis. To these facilities came specimens from hundreds of sites—361 of them annually by 1913. Among the practical recommendations that resulted from such applied research were continued calls for the use of nitrogen and phosphate fertilizers on northern plains soils.

In 1905, Hill hired Thomas Shaw, a former University of Minnesota specialist in animal husbandry and farm journal editor, to be his chief resident expert. When the GN set forth Shaw's opinions, they unfailingly carried the byline of "Professor," as did the advertisements for his numerous presentations for both the GN and the NP.

The northern railroads' research-promotional programs focused on both livestock and crops. Although concentrating mainly on the latter, Jim Hill continued his personal campaign, begun back in the 1880s, of importing blooded European bulls, as well as sheep and hogs, and distributing them either as gifts or for cheap service fees to improve the stock of farmers along his lines. For example, in 1913–14 alone, he brought in fifty Milking Shorthorn bulls. This undoubtedly did some good, although it could not begin to have much influence on the entire animal population of the area. He also played the key role in forming the American Milking Shorthorn Breeders' Association. Pondering the severe problem of hog cholera in the Midwest, Hill persuaded Abraham Flexner, of the Rockefeller Institute for Medical Research, to create a division of animal pathology, which John D. Rockefeller himself endowed with $1 million and to which Hill contributed $50,000.

The foundation of GN-NP support of crop agriculture lay in a network of model or demonstration farms, an idea pioneered by Seaman Knapp and his associates in the South and urged on Hill by his friend, the distinguished president of the University of Wisconsin, Charles Van Hise. After several initial attempts, Jim Hill sensibly concluded that fundamental research should be left to the state universities and the affiliated state-based experiment stations; the railroads could best muster their energies toward small, five-acre plots that they would lease from farmers and on which they would both demonstrate and test various crops in various soils. On Van Hise's recommendation, Hill hired F. R. Crane, of Wisconsin, to oversee this operation, and Crane soon had 151 such "farms" under lease across Minnesota and North Dakota.

On these demonstration plots, railroad and other experts worked with farmer-owners on a wide variety of experiments, testing tillage methods, fertilizers, seeds, and animal breeds. And from them came many useful recommendations, such as the reliability of durum wheat or of sugar beets for the well-watered bottomlands of the Red River valley, of crested wheatgrass and Sudan grass for high plains grazing lands, or of a corn variety called "Jim Hill," which did not in the end work out well. But experimentation provided no more than half the challenge; the other half involved how to disseminate the knowledge gained, during these years predating the creation of the national Cooperative Extension Service.

As noted, new seed varieties and breeding stock could be and were distributed widely by the railroad divisions and through the time-honored media of county fairs. As early as the late 1890s, the GN had begun using special trains to tour the hinterland, demonstrating the outcomes of research and development. In 1906 came a much larger and more elaborate "agricultural train," which the railroad advertised, interestingly, as an "agricultural college on wheels." Awards for best crops and finished animals also proved alluring: in that same year, the Hills began bestowing such ribboned awards in the amounts of $75–$300 in Minnesota and North Dakota. These ribbons festooned many farm and ranch dwellings and are still proudly shown by the children and grandchildren of those who received them.

The Hill lines promotion of farming entered a new, rapidly accelerated phase in about 1909, for a variety of reasons—all of which combined to foster the last great agrarian land rush in American history, into the semiarid western Great Plains and particularly into the northern plains. For one thing, the Milwaukee Road, completed in 1909, immediately began promoting the lands along its route, particularly the fertile Judith Basin of central Montana. In addition, Congress in that year enacted the Enlarged Homestead Act, which doubled the size of free land grants to 320 acres in selected regions of the arid West, including the plains. These doubled homesteads, which as fate would prove were still much too small for such dry lands, proved powerfully alluring to hard-pressed farmers on much smaller holdings back East. Also, American factories were pouring forth new machinery, such as steam tractors and grain drills, that could more easily work the larger acreages. Most important of all, a heady crusade now arose that took the name of "dry farming" and that made it seem indeed possible to turn the dry rangelands of the western Dakotas and eastern Montana, as well as other subregions like eastern Oregon, into fine croplands.

Apostles of dry farming, like Hardy Campbell, of South Dakota, believed that modern science and technology provided sound methods for raising abundant cereal grains, even in such semiarid locales as the northern plains. Farmers had merely to deep plow, which they could more easily do now with heavy steam-powered tractors, drawing precious moisture to the surface, and then to work the topsoil incessantly, maintaining a dust mulch that would serve to protect the precious moisture from evaporation. Both the NP and the Burlington heeded the fervid

Campbell's message and soon had him at work developing demonstration sites and preaching the message. Having already learned in eastern Washington that reliable rainfalls as minimal as eleven inches annually could produce good crops on fertile lands, the NP now saw a new value in the remaining eleven million acres of its land grant and began promoting the sale of these lands at prices ranging from two to twelve dollars per acre.

James J. Hill was not among the early converts to the gospel of dry farming. Rather, he long tended toward the conventional wisdom that, aside from irrigable lands along widely dispersed stream bottoms, the high plains were mainly suited only for grazing, and marginal grazing at that. Thus, he had long ago cautioned the GN general immigration agent, Max Bass, not to direct European and other farm immigrants west of Minot. Ever the instinctive promoter, though, Hill now made a zealous convert, telling a Bismarck gathering as early as 1903 that the GN was "unwilling to adopt the idea" that North Dakota was "an arid state."

Like his old associate and now U.S. senator from Montana, Paris Gibson, Hill was rethinking things, even to the point of concluding that unrealistic and ineffective giveaway land policies like the Desert Land Act and the Timber Culture Act should be discarded. Only the basic Homestead Act should be maintained, and it should be doubled in size to 320-acre parcels—as in fact it was by congressional action in 1909, with heavy lobbying support from the Hill organizations. Like his farm expert Thomas Shaw, Hill did not buy the most extreme arguments in favor of dry farming; but he did conclude that large portions of the high plains region could, through the new science of agriculture, be farmed productively. Simply put, this born promoter and perennial optimist simply could not abide the notion that these lands, which others called deserts, could not be made productive by his genius and the genius of the American farmer.

Once convinced, Hill as usual took up the cause with a full head of steam. He, son Louis, and their associates Shaw and NP Land Commissioner Thomas Cooper now lent their full support to the Dry Farming Congress, created in 1907 as a society of true believers. In 1909 the congress held a gala conference at Billings, Montana, the key rail hub where the Burlington joined the NP. The Hills showed up in grand style, Louis escorting sixty special guests in a private train and Jim brandishing five silver cups and a $1,000 farming award.

Jim Hill set forth his "Montana Dream," a vision of hitherto barren benchlands and plateaus luxuriant with waving fields of grain; but things turned unpleasant at the conference when he and his son insisted that the term "dry farming" was misleading and should be replaced with the more appropriate title "scientific farming." F. B. Linfield, director of the Agricultural Experiment Station at Montana State College, demurred, as did others, who were then cautioned "not to contradict Mr. Hill." But the Hills proved unable to win this point, and thereafter, they lost interest in the organization, although not in its cause.

The three Hill railroads, joined by the Milwaukee Road, now launched a mighty campaign to promote agricultural settlement in their open lands: primarily eastern Montana and the western Dakotas, as well as the central Oregon region served by the new Oregon Trunk Line and cutover timberlands in northern Minnesota. Their efforts focused both on a massive advertising campaign and on a vastly intensified immigration effort.

Each of the four railroads—the three Hill lines and the Milwaukee Road—sent exhibition trains into the eastern and midwestern states, showcasing the fine cereal grains, cattle, and sheep that could be grown in the Northwest. The railroads blanketed the northern states and northern Europe with posters, such as one by the Milwaukee Road showing a yeoman farmer whose horse-drawn plow opened a furrow across a map of the Northwest, out of which billowed gold coins. Another, by the GN, advertised a remaining 1.5 million acres of railroad land in the Red River valley and Park region. "No state presents a greater combination of advantages for the home-seeker than Minnesota," it grandly proclaimed. "The soil is deep, fertile and productive. It produces No. 1 hard wheat, the best in the world."

Promotional literature, especially from the railroads but also from state and local promoters, deluged eastern America and northern Europe; and it specialized in florid overstatement. The Milwaukee Road petitioned thirty thousand American farmers, claiming among other things that Fergus County in central Montana averaged yields of well over forty bushels per acre, an astronomical exaggeration. And the *Great Northern Bulletin* stated, incredibly enough, that new farms in eastern Montana were "the best in the United States." The *Bulletin* added, "320 acre homesteads are slipping away so rapidly that a young man back east had better wake up before his birthright slips away."

Even hard-nosed James Hill himself surrendered to the euphoria, writing about Montana to a correspondent in 1914: "The yields of most of the cereals are the highest per acre in the country. What she needs now is a larger population . . . it is upon the development of her agriculture that her future depends." He really had come to mean what he said, telling a *New York Sun* reporter in 1913: "Then there's Montana. That's a wonderful state." In a close study of Hill's promotion of Northwest agriculture, Howard Dickman correctly concluded, "Their advertisements, too, fell prey to bias, bombast, Pollyana-testimony, and a tinselly optimism." Like other northern plains drummers, Jim Hill was allowing the lure of a wet cycle and his unrestrained enthusiasm to overcome good sense.

In addition to its agricultural development program, the GN also had a long-standing colonization bureau; in fact, the two were joined into the Department of Agricultural Development in 1917. Based in Chicago, where he could best access the fertile recruiting ground of the Midwest, Hill's old friend Max Bass ran this program until his death in 1909, when his assistant E. C. Leedy replaced him. Now, armed with reams of literature, agents of the Hill lines fanned out in all directions, including northern Europe, where a booming population and a system of primogeniture, which vested family lands in the sole hands of oldest sons, sent thousands of young Norwegians and other nationalities in search of a kindred climate in the New World.

The GN and the NP arranged for the European immigrants to receive low transatlantic fares, which could bring them all the way to Duluth-Superior; and from Saint Paul on to the high

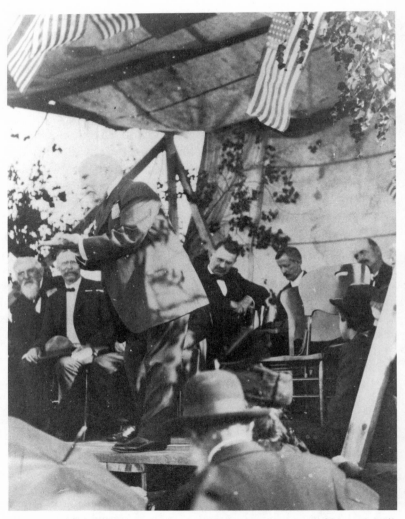
Jim Hill in characteristic exhortation, ca. 1914–15. Courtesy of James J. Hill Papers, James Jerome Hill Reference Library, Saint Paul, Minnesota.

plains, the railroads offered all immigrants even better deals. For rates ranging from $22.50 to $50, homesteaders could rent all or part of a boxcar, in which they could bring all their belongings, livestock, and family. Or, if they could afford it, they could ride in comfortable "Zulu" cars or even motor out in their own Model T Fords or Maxwells.

All these factors together—new farming technologies and methods, an enlarged homestead act, a massive promotion by regional railroads and their allies, commodity prices rising with global demand, and a wet cycle on the northern plains during the years after 1908—produced the last classic land rush in U.S. history. The rush focused especially on the vast eastern two-thirds of Montana and the neighboring and equally semiarid western one-third of North Dakota and adjoining northwestern South Dakota. Of all Jim Hill's major roles in history, his role in this promotion would prove not only the last but also the least fortunate.

The land rush abruptly transformed the new states of North Dakota and Montana. During the years 1898–1916, the GN, the NP, the Milwaukee, and the Soo lines nearly doubled the rail trackage of North Dakota, from 2,662 to 5,226 miles, much of it in the Drift Prairie–Missouri Plateau regions of the arid West; and in 1900, the GN opened its new, enlarged shop complex in Minot. Historian Elwyn Robinson estimates that approximately 250,000 settlers poured into the state during these years and that its overall population more than doubled, from 270,000 to 637,000. Thousands of these newcomers were products of the Hill promotion: Norwegians, German Russians, transplanted German Mennonites and Baptist "Dunkers," and of course a multitude lured out of the American Midwest and other regions. North Dakota now vied with Kansas for the honor of being named America's leading wheat state and in fact won the title for most of the thirty years after 1890.

In Montana, a mining-ranching domain, the homesteaders, or "honyockers" as they were called, had an even greater impact. Agriculture surpassed mining as the state's top industry in 1908, and over the next eleven years, nearly thirty-five million acres were homesteaded. Indeed, this became the most homesteaded state in the nation. The state's population mounted from 243,329 in 1900 to 376,053 in 1910 to 548,889 in 1920; and during the same time, the number of farms and ranches climbed from 13,370 to 26,214 to 57,677. During the first three months of 1910, the GN pulled over one thousand emigrant cars into its northern Montana depots. And on just one spring evening in Havre, Hill County, 250 homesteaders stepped off the train to greet the hard new world. Montana's wheat production, under eleven million bushels in 1909, soared to more than forty-two million bushels during the amazingly wet and productive year of 1915, when some fortunate farmers reaped forty to fifty bushels to the acre.

To old Jim Hill, it all seemed incredibly gratifying and providential, a dream come true. Even as abundant rains continued to fall, the outbreak of war in Europe in 1914, the peak year of homesteading in Montana, drove good prices even higher. He had confounded those, like the cowboy-painter Charley Russell of Great Falls, who had deprecated boosters such as Hill and his friend Senator Paris Gibson and who had argued that these men were feckless boosters destroying what was best left as good grazing land. Hill and the others had proven that the dry prairies could, in fact, be made into vast and productive granaries.

After a long haul through endless fields of standing grain and harvested stubble fields in late August 1915, Jim Hill wrote euphorically to his old friend Gaspard Farrer in England: "In the Northwest we have had a wonderful year for grain. On the lines of the Great Northern Railroad from the Twin Cities to the Rocky Mountains it is a grain field. All through Montana, where we used to hope the valleys would be cultivated and the bench-lands used for grazing, we have a continuous grain field, and the yield on the bench lands there is higher than that of the valleys. Fifty bushels of wheat and a hundred or more bushels of oats to the acre is not very uncommon."

A new and better world seemed to beckon, a world in which the food shortages Hill had feared would be eliminated from worry and a world in which his region and his railroad would share the prosperity that he had promised.

CHAPTER 8

The End of the Line

THE last years were, by about any standard, very good years. James J. Hill lived to what was then the venerable age of seventy-eight, supported by a wife who was, to the end as always, dutiful, dedicated, and supportive. All but one of his children, a daughter who died in infancy, outlived him. Although the pangs of old age visited him in full measure—rheumatism, enlarged prostate, the fits of congestion that periodically drove him to bed, painful dental problems, nagging hemorrhoids that he could not bring himself to have removed—these never combined to drive the willful old man to abandon his active, driven life-style. He did seem to become a bit more mellow, humorous, and solicitous with the passing years, though he appeared to fear death no more than he had feared life. The signature, grizzled Hill mien seemed more unkempt than ever. Photographs and, later in his life, motion pictures show him with discolored teeth, the always shaggy beard, and thinning hair turned snow-white; with a contented grin and with his thumbs looped in his lapels, he rocked back confidently in his stance. A large slice of the world was his: he had conquered it and successfully laid claim to it.

By now, both the rising value of his investments and the mounting pace of inflation were yearly multiplying his millions: he had become a true multimillionaire, one of America's wealthiest men. His yacht *Wacouta* remained docked almost year-around in Connecticut, and he spent far less time than most of his fellow investors at plush Jekyll Island on the Georgia coast. Yet more than ever, he spent his millions seemingly heedlessly.

As he finally began pulling away from day-to-day devotion to his railroads, he also spent less time at the Summit Avenue mansion in Saint Paul and more at his $1,500-per-month mansion at North Oaks and at his handsome home on East 65th Street in New York. In fact, now that his children had built lives and

Hill in 1910. Courtesy of James J. Hill Papers, James Jerome Hill Reference Library, Saint Paul, Minnesota.

families of their own, he and Mary spent more time at their homes as well. One favorite was "Maryhill," the superb summer estate that son-in-law Sam Hill built along the Washington bank of the Columbia and named in honor of three Mary Hills—wife, daughter, and mother-in-law.

It is impossible to know how he really felt about becoming a true American institution, the last of the railroad moguls. Surely, he must have relished it. When the organizers of the Panama-Pacific Exposition at San Francisco asked each state to name its outstanding citizen, a citizens' panel in Minnesota took little time to select James J. Hill as their choice. A leading manufacturer of men's hats featured his likeness, gazing out from under the brim of his trademark western homburg. When, in 1914, Hill publicly criticized the socialization program evolving in Great Britain, Chancellor of the Exchequer David Lloyd George deigned to respond formally and angrily.

To a number of requests that he write his reminiscences, he consistently replied that this should be done by others, after his death. One honor, however, brought a prompt and favorable response. When his old friend Thomas Lamont, of the House of Morgan, set out to raise an endowment for a "James J. Hill Professorship of Railroad Transportation" in the Harvard Business School, Hill matched it with $125,000 of his own, with the characteristic proviso that the occupant must have practical knowledge of the business and spend time learning the day-by-day working system of his lines.

Having retired as CEO of the Great Northern in 1907 and assumed the title of chairman of the board of directors, Jim Hill forfeited the latter title as well in 1912 and formally retired. He wrote to a friend in November: "For myself I do not wish to take up any new business. I am aiming to get out of active work and cannot succeed unless, as Greely [*sic*] said, 'The way to resume is to resume,' and the way for me to quit is to quit." This, as anyone acquainted with the man well knew, was poppycock; although Hill did devote more of his time to leisure after 1912, he remained highly active.

Loyal son Louis once again followed in his wake, assuming the

title of chairman of the board; as before, he proved quite competent but hardly the demanding world-beater that his father had
been. And as always, his compliant nature allowed the patriarch
to intervene selectively—and frequently—in management, even
in management of detail. Jim could now, however, focus even
more exclusively on grand strategy and on those new thrusts,
such as lumbering and especially the promotion of plains agriculture, that truly enticed him. Indeed, he could now find his extended family represented throughout the structure of his rail
empire. His eldest son, James Jr., had moved off to a well-heeled
semiretirement; but his eldest son-in-law, debonair Sam Hill,
remained affiliated. So did George Slade and Erasmus Lindley,
the husbands of two of his younger daughters.

Hill made, during these last years, perhaps the most important
of all his leadership recruitments for the GN, that of young
Ralph Budd. Another of Hill's main men, John Stevens, had first
hired Budd while on the Panama Canal project and had then
brought Budd along when he took over the Spokane, Portland,
and Seattle and the Oregon Trunk Line. Always watching for
young talent, James quickly took to this hawk-nosed, highly capable and personable young man and soon brought him to Saint
Paul as assistant to the president, which technically put him under Louis and Louis's subordinates but actually placed him at the
disposal of the grand old man himself.

Hill became so attached to Budd that he spent a good deal of
his private time with the young man, including leisurely automobile drives discoursing about his plans for the future, clearly
grooming Budd for top leadership after his own departure. He
expressed this wish to Louis and to others, and within a few years
of his death, Budd would occupy the presidency of the GN and
would, in fact, oversee its management as Louis took a more
relaxed role as chairman of the board. He would become perhaps
the most prestigious of all Hill's protégés, a key railroad leader of
the next generation.

With time now freed from direct management of his railroads,
Jim Hill turned his energies to an endeavor that had long interested him: banking. Thoroughly conversant with the world of

finance throughout his long career, he had long served on the boards of directors of no less than five financial institutions: the First National Bank of Saint Paul, the First National Bank of Chicago, the Illinois Trust and Savings Company, and two of the mightiest institutions of the nation's financial capital—the Chase National Bank and the First National Bank of New York. Like most of his industrial peers, he deplored America's decentralized and inefficient banking system, whose shortcomings had been underscored by the short but frightening Panic of 1907. And like many of his fellow midwesterners, he railed at the imperialistic financial reign of the Northeast over other regions.

In October 1912, Hill purchased two major financial institutions, the First National Bank and the Second National Bank, both of Saint Paul, and in 1913 he merged them under the name of the former. He poured nearly $4 million into the First National, enticing nearly all its stockholders to sell out to him with lucrative incentives; over the next four years, its deposits grew from $17 million to $55 million.

What he had in mind was to build his bank into a rock-solid anchor of fiscal stability for the Northwest, particularly to extend facile credit to farmers and ranchers who had long been racked by the need for flexible financial support in the seasonal vicissitudes of marketing their products. In this, he anticipated two primary new thrusts of the Woodrow Wilson administration: the Federal Reserve Act of 1913, which he lived to see, and the Federal Farm Loan Act of 1916, which he did not. If he had been given a few more years, he might have become a major leader in national banking.

Yet another project was the planning and construction of the new Great Northern Office Building, which he incorporated in 1914 and which was completed early in 1916. Characteristically, he doted on every detail of this thoroughly modern, fourteen-story, $4 million edifice, which occupied the half-block circumscribed by Jackson, Fourth, and Fifth Streets in central Saint Paul. The man definitely had a flair for architecture, as evidenced by the smooth, unadorned lines of the new building; and he watched with pride as his GN and NP corporate headquarters moved into the building, alongside his banking offices and his own personal staff of over a half-dozen busy workers, supervised as always by John Toomey. Atop the structure was a handsome penthouse "bungalow" for his personal convenience, but he showed little interest in it. Left behind was the old Great Northern General Office Building on Third Street, which had been his headquarters for nearly thirty years. The new building would stand as the largest building in the Twin Cities until, long afterward, the IDS Center would arise in Minneapolis.

The other building that occupied his waning years was the James J. Hill Reference Library in downtown Saint Paul, which he started work on in 1913 and modeled after the library that had been built as a memorial to J. P. Morgan in New York. This handsome, classical structure, fashioned in Italian Renaissance design, was once again planned by Hill himself, with the assistance of New York architect Electus Litchfield, who was ironically the scion of the Minnesota family that had started out in charge of the Saint Paul and Pacific and had caused him such grief so long ago. In turn, Mary and daughter Clara designed the interior, fashioned in beautiful pink marble.

True to form, Hill meant this to be, in fact, a reference library, not a general city library. It would focus on research and serious reading and not the general run of books for the public. More casual readers could go next door to the public library, to which his building was affixed. He placed his old editor war-horse J. G. Pyle in charge, having kept the man around for years since closing down his unprofitable *Saint Paul Globe*. This superb building, which is still an impressive structure and a going concern and now houses his personal papers, would not open until 1921, five years after his death and one month after Mary's.

He enjoyed, right to the end, the other avocations that great wealth had brought him, such as collecting the art of the French Barbizon school and, increasingly, donating these and other works to local exhibitors. And he continued to enjoy the perquisites of access to and influence on politicians at all levels. With the passing years, he devoted, naturally enough, less attention to the immediate concerns of state and local politics, which had drawn so much of his time and wrath on the long road upward, and more to the major personalities and issues at the national level, to which his hard-won eminence seemed to entitle him.

James J. Hill offers an especially gripping example, as W. Thomas White has revealed, of the frustrations even the most influential "captains of industry" felt in national politics. He had been very content, as a Democrat-turned-Republican, with President William McKinley, who appeared to that generation to have reintroduced prosperity to America. But then he found himself totally estranged from McKinley's successor, Theodore Roosevelt. Although he had much in common with TR, such as an attachment to the West and an erstwhile belief in conservation, the Northern Securities imbroglio embittered him, and the wound never healed.

Naturally enough, when Roosevelt declined to seek reelection in 1908, Hill followed the course of most businessmen and threw his support to TR's successful Republican designee, William Howard Taft. Now as before, he could not stomach the perennial, reformist Democratic nominee, William Jennings Bryan. And the Minnesotan got along reasonably well, if not intimately, with the portly president during the ensuing four years. Since his favorite national concern continued to be the enhancement of free trade between nations, he winced at the Taft administration's increase of duties with the controversial Payne-Aldrich Tariff of 1909. But on the other hand, he applauded Taft's moves toward a lowering of tariff barriers with Canada, a cause that he personally campaigned for, even though it was unpopular on the threatened turf of his home state. Like other advocates of reciprocity with Canada, he was saddened when his homeland rejected the issue before it could come to conclusive vote in the U.S. Congress.

In the critical election campaign of 1912, Hill kept his support with the president in Taft's unsuccessful bid for reelection. For the first time in many years, Jim Hill did not enter into a relationship, either positive or negative, with the president. He seemed pleased with Democrat Woodrow Wilson's successful move to lower trade barriers with the Underwood-Simmons Tariff of 1913 but not with the other reform measures of the president's "New Freedom" reform program. By 1914, in any event, Hill had become preoccupied with the overweening issue of war in Europe, to the near exclusion of all other issues.

Every bone in Jim Hill's body drew him toward an impassioned stand on the war between Britain, France, and Russia, on the one side, and Germany and Austria-Hungary, on the other. After all, he had been born in the British Empire, had been reared on English culture, and remained fondly attached to his native Canada. His closest friends included English capitalists like Gaspard Farrer and his peer associates Lord Mount Stephen and Lord Strathcona and Mount Royal, and his increasing role in international commerce led him naturally toward the English view of free trade and freedom of the seas. His rising status in the New York financial community served, as well, to imbue him with the values of the Morgans and other barons of Wall Street, values that included an affinity with London and Paris captains of banking and industry.

As soon as the horrors of modern war began to emerge in the summer of 1914, therefore, Jim Hill and his family became thoroughly absorbed and involved in coping with it. He and his daughter Clara threw themselves into the popular cause of providing relief for the Belgian victims of German invasion, the same cause that brought fame to young Herbert Hoover. Hill also involved himself heavily in the campaign, spearheaded by the House of Morgan and other old associates, to provide American "credits" to the financially strapped Anglo-French "Allies."

His own First National Bank of Saint Paul put up large subscriptions to the controversial loan. But, hailing from a region that questioned the neutrality of the credits, he proved more circumspect than most of his eastern colleagues, arguing futilely that the bankers should minimize their commissions and that the loans should not go toward the acquisition of war materials for American export, since the supplying of armaments to only one side was inherently unneutral and might draw America into the war.

These were, then, the issues that preoccupied the eventful days of 1914, 1915, and early 1916: the deepening, hopeless stalemate of war; the booming domestic prosperity that centered, in Hill's mind, on the great land rush to North Dakota and Montana; the excitement of seeing his monumental research library take shape and of moving into the Great Northern Office Building; and the growth of his bank. Like any other man, especially a man of those long-ago years, he also experienced the pangs that nearly eight full decades brought to a person, namely the pangs of failing health and of the death of friends. Old friends now passed yearly from the scene: his crony Henry Upham, John S. Kennedy, J. P. Morgan, Frederick Weyerhaeuser, Donald Smith, and in 1915 Sam Thorne, whose death of a heart attack occurred on one of the jaunts to the Saint John River and grievously disturbed Hill. Among the old associates, only stately George Stephen would outlive him.

Jim Hill's lifelong good luck served him well to the end, for when death came at age seventy-eight, it came quickly, although not without brief suffering. The spring of 1916 was a good and prosperous time, marred only by the rising fear of American involvement in a war that promised no early end, even after nearly two years of carnage. Although almost an octogenarian, the grand old man of American railroads enjoyed a pleasant life-style, spending a part of each workday at his new offices in the Great Northern Office Building and late afternoons and evenings at his homes at Summit Avenue and North Oaks.

Possibly knowing that the end was near, he spent more time now on philanthropy. He donated $25,000 to Catholic Marquette University at Milwaukee, and in a gesture that was interpreted as a peace offering to the city of Tacoma, his·longtime nemesis, he gave $50,000 to the College of Puget Sound. Indeed, his friends noticed other signs that he felt the imminence of death. After a visit with Hill at his New York office in the fall of 1915, John Stevens recalled how the old man walked with him out to the elevator and, uncharacteristically, placed a hand on his shoulder, saying: "John, is there anything in the world that I can do for you? If there ever is, you know where to find me." Stevens wrote, "I left him with the sad foreboding that I would never see him again."

For about a year, Jim had suffered the mounting symptoms of serious trouble, namely painful indigestion and the agony of a long-term hemorrhoidal irritation that his pride and compulsive sense of privacy kept him from dealing with through surgery. By mid-May, amid unseasonably cold weather, he was feeling worse and worse; he quit going to the office and took to bed. Even so, Toomey and the staff continued to bring him his work. But, as day followed day, his situation deteriorated, and by May 23, he fell into excruciating pain.

The family, now thoroughly frightened, brought in Dr. Stanley Zager and his old friend from New York Dr. Herman Biggs and then the increasingly famous Mayo brothers—Charles and William—from Rochester, Minnesota, to work with Hill's personal doctor, James Gilfillan. This was, incidentally, the first time that the Mayos had ever practiced medicine beyond the confines of their Rochester, Minnesota, clinic. At first, it appeared that the fever would pass, but then Hill again deteriorated with a high fever. The doctors now realized that they confronted a hopeless situation. Hill lay in critical condition from what they termed "intestinal catarrh"; in addition, his hemorrhoidal condition had erupted into a raging infection, with gangrene spreading along his left side.

They could do little more for him than to drain the resulting lesions. Clearly, the old man was beyond help, and mercifully, he finally fell into a coma that relieved his suffering. At midmorning on a radiant sunny day, May 29, 1916, James J. Hill died, with all his children except one, daughter Ruth, at his side. Dr. Gilfillan publicly stated: "Mr. Hill was a game fighter. Blood poisoning caused his death. He complained little during his illness, which was rather painful. He was conscious most of the time."

At the hour of his funeral, on the afternoon of May 31, every train on each of the "Hill lines" ground to a stop and rested for five minutes in a poignant salute to the man who had welded them into one of the world's great transportation empires. Soon afterward, a small cluster of family and friends gathered at his burial place, on a beautiful elevation at North Oaks, where he would lie for two decades before he and Mary were reinterred in the Saint Paul Resurrection Cemetery.

As so often happens in the passing of a man who had become a monument in his own lifetime, past criticisms were now forgotten, and everyone remembered his remarkable achievements. Minnesota Governor J. A. A. Burnquist saluted Jim Hill as "the greatest constructive genius of the Northwest" and ordered flags on state buildings flown at half-mast, as they were in states all the way to Oregon. His friend Archbishop John Ireland of Saint Paul termed him "a man of rarest talent of mind, a genius such as is seldom to be seen . . . but also one who . . . put his wondrous talent to the service of fellow men, whose whole career was marked with strict integrity and highest sense of honor."

The *New York Times* typified the obituaries: "Greatness became him, and was a condition of his errand here. Whatever he had done, it had been greatly done. He trusted democracy perhaps more than it trusts itself. He believed in its economic destiny. Giving much, he received much. We salute the memory of a great American." Commenting on "James J. Hill and His Empire," the *Philadelphia Evening Ledger* noted, "If he built an empire he joined it to a republic." And the *World's Work* saluted him grandly as the "foremost practical master of the large problems of progress of his time; the railroad-building genius who opened up the great northwestern wilderness."

Out in his own part of the world, the *Minneapolis Tribune* commemorated him: "There was nothing of the stand-patter about James J. Hill. He believed in pushing out the boundaries of his world. . . . It could not be said with conviction that the Northwest of to-day would be the prosperous section that it is if he had not lived. His public record is that of a builder, a pioneer, a conservator." And in faraway Great Falls, Montana, where the Hill-sponsored homestead boom was now cresting, that city's *Tribune* remembered how others had scoffed at his dream of turning grasslands into wheat fields: "The title of Mr. Hill to greatness is that he achieved great things in the way of making the world in which he lived a better place to live in. He made gardens grow where desert land existed before. He made available for habitations millions of homes where only gophers and wild animals before had their habitations. He added greatly to the sum total of human happiness."

His seaport city of Seattle eulogized Jim Hill every bit as
fervently. The bronze bust of Hill that had been erected at the
University of Washington after his speech at the opening of the
1909 Alaska-Yukon-Pacific Exposition was draped in a floral
wreath. With complete sincerity, Judge Thomas Burke commented, "It would be impossible to overestimate the value of Mr.
Hill's influence in making Seattle the city that she is today." The
Seattle Times concurred, noting that although his death was a
"loss to the entire country," he would be mourned especially by
"the Puget Sound metropolis" that he had done so much to
build.

How close were the eulogists to capturing the real meaning of
the man and his accomplishments? They were certainly correct in
viewing him as larger than life, as a man whose opportunities and
deeds could never again be matched—if not because of his sin-
gularity, then at least because such land-opening opportunities
would never appear again. The truth was that the breadth of his
reach and of his influence extended so far that he must be viewed
in multiple contexts, with varying and even contradictory con-
clusions about who he was and what he left behind.

Certainly, he fulfilled many times over his dream of early manhood: to achieve the modest fortune of $100,000. In fact, he
amassed one of the great American fortunes. When his estate was
filed in Saint Paul Probate Court in 1917, its value, rapidly compounding due to wartime inflation, stood at $52,888,519. Of this,
$16,668,000 went to his widow; $3,704,000 went to each of his
children; and only a paltry $1,535,000 went to the undemanding
income and inheritance taxes of those days. When one considers
that, adjusting for future inflation, this sum was worth many
times over that amount in current dollars, it is even more obvious
how much he had made. Moreover, he passed on the spirit of
wise stewardship and of philanthropy to his children, so that the
Hill family fortune would sustain and grow. In later years, the
Hill Family Foundation and its successor, the Northwest Area
Foundation, have set a national example in intelligent investments in regional philanthropic giving.

On the other hand, his sweeping influence could also lead to wholesale failure. Such was the case with the homesteading promotion of 1909–18 on the northern plains. The mighty land rush that seemed to crest during the wet years of 1915–16 took on a new frenzy as a result of the artificially high commodity prices and the government promotion of World War I but then crashed amid drought and plummeting prices during 1919–21. As wheat prices skidded from over two dollars to around one dollar per bushel, and as high winds blew away the parched topsoil, at least seventy-five thousand farmers and family members fled the plains expanses of both North Dakota and Montana; and in each state, over half the banks failed during the years 1919–25.

In the 1940s, polemical journalist-historians, like Joseph Kinsey Howard in Montana and Bruce Nelson in North Dakota, vilified Hill as the architect of disaster, and for years, schoolchildren sang a popular jingle:

> Twixt Hill and Hell there's just one letter:
> Were Hill in Hell, we'd feel much better.

Such personification of major historical events is, of course, common to western history, especially to the heroes of the "Wild West" but also to the villainization of industrialists by the "Plundered Province" school of writers, of whom Howard and Nelson are virulent examples. Jim Hill does deserve considerable criticism for his overpromotion of intensive, homestead agriculture on the semiarid plains, and certainly the abandoned farms and dwindling small towns of the region are mute testimony to his misguided efforts. In a frenzy of promotion, he failed to take environmental limitations into account. But so, after all, did most of his contemporaries, thousands of whom were also promoters, just like he was.

The salient fact is, in objective hindsight, that the application of humid-area, intensive agriculture to the dry western plains was probably as inevitable as it was hopeless. Jim Hill's leadership in promoting the big boom did not cause it, but his leadership certainly did exacerbate it and thus exacerbated its inevitable bust. It must be realized, though, that the region has indeed become a great granary, just as Hill and the others thought it would; and thus a balanced perspective concludes that the great land-taking was not a chimera, only an overpromotion. For that, the human cost has been high, and Hill's deprecation by the descendants of the homesteaders is, at least to some extent, both understandable and, at the level of group memory, appropriate.

In this, as in so many other ways, he was without peer, the preeminent builder of the frontier economy of the Northwest. By controlling the transportation structure of the region—a near-monopoly railroad that, at the time of his death, was only beginning to feel the competition of automobiles and public highways—he exercised more sweeping economic power than did any other industrialists, even the lumbermen and mining barons. The fact that, viewed from the distant perspective of an elapsed century, things often turned out differently than he had anticipated should not obscure his remarkable influence. For instance, the iron ores of the great Mesabi deposits have now played out, and the "Iron Range" country of Minnesota is a depressed area. But the historic facts remain that these iron mines represented one of the most graphic of all examples of American abundance, to a large extent fueling the great industrial revolution of the twentieth century, and that Hill and the GN led in their efficient utilization.

Similarly, the glory days of the Pacific Northwest lumber industry now lie well in the past—in those early decades of this century when Oregon and Washington ranked as the nation's leading wood products states. But one would have to strain to exaggerate Hill's influence in transplanting this key industry from his home region to the new one that he was building. Truly, Jim Hill made it happen by promising and delivering low rates on eastbound lumber, rates that facilitated the hauling both of the lumber itself and of the balancing westbound ladings. Thus, although the luxuriant, old-growth timber stands are now nearly gone, and although the industry is today imperiled, the strategy of Jim Hill in developing it remains a key historic factor in the past one hundred years of regional growth and change.

Hill's grandiose dreams of initiating maritime commerce on

the Pacific and of opening the markets of Asia to America's bounty of natural products seem, from today's perspective, at once both fanciful and farsighted. True enough, he failed—due to his own inexperience in this realm, to the fact that national policy ran counter to his vision, and to the unalterable fact that, except for Japan, Asian markets were not nearly developed enough to be receptive. But his belief in the idea of using superships, and of applying the lessons he had learned in railroading about the profitability of massive tonnages, is impressive from a modern vantage point. And so is his belief that the cornucopia of America's harvests of crops, metals, and other products would one day find an enormous demand and market in Asia. Even in failure, his dreams would live on.

Of course, his primary legacy lies in his railroads, the GN especially but also the NP, the Burlington, and the Spokane, Portland, and Seattle, which remained—after the Northern Securities decision—bound by a loose community of interest although not by a direct affiliation. The long shadow of his influence over the Hill lines has proven quite remarkable. Son Louis remained chairman of the GN board until 1929 and a member until 1948; son James Norman served as a member of the NP board until 1922; Hill's righthand man Edward Nichols was on the GN board until 1934; and his most influential disciple, Ralph Budd, would occupy leadership positions, especially of the Burlington, until well past midcentury. Much more important, his philosophy of railroading—with its emphasis on infrastructure and the primacy of freight—would live on, not only in these lines but in most others as well.

Had he lived another decade or two, Jim Hill would have experienced more frustration than satisfaction with the railroading business. Although he would have heartily approved the new technologies of railroading, such as diesel engines and modern grading machinery, he would have raged at the federal takeover of railroads during World War I and the ICC controls placed over them when they returned to private ownership afterward. And he would have realized his earlier misjudgment and comprehended the threat that the now ubiquitous cars and trucks, traveling on publicly maintained highways, posed to the freight trains that he had considered destined always to be the backbone of American commerce. Most of all, he would have chafed again at the repeated failures of his minions to secure a full merger of his railroads.

In the mid-1920s, as the turmoil of wartime regulation and reprivatization of the railroads faded into the background, the executives of the four Hill lines, led by Ralph Budd, went to the ICC with a proposal for a new merger called the Great Northern Pacific Railway Company, in which the GN and the NP would formally merge and which would then control the stock of both the Burlington and the Spokane, Portland, and Seattle. The ICC approved the merger, but only with the unacceptable provision that the Burlington must be divested, and so in 1931 the application was withdrawn. One frustration followed another, and not until long into the future—in 1970, amid a new wave of rail mergers—did the lines once gathered together by Hill into Northern Securities finally gain Supreme Court approval to meld their corporate identities into a new corporation, Burlington Northern. Under this new identity, the dream of Jim Hill lives on.

Burlington Northern, Inc., embodies the business achievements of James J. Hill as few corporations today embody the work of any individual. In the wake of the demise of the Milwaukee Road in the mid-1980s, the "BN" system dominates the Northwest about as it did before the Milwaukee's late construction, with major competition from the Union Pacific on the western end and some competition from the Soo Line and others to the east. Hill would wince, however, at the location of the corporation headquarters in Fort Worth, Texas, rather than the Twin Cities or Seattle.

Like other American railroads, this one continues to operate on the principles first advocated by James Hill and E. H. Harriman—that a well-built and heavily utilized railroad is still the best system for heavy loads and, conversely, that freight cannot and should not subsidize passenger traffic, which has long since mainly gone to other modes. He would nod an emphatic

The crack passenger train named for the Great Northern's architect. Courtesy of Montana Historical Society, Helena.

approval at how BN and other "container," "unit," and car-rack trains have recaptured the bulk cargoes that were earlier lost to trucks and canal-based barges and thus at how the basic freight train has enjoyed a rebirth.

Like most of the other "robber barons" or "captains of industry," and like most dynamic individuals of any generation, James Jerome Hill displayed what Allan Nevins once called "a sort of lunar dualism." Beyond dispute, his positive traits were quite remarkable: a quick intelligence and power of analysis, an incredible power of will and personality, and an unparalleled work ethic and commitment. His negative attributes, simply enough, were mirror images of the positive: an extreme irascibility that sometimes exploded into rage, a willfulness that could turn into outright ruthlessness, a cold manipulativeness that he used on politicians and other adversaries, and such a preoccupation with the purpose at hand that he sometimes lost sight of the broader perspective.

What does one conclude, in the final analysis, about this remarkable man? Surely, the Northwest will never again witness an individual with such sweeping power, simply because the unique opportunity provided by an opening frontier and a transportation monopoly will never again appear. It is entirely appropriate that the prime passenger train from Chicago to Seattle is called the "Empire Builder" in his memory; for his hand reached into every aspect of building the regional economy and social order, from transportation to agriculture, mining, lumbering, maritime trade, and, not to be forgotten, town and city building.

His larger-than-life stature is well attested by the persistence, nearly eighty years after his death, of his memory and legend. Today, his name is a byword in the Twin Cities, of which he was the most important frontier builder, in large part because his research library and tourist-site home in Saint Paul and his family philanthropy, the Northwest Area Foundation, are so well-known but also because time has done little to tarnish his legend. Much farther west, in Spokane, the Hillyard community annually celebrates its "Jim Hill Days," with the usual foot races and festivals.

And at Havre, in Hill County, Montana, a new statue of Hill faces the city.

The various determinists no doubt are correct that events shape people more than people shape events, but the life of James J. Hill certainly demonstrates the impact one willful individual can have on the course of history. We shall never see his like again, and that simple fact adds yet another dimension to the fascination his life will afford to each new generation.

Bibliographic Essay

THE voluminous Hill Papers, which were generally closed to scholars until 1982, are gathered and indexed at the James J. Hill Reference Library in Saint Paul, Minnesota. I used this large collection only selectively, since my book is part of a series that consists of brief volumes interpretative and introductory rather than lengthy and authoritative in nature.

Two large biographies offer the starting points for any new study of Jim Hill. The standard work is Albro Martin's *James J. Hill and the Opening of the Northwest* (New York: Oxford University Press, 1976), which, although highly laudatory, is also packed with information and insights found nowhere else. The recent paperbound edition of this work, published by the Minnesota Historical Society Press at Saint Paul, contains a valuable introduction by W. Thomas White. Less valuable, but still informative, is the obsequious "authorized" biography by Hill's media man Joseph G. Pyle, *The Life of James J. Hill*, 2 vols. (New York: Doubleday-Page, 1916–17). Stewart Holbrook's *James J. Hill: A Great Life in Brief* (New York: A. A. Knopf, 1955) is entirely superficial. Clara Hill Lindley penned a sketchy *James J. and Mary T. Hill: An Unfinished Chronicle by Their Daughter* (New York: North River Press, 1948), which has limited value for family history.

On Hill's rail empire, the most worthwhile source is the elaborate and beautifully published *The Great Northern Railway: A History* (Boston: Harvard Business School Press, 1988), which was the culmination of a lifetime effort by the late Ralph W. Hidy and Muriel E. Hidy and which was finished by Roy BV. Scott, Don L. Hofsommer, and Elizabeth A. Burnham. Copies of the much larger manuscript from which this volume was distilled are available at several archives. It is hereafter cited as *GN Manuscript*. I benefited much from using the copy at the K. Ross Toole Archives of the University of Montana.

Other histories of Hill's rail empire tend to be either very brief works or pictorial overviews. In the former category is Duncan J.

Kerr, *The Story of the Great Northern Railway Company—and James J. Hill* (Princeton, N.J.: Princeton University Press, 1939). In the latter group are Charles R. Wood, *Lines West: A Pictorial History of the Great Northern Railway* (Seattle: Superior Publishing, 1967), and Bill Yenne, *The History of the Burlington Northern* (New York: Brompton Books, 1991).

Jim Hill's family history and early years are best addressed by Martin, *Hill;* Pyle's account and that of Hill's daughter Clara Lindley, both noted above, each rely heavily on Hill's own and his wife's recollections. He offered further recollections, as rendered by Annabel Lee, in "The Beckoning Northwest," *Collier's,* November 20, 1915, pp. 27–28, and in other, similar interviews. A fascinating description of early Saint Paul, and of the Hills' role in it, is Robert M. Frame III, *James J. Hill's St. Paul: A Guide to Historic Sites* (Saint Paul: James J. Hill Reference Library, 1988). See also Richard Moe, *The Last Full Measure: The Life and Death of the First Minnesota Volunteers* (New York: Henry Holt, 1993).

James Hill offered further reminiscences on his early business career in testimony presented in the case of *Jesse P. Farley* v. *Norman W. Kittson et al.,* July 6, 1887, U.S. Circuit Court, Minnesota District. On his early steamboat business, see also Vera Kelsey, *Red River Runs North* (New York: Harper and Brothers, 1951). For Minnesota and regional background, I relied especially on William E. Lass, *Minnesota: A Bicentennial History* (New York: W. W. Norton, 1978); Theodore C. Blegen, *Minnesota: A History of the State* (Minneapolis: University of Minnesota Press, 1963); John R. Borchert, *America's Northern Heartland* (Minneapolis: University of Minnesota Press, 1987); and Stanley N. Murray, "Railroads and the Agricultural Development of the Red River Valley of the North, 1870–1890," *Agricultural History* 31 (October 1957): 57–66.

Among the many histories and interpretations of American railroading, I found particularly helpful John F. Stover's *The Life and Decline of the American Railroad* (New York: Oxford University Press, 1970); Albro Martin, *Railroads Triumphant: The Growth, Rejection, and Rebirth of a Vital American Force* (New York: Oxford University Press, 1992); Robert E. Riegel, *The Story of the Western Railroads* (New York: Macmillan, 1926); Julius Grodinsky, *Transcontinental Railway Strategy, 1869–1893* (Philadelphia: University of Pennsylvania Press, 1962); and John R. Stilgoe, *Metropolitan Corridor: Railroads and the American Scene* (New Haven, Conn.: Yale University Press, 1983). Among several studies of the Northern Pacific and its dominant figures, see especially James B. Hedges, *Henry Villard and the Railways of the Northwest* (New York: Russell and Russell, 1930), and Robin W. Winks, *Frederick Billings: A Life* (New York: Oxford University Press, 1991).

The large question of railroad land grants is treated in many studies, including Lloyd J. Mercer, *Railroads and Land Grant Policy: A Study in Government Intervention* (New York: Academic Press, 1982), and William S. Greever, "A Comparison of Railroad Land-Grant Policies," *Agricultural History* 25 (April 1951): 83–90. Especially illuminating of this subject is John B. Rae, "The Great Northern's Land Grant," *Journal of Economic History* 12 (Spring 1952): 140–46.

Martin, *Hill,* and Hidy et al., *Great Northern,* offer in-depth perspectives on the creation of the Manitoba Railroad. Pierre Berton offers an interesting further perspective in his readable *The Impossible Railway: The Building of the Canadian Pacific* (New York: A. A. Knopf, 1972). On the "associates," see Saul Engelbourg, "John Stewart Kennedy and the Scottish American Investment Company," in *Essays in Economic and Business History,* ed. E. J. Perkins (Los Angeles: University of Southern California Department of History, 1988), pp. 37–54; Heather Gilbert, *The End of the Road: The Life of Lord Mount Stephen,* 2 vols. (Aberdeen, Scotland: Aberdeen University Press, 1977); Heather Gilbert, "The Unaccountable Fifth," *Minnesota History* 7 (Spring 1971): 175–76; and John Moody and George Kibbe Turner, "The Masters of Capital in America," *McClure's* 36 (December 1910): 123–40. The Hill Papers offer much material on the *Farley* case.

Regarding the Canadian Pacific, in addition to Berton, *The Impossible Railway,* consult John A. Eagle, *The Canadian Pacific Railway and the Development of Western Canada, 1896–1914* (Kingston, Montreal: McGill-Queen's University Press, 1989); Gerald Friesen, *The Canadian Prairies: A History* (Toronto: University of Toronto Press, 1984); J. Arthur Lower, *Western Canada: An Outline History* (Vancouver: Douglas and McIntyre, 1983); and W. A. Waiser, *The Field Naturalist: John Macoun, the Geological Survey, and Natural Science* (Toronto: University of Toronto Press, 1989).

The other regional roads that Hill had to deal with are addressed in Richard C. Overton, *Burlington Route: A History of the Burlington Lines* (New York: A. A. Knopf, 1965); August Derleth, *The Milwaukee Road: Its First Hundred Years* (New York: Creative Age Press, 1948); and H. Roger Grant, *Corn Belt Route: A History of the Chicago Great Western Railroad Company* (DeKalb: Northern Illinois University Press, 1984). Grant provides more insights in the following: "The Mason City Road: From Iowa Shortline to Chicago Great Western Affiliate," *Annals of Iowa* 46 (Summer 1982):

323–36; "A. B. Stickney and James J. Hill: The Railroad Relationship," *Railroad History* 146 (Spring 1982): 9–21; and "The James J. Hill Papers: An Untapped Source for the Study of Iowa History," *Annals of Iowa* 46 (Summer 1982): 373–76. The Chicago hub is superbly depicted by William Cronon in *Nature's Metropolis: Chicago and the Great West* (New York: W. W. Norton, 1991).

The westward extension of the Manitoba Road into North Dakota is described in Elwyn B. Robinson, *History of North Dakota* (Lincoln: University of Nebraska Press, 1966); Robert P. and Wynona H. Wilkins, *North Dakota: A Centennial History* (New York: W. W. Norton, 1977); Harold E. Briggs, "The Great Dakota Boom, 1879 to 1886," *North Dakota Historical Quarterly* 4 (January 1930): 78–108; Ross R. Cotroneo, "Northern Pacific Officials and the Disposition of the Railroad's Land Grant in North Dakota after 1888," *North Dakota History* 37 (Spring 1970): 77–103; and Hiram M. Drache, "The Economic Aspects of the Northern Pacific Railroad in North Dakota," *North Dakota History* 34 (Fall 1967): 321–69.

Much has been written recently about the Montana Extension. See W. Thomas White, "Paris Gibson, James J. Hill, and the 'New Minneapolis': The Great Falls Water Power and Townsite Company, 1882–1908," *Montana: The Magazine of Western History* 33 (Summer 1983): 60–69; W. Thomas White, "Commonwealth or Colony? Montana and the Railroads in the First Decade of Statehood" *ibid* 38 (Autumn 1988): 12–23; Richard B. Roeder, "A Settlement on the Plains: Paris Gibson and the Building of Great Falls," *ibid* 42 (Autumn 1992): 4–19; William L. Lang, "Charles A. Broadwater and the Main Chance in Montana," *ibid* 39 (Summer 1989): 30–36; William L. Lang, "Corporate Point Men and the Creation of the Montana Central Railroad," *Great Plains Quarterly* 10 (Summer 1990): 152–66; and Michael P. Malone, *The Battle for Butte: Mining and Politics on the Northern Frontier, 1864–1906* (Seattle: University of Washington Press, 1981).

Informative on gaining access through the North Dakota and Montana Indian reservations is Dennis J. Smith, "Procuring a Right-of-Way: James J. Hill and Indian Reservations" (graduate research paper, University of Montana, 1983). Similarly instructive regarding the decision to build on to the sea is N. S. B. Gras and Henrietta M. Larson, *Casebook in American Business History* (New York: F. S. Crofts and Co., 1939), pp. 403–32.

The remarkable John F. Stevens and his discovery of Marias Pass have attracted a lot of attention. See John F. Stevens, "An Engineer's Recollections, V: The Discovery of Marias Pass," *Engineering News-Record* 114 (May 9, 1935): 672–75; Ralph W. Hidy and Muriel E. Hidy,

"John Frank Stevens: Great Northern Engineer," *Minnesota History* 41 (Winter 1969): 345–61; and Earl Clark, "John F. Stevens: Pathfinder for Western Railroads," *American West* 8 (May 1971): 28–33, 62–63.

Glenn C. Quiett presents an interesting depiction of the situation in Spokane, and that in Seattle and Portland as well, in *They Built the West: An Epic of Rails and Cities* (New York: D. Appleton-Century, 1934). On rail rivalries in the Columbia Valley, see Maury Klein, *Union Pacific: The Birth of a Railroad, 1862–1893* (Garden City, N.Y.: Doubleday, 1987); and Hedges, *Henry Villard.* The rivalry between Puget Sound cities is described in Norman H. Clark, *Mill Town: A Social History of Everett* (Seattle: University of Washington Press, 1970); Roger Sale, *Seattle: Past to Present* (Seattle: University of Washington Press, 1976); Nard Jones, *Seattle* (Garden City, N.Y.: Doubleday, 1972); and especially, Robert C. Nesbit, *"He Built Seattle": A Biography of Judge Thomas Burke* (Seattle: University of Washington Press, 1961).

The labor situation is well addressed by W. Thomas White in the following: "Race, Ethnicity, and Gender in the Railroad Work Force: The Case of the Far Northwest, 1883–1918," *Western Historical Quarterly* 16 (July 1985): 265–83; "The Pullman Strike in Montana," *Montana: The Magazine of Western History* 29 (August 1979): 2–13; "Railroad Labor Protests, 1894–1917: From Community to Class in the Pacific Northwest," *Pacific Northwest Quarterly* 75 (January 1984): 13–21; "Protest Movements on the Northern Tier: A Comparative Look at Railway Workers in the Pullman Strike of 1894 and the 1922 Shopmen's Strike," in *Centennial West: Essays on the Northern Tier States,* ed. W. L. Lang (Helena: Montana Historical Society Press, 1991); and "A History of Railroad Workers in the Pacific Northwest, 1883–1934" (Ph.D. diss., University of Washington, 1981). *GN Manuscript* also describes GN labor policies in detail. See Yuji Ichioka, "Japanese Immigrant Labor Contractors and the Northern Pacific and Great Northern Railroad Companies, 1898–1907," *Labor History* 21 (Summer 1980): 325–50.

Horace S. Merrill offers a fascinating profile of Hill's involvement in Minnesota politics in "Ignatius Donnelly, James J. Hill, and Cleveland Administration Patronage," *Mississippi Valley Historical Review* 39 (December 1952): 505–18. W. Thomas White provides an informative national perspective in "A Gilded Age Businessman in Politics: James J. Hill, the Northwest, and the American Presidency, 1884–1912," *Pacific Historical Review* 57 (November 1989): 439–56. See also Matthew Josephson, *The Politicos* (New York: Harcourt, Brace and World, 1938). For other state perspectives, see Robinson, *North Dakota;* Michael P. Malone, Richard B. Roeder, and William

L. Lang, *Montana: A History of Two Centuries*, 2d ed. (Seattle: University of Washington Press, 1991); W. Thomas White, "The War of the Railroad Kings: Great Northern–Northern Pacific Rivalry in Montana, 1881–1896," in *Montana and the West: Essays in Honor of K. Ross Toole*, ed. R. C. Myers and H. W. Fritz (Boulder: Pruett, 1984), pp. 37–54; Nesbit, *"He Built Seattle"*; and John Fahey, *The Inland Empire: Unfolding Years, 1879–1929* (Seattle: University of Washington Press, 1986).

The GN's move into lake and ocean transportation is well covered in *GN Manuscript* and also in Howard B. Schonberger, "James J. Hill and the Orient Trade," *Transportation to the Seaboard: The "Communication Revolution" and American Foreign Policy, 1860–1900* (Westport, Conn.: Greenwood, 1971), chap. 8; W. Kaye Lamb, "The Trans-Pacific Venture of James J. Hill," *American Neptune* 3 (April 1943): 185–204; C. M. Keys, "The Contest for Pacific Traffic," *World's Work* 10 (August 1905): 6503–9; and Mary H. Severance, "James J. Hill: A Builder of the Northwest," *American Monthly Review of Reviews* 21 (June 1900): 669–78.

Hill's role in fostering the Pacific Northwest lumber industry needs much further study, but see Carlos A. Schwantes, *The Pacific Northwest: An Interpretive History* (Lincoln: University of Nebraska Press, 1989); Gordon B. Dodds, *The American Northwest: A History of Washington and Oregon* (Arlington Heights, Ill.: Forum Press, 1986); and Ralph W. Hidy, Frank Ernest Hill, and Allan Nevins, *Timber and Men: The Weyerhaeuser Story* (New York: Macmillan, 1963). On the Mesabi venture, consult David A. Walker, *Iron Frontier: The Discovery and Early Development of Minnesota's Three Ranges* (Saint Paul: Minnesota Historical Society Press, 1979); Joseph Wilmer Thompson, "The Genesis of the Great Northern's Mesabi Ore Traffic," *Journal of Economic History* 16 (December 1956): 551–57; and Joseph Wilmer Thompson, "An Economic History of the Mesabi Division of the Great Northern Railway Company to 1915" (Ph.D. diss., University of Illinois, 1956).

Both Martin, *Hill*, and *GN Manuscript* illuminate the imbroglio over the Northern Pacific takeover. Further insights are in Ron Chernow, *The House of Morgan: An American Banking Dynasty and the Rise of Modern Finance* (New York: Touchstone Books, 1991); Vincent P. Carosso, *The Morgans: Private International Bankers, 1854–1913* (Cambridge: Harvard University Press, 1987); and Moody and Turner, "Masters of Capital."

The best place to get acquainted with the highly articulate Jim Hill is in his volume of collected essays on a multitude of subjects: *Highways of Progress* (New York: Doubleday, 1910). Over the years, he poured forth his ideas to journalists, a good example being Lee, "The Beckoning Northwest." Howard L. Dickman presents and assesses Hill's thinking on agriculture in "James Jerome Hill and the Agricultural Development of the Northwest" (Ph.D. diss., University of Michigan, 1977).

Historians have devoted much attention to the subject of rail regulation. I have learned especially from Edward S. Purcell, Jr., "Ideas and Interests: Businessmen and the Interstate Commerce Act," *Journal of American History* 73 (December 1986): 561–78; Albro Martin, "The Troubled Subject of Railroad Regulation in the Gilded Age: A Reappraisal," *ibid* 61 (September 1974): 339–71; Robert B. Carson, "Railroads and Regulation Revisited: A Note on Problems of Historiography and Ideology," *Historian* 34 (May 1972): 437–46; and Gabriel Kolko, *Railroads and Regulation, 1877–1916* (Princeton, N.J.: Princeton University Press, 1965). Spokane's struggle over freight rates is assessed in Douglas Smart, "Spokane's Battle for Freight Rates," *Pacific Northwest Quarterly* 45 (January 1954): 19–27.

Martin, *Hill,* provides the best focused insight into the struggle over the Burlington Road and the *Northern Securities* case. For other perspectives, consult Overton, *Burlington Route;* Chernow, *The House of Morgan;* Lloyd J. Mercer, *E. H. Harriman: Master Railroader* (Boston: Twayne, 1985); the still valuable Balthusar H. Meyer, *A History of the Northern Securities Case* (Madison: University of Wisconsin, 1906); and Walter Rosenbarry, "The Political and Economic Significance of the Northern Securities Company" (honors thesis, Harvard University, 1953). Among many national perspectives, an especially insightful one is offered by Martin J. Sklar, *The Corporate Reconstruction of American Capitalism, 1890–1916* (Cambridge: Cambridge University Press, 1988). For an example of regional response, see Carl H. Chrislock, *The Progressive Era in Minnesota: 1899–1918* (Saint Paul: Minnesota Historical Society, 1971).

The debate over capitalization of the GN is presented by A. B. Stickney, "Railway Overcapitalization: I.—A Defense of the Great Northern," and William L. Snyder II, "The Case against the Great Northern," *Outlook,* March 9, 1907, pp. 558–63. Martin, *Hill* and *GN Manuscript* offer good overall assessments of GN struggles with the Canadian Pacific; supplement these with Eagle, *Canadian Pacific;* and for the Milwaukee Road, Derleth, *The Milwaukee Road.* John C. Hudson expertly assesses the Soo rivalry in "North Dakota's Railway War of 1905," *North Dakota History* 48 (Winter 1981): 4–19, and in *Plains Country Towns* (Minneapolis: University of Minnesota Press, 1985).

Hill's struggle with Harriman in the Columbia Valley is well described in *GN Manuscript* and in Quiett, *They Built the West;* see, especially, Carlos A. Schwantes, *Railroad Signatures across the Pacific Northwest* (Seattle: University of Washington Press, 1993). Also see Mercer, *Harriman;* Charles Wood and Dorothy Wood, *The Spokane, Portland, and Seattle Railway: The Northwest's Own Railway* (Seattle: Superior Publishing, 1974); John F. Stevens, "Engineer's Recollections: Railway Invasion of Central Oregon," *Engineering News-Record* 114 (June 27, 1935): 917–19; and Don L. Hofsommer, "Rivals for California: The Great Northern and the Southern Pacific," *Montana: The Magazine of Western History* 38 (Spring 1988): 58–67.

John Kimberly Mumford's assessment of Hill is in "The Land of Opportunity: The Great 'One-Man Railroad' of the West," *Harper's Weekly,* October 31, 1908, pp. 24–25. Hill's promotion of iron and lumber industries, and of Pacific commerce, is referenced above. On tourism, see Michael G. Schene, "The Crown of the Continent: Private Enterprise and Public Interest in the Early Development of Glacier National Park, 1910–17," *Forest and Conservation History* 34 (Spring 1990): 69–75, and Warren L. Hanna, *Stars over Montana: Men Who Made Glacier National Park History* (West Glacier, Mont.: Glacier Natural History Association, 1988).

On Hill's agricultural promotion, see Hidy et al., *Great Northern;* Dickman, "James Jerome Hill"; Fahey, *Inland Empire;* Mary W. M. Hargreaves, *Dry Farming in the Northern Great Plains, 1900–1925* (Cambridge: Harvard University Press, 1957); Roy V. Scott, "American Railroads and Agricultural Extension, 1900–1914: A Study in Railway Developmental Techniques," *Business History Review* 39 (Spring 1965): 74–98; Roy V. Scott, *Railroad Development Programs in the Twentieth Century* (Ames: Iowa State University Press, 1985); David H. Hickcox, "The Impact of the Great Northern Railway on Settlement in Northern Montana," *Railroad History* 148 (Autumn 1983): 58–67; Dave Walter, "Simon Pepin: A Quiet Capitalist," *Montana: The Magazine of Western History* 39 (Winter 1989): 34–38; and, for two polemical flourishes, Bruce Nelson, *Land of the Dacotahs* (Minneapolis: University of Minnesota Press, 1946); and Joseph K. Howard, *Montana: High, Wide, and Handsome* (New Haven, Conn.: Yale University Press, 1943).

On Hill's final years, see especially Martin, *Hill;* "James J. Hill's Letter to the Stockholders on Retiring from the Chairmanship of the Board of Directors, July 1, 1912," in *Memoirs of Three Railroad Pioneers,* ed. Stuart Bruchey (New York: Arno Press, 1981); Albro Martin, "Ralph Budd," in *Railroads in the Age of Regulation, 1900–*

1980, ed. Keith L. Bryant (New York: Facts on File Publications, 1988); White, "A Gilded Age Businessman in Politics." On the Hill estate, see Gustavus Myers, *History of the Great American Fortunes,* rev. ed. (New York: Random House, 1937); on later merger efforts, see Hidy et al., *Great Northern,* and Gras and Larson, *Casebook in American Business History.*

The obituary quotations are from *World's Work,* July 16, 1916, p. 243; *Literary Digest,* June 10, 1916, p. 1689; *Minneapolis Tribune,* May 30, 1916; *Great Falls Tribune,* May 30, 1916; and *Seattle Times,* May 30, 1916.

Index